Based on the
Award-winning
Computer Games
Myth: The Fallen Lords
and
Myth II: Soulblighter.

Written and Produced by
GENE SEABOLT

Edited by
ALAIN DAWSON
and SEAN PUNCH

Illustrated by
MARK BERNAL,
JOHN BOLTON,
PAUL CLIFT,
GARY MCCLUSKEY,
ROBT MCLEES,
FRANK PUSATERI,
and JUAN RAMIREZ

Cover by
JOHN BOLTON

Playtesting by
ALLEN TURNER and
THE CREW AT BUNGIE,
JOSH FLACHSBART, and
ANDREAS WICHTER

Additional Support by
PAUL CLIFT and
DOUG ZARTMAN

Based on the Setting by
ROBT MCLEES

GURPS
Myth

Roleplaying in the World of the Fallen Lords

GURPS System Design † STEVE JACKSON
Managing Editor † ALAIN H. DAWSON
GURPS Line Editor † SEAN PUNCH

RUSSELL GODWIN † Print Buying
MICHAEL BOWMAN † Errata Coordinator
ROSS JEPSON † Sales Manager

ISBN 1-55634-413-9   1 2 3 4 5 6 7 8 9 10

STEVE JACKSON GAMES   **BUNGIE**®

GURPS MYTH
CONTENTS

About GURPS

Steve Jackson Games is committed to full support of the *GURPS* system. Our address is SJ Games, Box 18957, Austin, TX 78760. Please include a self-addressed, stamped envelope (SASE) any time you write us! Resources now available include:

Pyramid (**www.sjgames.com/pyramid**). Our online magazine includes new rules and articles for *GURPS*. It also covers the hobby's top games – **Advanced Dungeons & Dragons, Traveller, World of Darkness, Call of Cthulhu, Shadowrun,** and many more – and other Steve Jackson Games releases like **In Nomine, INWO, Car Wars, Toon, Ogre Miniatures,** and more. *Pyramid* subscribers also have access to playtest files online, to see (and comment on) new books before release.

New supplements and adventures. *GURPS* continues to grow, and we'll be happy to let you know what's new. A current catalog is available for an SASE. Or check out our Web site (below).

Errata. Everyone makes mistakes, including us – but we do our best to fix our errors. Up-to-date errata sheets for all *GURPS* releases, including this book, are available from SJ Games; be sure to include an SASE. Or download them from the Web – see below.

Q&A. We strive to answer any game question accompanied by an SASE.

Gamer input. We value your comments, for new products as well as updated printings of existing titles!

Internet. Visit us on the World Wide Web at **www.sjgames.com** for an online catalog, errata, updates, and much more. We also have Compuserve and AOL conferences. *GURPS* has its own Usenet group, too: rec.games.frp.gurps.

GURPSnet. This e-mail list hosts much of the online discussion of *GURPS*. To join, mail majordomo@io.com with "subscribe GURPSnet-L" in the message body, or point your browser to **http://gurpsnet.sjgames.com/**.

The *GURPS Myth* web page is at **www.sjgames.com/gurps/books/myth**.

Page References

Any page reference that begins with a B refers to *GURPS Basic Set, Third Edition Revised;* e.g., p. B144 refers to page 144 of *Basic Set.* CI refers to Compendium I, CII to Compendium II, G to Grimoire, M to Magic, P to Psionics, and UN to Undead. For a full list of abbreviations, see p. CI181 or **www.sjgames.com/gurps/abbrevs.html**.

Introduction

Let's be honest. At its core, roleplaying's about indiscriminately whacking things. We can layer all the verisimilitude that we like onto our core rules; we can tear apart the motives and ethics of dungeon-crawling; we can draw lines between "real" roleplaying and "munchkins." It doesn't matter; people don't enter imaginary worlds to accept the same social bonds with which real life enwraps us. They do so to explore shattering those bonds without risking jail in the process.

Designers of computer roleplaying games understand this. Even as their products lead more and more players into more and more fantasies, behind all the accelerated graphics and elaborate polygon models the majority still possess a simple core concept: Here's the target. It's shooting back.

GURPS grew out of a set of arena-combat rules (here's the target), but has spent the rest of its life not looking back. For the most part *GURPS* embraces verisimilitude,

sophistication . . . restraint. There's nothing wrong with this, but it's good to revisit the roots, to remember what it is that brought most of us into this pastime in the first place.

We can't think of a better setting to do that in than the no-holds-barred world of *Myth: The Fallen Lords* and *Myth II: Soulblighter*. It embraces what it is – a fantasy free-for-all – with charm and a wink. It's dark and epic, but grimly comic at times. The ghouls are cool, the hardware hardcore, and the setting unsettling. It's hack and slash at its finest and funnest.

Then there's *Fear* and *Loathing*, the character and map editors for *Myth II*. These are simply the sexiest and most exciting tools to hit roleplaying in a long time. We think tools like these will define 21st-century roleplaying, that the literate end of the hobby represented by *GURPS* will synthesize with the computer end represented by *Myth* through GM-level controls such as these. We know *GURPS* players are sophisticated enough to use them. We just had to introduce you.

There's two good reasons for this book. Here's one more: If you're a *Myth* fan new to *GURPS* upon opening this book, let me be the first to welcome you. We have an exciting game system that allows you to tweak your character to your heart's content, then 'port him to a starship, the Battle of Hastings, or Victorian London with nary a blink. This book and the free rules at **www.sjgames.com/gurps/lite/** should get you started.

About Bungie

Based in Chicago, Bungie Software is a leading developer and publisher of games for Windows, Macintosh, and other computer platforms. Learn more about Myth and Bungie's latest offerings at **www.bungie.com**.

About the Author

Gene Seabolt has filled many production and administrative roles as a Steve Jackson Games employee. He lives in Austin, TX, with his wife, Lee, and son, Shane. He rarely makes public appearances without an extensive entourage.

I. The World of Myth

There are laws that govern the workings of the universe that have remained immutable for countless aeons. According to these laws, the forces of Light and Dark hold dominion over the world successively, the land belonging in turn to men, or to monsters.

ELVENS HAVE LEFT THE BUILDING

The Myth setting lacks a few stock fantasy features, most prominently Elves. This denies that one player in every roleplaying group the chance to act over-the-top fey, and is no accident of omission.

The cultural backdrop and dynamics of Myth deliberately ignore many fantasy staples that the designers found disagreeable. Along with Elves, creatures not seen in Myth include Goblins, likely because little, clever creatures have no business mixing it up with the big boys. Also omitted are Golems and Elementals, which in most settings have all the personality of dirt (admittedly sort of appropriate for the Golems and Earth Elementals . . .).

Cunning Trolls staging puzzles won't be found, either. And while the lowliest NCO needs excellent tactics to survive long in Myth, both computer games lack the puzzles-for-their-own-sake that thrive in many of their contemporaries. Perhaps the evil overlords of Myth know better than to build intricate death traps to show off how smart the heroes are with the intention of showing off how clever the evil overlord is.

Something else that won't be found in Myth is bad poetry. Presumably, centuries ago the Myrkridia ate all the bards traveling from town to town, bards started settling down in one place, the residents of those places realized how awful their fare was on hearing it for the 17th time in a week, and they kicked the bards out to take their chances on the road again . . .

Individual GMs may feel free to introduce any of these elements into their own Myth campaigns, of course. The above merely serves to illustrate the original mind frame in which Myth was developed. Its cultural roots have far more to do with the Black Company than the Lord of the Rings.

Each cycle would be presaged by the appearance of a great comet, foretelling the rise of savior or destroyer. Each golden age would give way to one of darkness, when foul things would stir beneath the earth, and evil spirits would plague the land. In turn, each Dark age would fall to one of Light; the evil would pass from the land just as the comet from the sky.

– from the lore of Myth

Setting the Tone

Myth takes place on a continent with no name, a land with a central, easily grasped agenda: The forces of Light grapple with the forces of Dark in a cyclical, epic struggle for control over all of the known world.

For untold centuries the upper hand in this struggle has exchanged places in 1,000-year cycles. Dozens of generations suffer under the terrors of the dark and undeath (or the choking laws of civilization) till a fiery comet heralds the arrival of a new champion. He leads his forces into a war of conquest that escalates into a sort of renewable armageddon, blasting the opposition back into the core territories from which they sprang and ushering in a new age, 1,000 years in which his formerly oppressed races become the oppressor. Till the comet next arrives.

This much is known by all. This destiny shapes the inhabitants of Myth into warriors without qualms. Most don't question their motives because the motive is to overcome or die – or, worse yet, suffer tyranny. There are no sidelines in Myth. To suggest diplomacy, an attempt at peaceful coexistence, in this ageless struggle would be to gain the reputation of an amusing madman. The struggle is destiny – the very reason for existence. How could it possibly maintain such a regular rhythm if it were not so? In Myth, man was born to take up arms and rarely die in bed.

At the same time, a sense of dark humor can punctuate the proceedings. After all, the outcome of these end-of-epoch cataclysms is preordained. Light or Dark will win in its turn despite the individual fortunes of lowliest swordsman or mightiest Trow. Far too often, the best a combatant can hope for is a death of the quick and painless sort. To make a difference would be to cross blades with destiny itself.

Or would it? A kernel of doubt must exist, for men and monsters still take up weapons though destiny says their cause is lost, or – harder still – destiny says their cause will prevail and they risk becoming a casualty who will reap no rewards. Perhaps even destiny can be overcome with stout enough heart and arm . . .

As the Smoke Clears

At present, the world of Myth is recovering from the latest epoch-changing confrontation between Light and Dark – the Great War waged just over six decades ago – as well as a Dark lieutenant's unprecedented return, thrown back just one year ago.

The Light has prevailed in both wars, though it has been a near thing in each case. The original Dark lord – Balor the Leveller – is destroyed and his lieutenant – the bloodcurdling Soulblighter – has shared his fate. A hard-earned peace and prosperity seem the immediate outlook, if one can overlook one simple detail.

It wasn't the Light's turn to win.

THE LIGHT

The saviors of each golden age were men who had risen to face the Dark and never turned away. They were men of unflinching heroism who would not rest until they had loosened the bloodless grip of wicked things which had dominated their lands. Many of these heroes were doomed to return in the following age as Fallen Lords, destroying all they had fought so hard to preserve.

– from the lore of Myth

The Light is the cause of life, civilization, prosperity, and law – though rarely all at once. It forms a coalition of societies – some uncivilized, some chaotic and undisposed toward the rigid self-discipline of law, and some as prone to wage war on their own time as in service against the Dark. The Light could form no "party platform" without at least one society or race in its coalition objecting to each item within it.

The forces of Light have their differences, but set them aside for the common good when the Dark threatens. Even the most stubborn understand that piecemeal they represent nothing more than prey.

Races and Units

Humans and Dwarves form the backbone of the Light, humans by virtue of their numbers and the relatively few Dwarves with their expertise in explosives.

The primary human military force is the Legion, ordinary Warriors (see p. 76) with crack training who understand (if not always accept) that their duty often includes paving other units' victories with their lives. They often work in tandem with Bowmen (see p. 71) who employ irregular tactics. The warlike, barbarian Berserks (see p. 70) provide a ferocious punch. The Heron Guards (see pp. 73-74) form an elite force, though in the Great War they served as healing support in their penitent role as Journeymen.

The Dwarves (see pp. 38-39) use their pyrotechnic weapons exclusively, though they once wielded traditional melee weapons.

A few other groups and races – the Warlocks (see p. 75), the all-but-human fir'Bolg (see p. 71), and the reclusive Forest Giants (see pp. 42-43) primary among them – embrace Light's cause as it suits them, but when push comes to shove it's the selfless human forces and fearless Dwarves that the Light depends upon to carry the day.

Society

For much of recent history the Light was led by the Avatara (see pp. 97-98), a circle of archmages of whom the most powerful was Alric. Alric has revived the Cath Bruig empire (see p. 13) with himself on its throne. The empire encompasses most of

(see p. 76) ... (see p. 71) ... (see p. 70) ... (see pp. 73-74) ... (see pp. 38-39) ... (see p. 75) ... (see p. 71) ... (see pp. 42-43) ... (see pp. 97-98) ... (see p. 13)

GOOD VS. EVIL

Order vs. chaos, light vs. dark – under any sobriquet Myth has embraced the standard device for conflict employed by most fantasy genres. It offers many advantages: The good/order/light guys can slash away at the evil/chaotic/dark minions without remorse or self-incrimination. (And vice versa, though presumably the bad guys don't get to feel as smug afterward. Sometimes they do enjoy better looting.) This becomes even more convenient in a setting such as Myth, where each side can pretty much always identify the other on sight.

While the cataclysmic clashes ending/beginning each age usually should be played straight-up in this fashion, the Myth setting offers a variety of opportunities for more morally ambiguous conflict. The Light includes many races that don't get along all that well, especially now that the Trow have left their allegiances in doubt. Even when united under some awesome dark lord, the forces of Dark skirmish among themselves as vigorously as they would against Light.

An interesting cultural note is that neither side displays overwhelming self-righteousness in its cause. The Heron Guards represent the closest thing to a holy order of knights in Myth, but their recorded comments have little to do with "crusades" or "infidels" and mostly portray the Dark as a more-than-respectable threat which they're fortunate to have dodged this time. The Dark doesn't spout off about "entropy" or "decadent civilization" – it's mostly too busy doing to be philosophizing.

The only culture smacking of self-assessed superiority is the Trow, who also represent perhaps the one truly neutral society in Myth. They simply look down on anything non-Trow.

GMs may feel free to introduce insufferable paladins and evil overlords spouting twisted Darwinism as they wish, but the general undercurrent in Myth is that everyone realizes the other side does what it does simply because that's what they are. Proselytisation and sermons just waste time when extermination is the only real cure . . .

Religion

The inhabitants of Myth practice many religions. Most of these are polytheistic, springing from a core set of legends shared by many races.

In these legends, before the world there existed the dark gods. Today only the Ghôls remember their names and still offer them bloody sacrifices.

The world began with an epic battle between two gods, Wyrd and Nyx. Wyrd created the world, but the battle left a wound in his work, the huge volcano Tharsis (see p. 11). To this day the Trow choose to worship the "loser" in this conflict, Nyx, perhaps reflecting their judgment of Wyrd's craftsmanship.

Thinking that Wyrd tricked them, the dark gods beheaded Wyrd's son, Segoth. His head was preserved such that it will never die, nor lose its power of speech . . .

Wyrd drew his power from the One Dream, which remains the goal of any self-respecting archmage in Myth (see pp. 95-96). Most races think of the known regions (portrayed in the map on p. 10) as defining the field of Wyrd's vision when he first awoke from the One Dream. Everything beyond that doesn't really exist, because Wyrd could not see it.

The legends differ at this point, but apparently the dark gods (also referred to as the old gods) finally gained their revenge on Wyrd himself. They shattered the One Dream into the Forty-Nine Dreams of Wyrd and scattered them across the world of Myth. Rune Stones mark these sites, and desecrating or destroying one would cause that fragment of the dream to be forever lost.

It's unclear whether the Ghôls' gold idol to the dark gods – called Crom Cruach by humans – also serves as one of these Rune Stones. What is known is that the Ghôls sacrifice children there to beg favor from the dark gods. Its location is not known among humans or Dwarves, either of whom would mount a great effort to destroy it in vengeance for this bloody ritual.

Spirit worship isn't common, but does exist in isolated examples. The bre'Unor (see pp. 36-37) display fanatical devotion to the profane b'Y'laggo.

Continued on next page . . .

the lands of humanity, stretching east from Tandem on the northwestern and Covenant on the southwestern shores, to the Dire Marsh in the northeast and dwarven lands in the southeast. (See map on p. 10.)

The empire practices feudalism, recognizable from medieval examples but with a stronger emperor and weaker nobility. Historically, the affluent Province has possessed its own king, based in Madrigal and not always answering to the emperor in Muirthemne. Currently Alric holds both titles.

The empire's people primarily practice agriculture, with the vast majority farming in the interior or fishing on the coasts.

On parchment, these lands include the two great forests The Ermine and Forest Heart (see p. 15). In practice, the new Cath Bruig's law penetrates the arbors as little more than sound suggestion. The fir'Bolg practice their own tribal society and the Forest Giants lead simple lives untouched by anything resembling government. The

Berserks enjoy similar inaccessibility. They maintain a tribal community stretching along the mountainous northern coast. Their fishing, farming, and raiding is little touched by imperial administration.

The Dwarves are rebuilding their own kingdom once centered on Stoneheim and Myrgard (see p. 14). It maintains close contact with Cath Bruig.

The Dark

. . . and the gates of the Underworld will be torn asunder to let the hungry dead spill forth and eat the living.

– from the lore of Myth

The Dark represents rapine and rage, death and destruction. Its forces include the mindless undead, self-aware undead, living races too reprehensible for redemption, and a few races and human outcasts who haven't been able to reach an accord with the existing Light societies.

The Dark suffers roughly the same internal discord as the Light; outlooks actually differ more than with the Light, but the fact that most anything goes balances this out. Though motives vary from simple churlishness to obsessive quests to destroy the world, Dark forces all have evil in common.

Races and Rank Things

The Dark encompasses so many creatures that no one sort predominates as humans do in the Light. The undead form the largest component in its forces. Thralls (see pp. 62-63) provide a backbone of melee troops around which work the Soulless (see pp. 58-59) with their putrid spears and the Wights (see pp. 66-67) with their the-second-time's-the-charm suicidal forays. Ghasts (see pp. 44-45) provide the cannon fodder, Stygian Knights (see pp. 60-61) the heavy infantry, and Shades (see pp. 54-55) the wizardly support arm. Shadows (see pp. 56-57) are a form of ghostly undead.

Living creatures working alongside the decaying cohorts include the long-limbed Ghôls (see pp. 46-47) and low-browed Mauls (see pp. 48-49). Priestesses plucked from another dimension, the Fetch (see pp. 40-41) provide literal shock troops. More ferocious and fearsome than all are the Myrkridia (see pp. 50-51).

The line between life and death can blur in service to the Dark. Rumors have it the mysterious bre'Unor (see pp. 36-37) are more undead than alive. The profane Myrmidons (see pp. 52-53) gave up life itself in exchange for a grim immortality.

Perhaps most contemptible of all are the human Brigands and Dark Archers (see p. 72) who have gone over to the Dark.

Finally, loom the mighty Trow (see pp. 64-65), whose allegiance shifted to the Light but has now expired, leaving their status uncertain.

Anti-Society

The Dark rarely governs. Some Dark lords, such as Balor, have seemed to desire an iron-fisted rule, but even those who won their war have lost that battle and died in the process of securing a chaotic Dark reign. Other Dark leaders such as Soulblighter have sought nothing more than destruction.

Among themselves, Ghôls and Mauls possess rough tribal societies. The Ghôls are defying the Dwarves at Stoneheim and all points around Myrgard. (See map on p. 10.) The Mauls wander northeast of the Dire Marsh (see p. 16), toward their homeland the Blind Steppe (see p. 17). Bands of Ghôls range far from home on raids, and pockets of disoriented Mauls may still be encountered far west of their usual haunts.

The Myrkridia now practice nothing more than running in packs. Though they once overran all the continent, they now are few in number and far less organized. Despite having been all confined to the Tain (see p. 85) at one point, the survivors may once again be found just about anywhere. They advanced along all fronts in Soulblighter's campaign, and without really meaning to a pack of Myrkridia can roam 100 leagues between two full moons.

The Fetch probably have a perverse but sophisticated culture in their home dimension; too few exist on this plane to form a society. The Trow retain fragments of a once thriving civilization, which they secure from Dark influences as forcefully as from Light.

Most of the undead have no concept or need for societies. The Shades might be prone to establish cancerous tyrannies wherever they might seize control. Most of their brethren simply serve their masters.

The Forest Giants practice a form of nature worship. The story goes that a human priest asked them of their faith on the last day of the siege at Seven Gates. The elder giants ignored him as is their wont, but a younger giant struck the wall of the canyon with an open palm, showering the priest with chips of stone. "The earth is our faith," he explained.

Reincarnation is a common theme. Most religions limit the potential for reincarnation to great heroes or villains, who tend to be alternate aspects of the same reincarnated soul. The Skrael – a reclusive, amphibious race found in the Deep Mire (see p. 17) – believe that their warriors who die in battle are reborn seven times, each time to avenge themselves upon their destroyer, and that each of these incarnations may give rise to seven more, and that in this way their race is perpetuated.

The only race displaying a variety of religious beliefs is humanity. Several religions based in the southern lands have become popular. Obscure cults are not uncommon, if rarely found in the public eye. Any of the elements discussed above might be found in a human religion. One cult of particular note is the spider-cult of ancient Muirthemne (see p. 13).

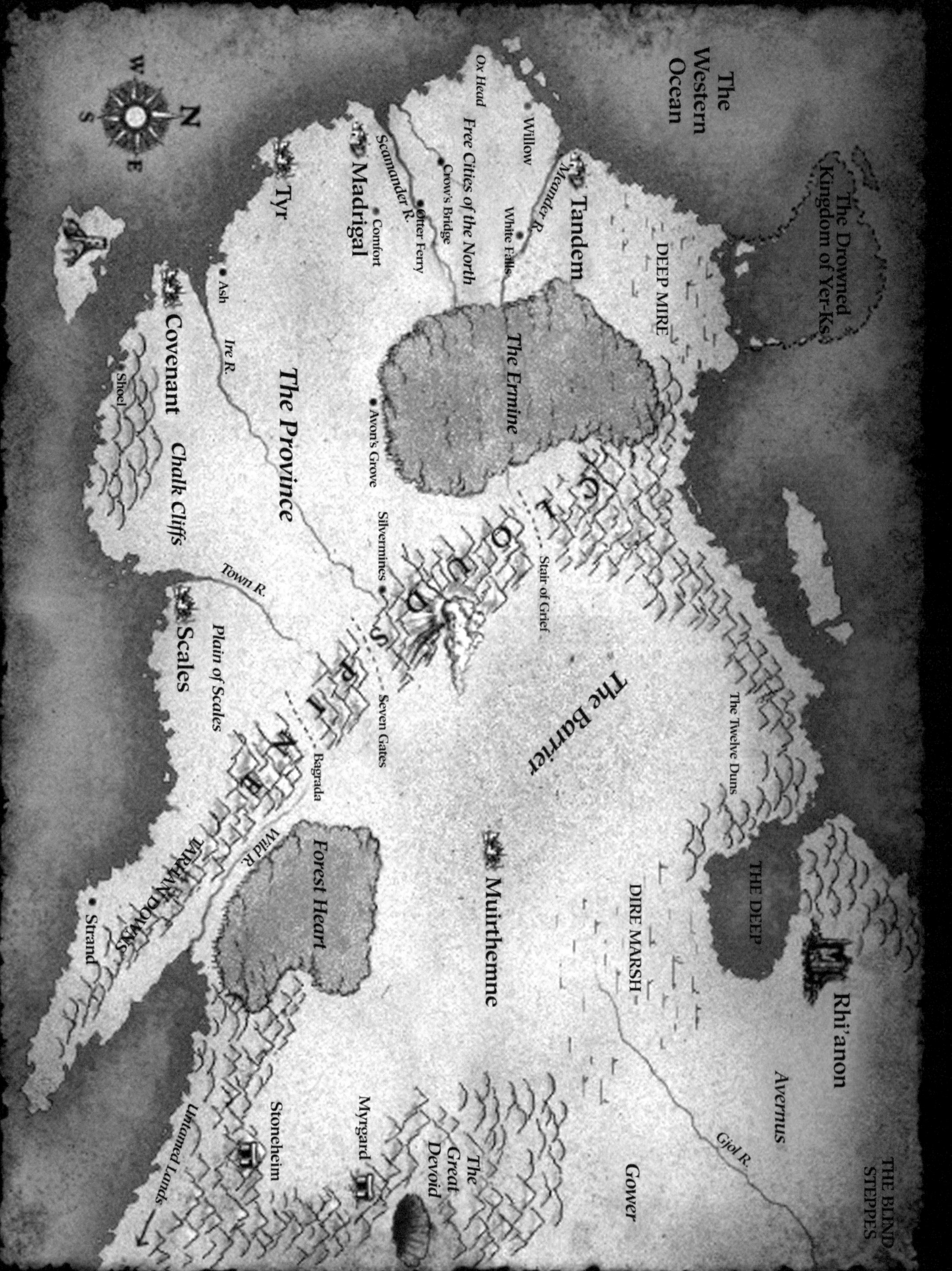
The Western Ocean
The Drowned Kingdom of Yer-Ks
DEEP MIRE
Tandem
Meander R.
Willow
White Falls
Ox Head
Free Cities of the North
Crow's Bridge
Otter Ferry
Scamander R.
Madrigal
Comfort
Tyr
Ash
Covenant
Ire R.
Shoel
The Province
The Ermine
Avon's Grove
Chalk Cliffs
Silvermines
Stair of Grief
CLOUDSPINE
Town R.
Scales
Plain of Scales
Seven Gates
The Barrier
The Twelve Duns
Bagrada
Wild R.
Forest Heart
TARRIN DOWNS
Strand
Muirthemne
THE DEEP
DIRE MARSH
Rhi'anon
Avernus
Gjol R.
Gower
The Great Devoid
Myrgard
Stoneheim
Untamed Lands
THE BLIND STEPPES
N
S
E
W

Sites to See and Sack

This is the path of the sun's journey by night.
— ironic Legion expression about eastward campaigns

The following pages succinctly describe the lands of Myth, as illustrated on the facing page's map. Cultural information will usually be found in the racial or character templates of a region's native inhabitants. These can be found in Chapter 3, *Denizens of Myth*.

CLOUDSPINE

The mountain range bisecting the land of Myth defines it in many ways. To its west lies the heart of human civilization, the rich farmlands of the Province, the timber resources of the Ermine, and the abundant fishing of the west coast. To the east stretch the now-blasted plains that once sustained herds of horses and cattle, and beyond them lurk the lands of the Dark.

At most times, the Cloudspine protects the western lands more effectively than any city wall, since it allows approach from the east only in three easily defended passes (see sidebar). Without its buffer, the last two wars might have ended differently. It also serves as a sort of score card for the battle between Light and Dark. Light is prospering when its rule extends to the Dire Marsh; equilibrium rests on the Cloudspine; the Dark ascends once it crosses into the west.

Few creatures live among the Cloudspine's lofty peaks at its center. Intelligent inhabitants number only miners and a few reclusive mages, hermits, and outdoorsmen seeking the finest falcon eggs.

The fir'Bolg explore the smaller peaks that brush the Ermine to the north, and the Berserks prowl the extended eastern range forming the northern coast.

Strand

The Cloudspine forms the Tarhan Downs peninsula to the south. The region housed fishing villages, resorts, private villas, a bit of mining, and countless vineyards. The population centered on Strand, a city of some 20,000 souls.

Soulblighter completely depopulated the region during his invasion. Resettlement has begun, slowed by pestilence and rocky soil ill-suited for grave-digging. Travelers report the stench of death has almost left the air once known for its restorative powers.

THE THREE PASSES

Ordinary travelers can only cross Cloudspine at its three passes. The easiest to cross and most difficult to defend is the northern Stair of Grief. The middle pass Seven Gates and southern Bagrada average a considerably higher elevation, but don't require a lengthy trip through the Barrier (see p. 14) to reach them.

The Stair of Grief amounts to 125 miles of bad terrain (see pp. B187-188). Use the worst encumbrance level in a party to determine travel time. In winter, it's very bad terrain. One guide for every 10 travelers must make a Survival (Mountains) roll each day, at -5 in winter, or everyone suffers 1d damage.

Either southern passage amounts to 175 miles of bad terrain in summer, or very bad terrain in fall or spring. For most of the winter they can't be crossed. Bagrada also requires an Area Knowledge roll, as it is a maze of tiny canyons named things like Fool's Pass and Devil's Overlook, for good reason. Huge carved throne-idols – their origins lost in time – serve as landmarks for experienced guides in Bagrada.

In mass combat (see p. CII119), the Stair of Grief provides defenders a +3, the other two passes a +5. Seven Gates features seven chokepoints and Bagrada has about 30 critical but small junctures.

Flying creatures able to reach 15,000 feet or Dwarven balloons can attempt to cross Cloudspine without using a pass. The trip is very cold, very dangerous due to high winds, and very fatiguing due to altitude. Few dare it.

THARSIS

Tharsis, also known as the Forge of the Trow, is the huge volcano near Seven Gates. Soulblighter met his end there.

Though never dormant, Tharsis has only erupted at the close of each 1,000-year age till recently. It figures prominently in religion (see sidebar, p. 8) as well as magery.

NEW CENTER OF CIVILIZATION

More than a century has passed since the old empire of Cath Bruig fell; little more than a year has passed since Alric declared the new Cath Bruig (see p. 13). In that interval, the Province housed most of humanity, and its king in Madrigal governed them, making him the foremost ruler of human lands. For much of the period that king was Alric himself.

Reviving Cath Bruig proper would require moving vast amounts of administrative apparatus and influence from Madrigal to Muirthemne, a challenging bit of logistics at TL3 and a move that would send ripples throughout human society. Western nobles would lose influence and access to the imperial court; eastern nobles would gain proportionately. An emperor based in Muirthemne will find it harder to keep an eye on his western-coast nobility, but he will find it easier to keep current on Dark risings in the east.

The move is not one undertaken lightly, and Alric hasn't made great haste in relocating his court the 200 leagues eastward to Muirthemne. This has prompted rumors that Alric is considering basing his incarnation of Cath Bruig in Madrigal, the city he's called home for decades. Such a decision would cause political trouble with eastern nobles, just as moving would dismay western nobles, and staying put would create dissent among Alric's wizardly allies as well. As described in the sidebar on p. 13, one aspect in which Muirthemne greatly outranks Madrigal is thaumatological history and resources. Mages serving the throne in Madrigal would advance their knowledge far less rapidly than those based in the ruined splendors of the former capital.

Some observers believe this factor alone will prompt Alric to move to Muirthemne. Until he finally and firmly commits to that decision, political intrigue, magical espionage, and even measures as extreme as assassination may take place in an attempt to sway his decision.

THE PROVINCE

Here lies the heart of humanity, the wealthiest and most populous region of the lands of Myth. Villages rarely sit more than two miles apart in its rich southern farmlands, and are packed tighter still along the Ire River. Fishing villages ring the western coast, interspersed with great cities that serve as transportation hubs for coastal shipping. (Higher priority needs can be met with World Knots; see p. 85.) The southern and western fringes of The Ermine fill the region's timber needs. Left alone, the Province's population invariably prospers and mushrooms. The region can sustain 12 million inhabitants at TL3 in good times. No one knows for certain what the current, war-decimated population is – no more than half of that, certainly.

Traditionally, a king rules the Province from the capital Madrigal. Alric currently holds that title in tandem with his throne as emperor of Cath Bruig, and of late has spent more time at the empire's traditional capital, Muirthemne. In the past, the Province's king has been the one noble who often held the power to check the emperor.

The Great Cities of Man

The five metropolises of the Province average 40,000 inhabitants each, with Madrigal perhaps twice that size. They currently are the centers of human culture and industry. Tandem harvests whales from the Western Ocean and exports the oil across human lands. Madrigal imports Ermine timber and exports finished goods in addition to its extensive governmental structure of viziers and courtiers. Tyr serves as a central market for livestock and fishing, exporting leather goods, dried meats, and salted fish in quantity. Covenant boasts thriving textiles, and Scales is a center of pottery, ceramics, and the wholesale of wine.

Their westernmost locations and scars of war provide all the evidence necessary of how closely fought the last two wars were. The Dark overran the great cities in both Balor's and Soulblighter's onslaughts, and great wards still consist of burnt timbers and rubble. In all of them, debate rages over improving the walls and other defenses. One faction seeks to forestall a repeat of these tragedies. The other insists the danger has passed, at least for generations to come.

The wars left roving bandits in the countryside, Brigands and Dark Archers who served with Soulblighter and now cannot return to civilized society. Ghôls and other dark creatures have yet to be exterminated, as well. Most travelers within the Province's interior encounter no trouble, but setting off on long trips ill-armed is ill-advised.

THE REKINDLED EMPIRE

To the immediate east of the Cloudspine stretch the plains that once served as home to the greatest human civilization ever known – the old empire of Cath Bruig. Although Alric has declared a new Cath Bruig, he has far to go before equaling the old glories – and far fewer resources to do so.

In its heyday, this vast plain supported immense herds of cattle and horses, some agriculture, and orchards toward the southern hills. A web of well-maintained roads led from all points of the compass to mighty Muirthemne, the capital, which once boasted 100,000 inhabitants.

Currently the roads – ravaged by countless legions, hordes of undead, and no maintenance – are being slowly repaired. The orchards and lush farmlands of the south are recovering nicely. The great plain itself has further to go.

Muirthemne

Muirthemne – originally called Llancarfan – prospered for nearly three millennia before Balor overcame its awesome defenses, burned it, and buried much of it beneath stone and sand.

For most of its history Muirthemne served as capital of the Cath Bruig empire. The city currently houses about 25,000 souls among the few remaining splendors testifying to centuries of dominating the lands of Myth.

The center of the city is a forum, over which still towers the golden Bleeding Tree. For centuries a grand bazaar was held there at every harvest. A dazzling array of spired palaces and monuments filled the city center before Balor arrived.

Though Muirthemne survived the onslaught of Myrkridia during the Wind Age (see pp. 19-20), the circumstances of those victories led to the creation of several fearsome Myrkridian ghosts, some of which may haunt it to this day.

For centuries the city housed a strange spider-cult founded by the Smiths, a group of enchanters who would work the weapons they created with eerie motifs. Even when the cult began abducting commoners, its atrocities were overlooked, apparently for political reasons. Finally, as the disappearances increased, Connacht (see p. 20) faced the issue and assaulted their shrines, but the Smiths and their followers had disappeared in turn. Their fate is unknown.

ANCIENT GLORIES

If all roads led to Muirthemne for centuries, then even more certainly did all magical paths of knowledge. The Cath Bruig capital served as the center of wizardly learning for millennia, and retains that distinction to this day.

Though many great libraries were lost when Balor conquered and burned the city decades ago, in the 60 years since that war ended many of these repositories have been partially restored. Teams of mages and librarians carefully excavate and sift the ashes, applying Repair and Copy spells where possible. The work will continue for decades more.

The city retains several small magical colleges and medium-sized enchanting circles. Several guilds call it home and compete for influence and resources. A competent mage new to the city would likely be courted – or pressured to join – by a variety of these groups.

Among the many quarters of the city that remain charred and ruined, an explorer might come across the home and possessions of a decades-dead mage – and perhaps below that the remains of a centuries-dead mage! Magical items might lie unnoticed among the ash and debris. Centers of magical power – such as the spider shrines mentioned in *Muirthemne* to the right – might stand forgotten and undisturbed by Balor's flame.

Alric well knows the temptations that the city presents to fortune-hunters. He has made unauthorized combing of the ruins a serious offense, and posted sentries. But the debris offers many hiding places, and the emperor's guards often hesitate to patrol very deeply into these untamed reaches of a city steeped in so much magical history . . .

The Dwarven Strongholds

Southeast of Muirthemne and east of Forest Heart stand the Dwarven mountains, home to that strange little race and their kingdom, which is traditionally anchored on the twin capitals of Myrgard and Stoneheim.

The two cities are marvels of architecture, having incorporated sophisticated mining techniques and/or powerful earth magic to make many of the buildings and public features seem to rise from the very stone of their mountain settings.

The immense walls of these strongholds withstood all attacks for centuries, till the Ghôls in Balor's forces overwhelmed the defenders with sheer body count, seizing both cities 111 years ago.

Five decades later, near the conclusion of the Great War, the Dwarves took back Myrgard. They now base their kingdom upon it and the mountains around it stretching roughly to the Great Devoid.

They have yet to retake Stoneheim, finding that their exquisite defenses perform as well for simpleminded Ghôls as stalwart Dwarves. Travelers between Myrgard and Stoneheim will almost certainly encounter Dwarven or Ghôl forces, or a battle between the two.

Those tempting fate and exploring the vicinity may discover huge labyrinthine Dwarven mines or towering waterworks . . . or their ruins in which a Ghôl ambush lurks. The constant hostilities have made both sides extremely suspicious of travelers . . . and neither was known for their hospitality to begin with. The region is best avoided if at all possible.

The Barrier

Stretching from the region of Muirthemne in a great swath to the northwest, these badlands claim what was once prime pastoral land. Now nothing less hardy or more useful than a weed thrives in the Barrier's barren soil. The ground itself gives off heat, making the Barrier much hotter than surrounding lands. Some say this is created by rare earths normally bound to their place by the net of grasses. Some say it's a curse.

Balor created the Barrier over a century ago in a great magical conflagration centered on Muirthemne and spread by the prevailing winds. Alric and mages in his service are seeking a way to reverse the damage.

Because of its inhospitality, the Barrier houses a variety of bandits seeking to escape human attention, and wandering undead who simply don't notice the grim conditions that have kept them from being encountered and destroyed.

The Barrier represents a large difficulty for restoring Cath Bruig, because roughly 200 miles of it separate the Stair of Grief (see sidebar, p. 11) and Muirthemne. Travelers through the two southern passes face shorter stretches, but all seeking Muirthemne must endure some amount of passage. For Survival rolls and general conditions, treat the Barrier as a particularly hostile desert.

The Berserk Lands and Twelve Duns

The great plain is bound to the north by a mountain range that forms a somewhat smaller (though still formidable) spur to the Cloudspine. Beyond this lies a narrow coastal region, bitter and cold but profitable in fishing and tending sheep. The Berserks claim most of these lands, and for most of history have maintained military service to Cath Bruig in exchange for self-rule. They also inhabit the large island and its smaller companions in the northern sea, known by a variety of names but most commonly referred to in the Berserk tongue as "Strainer of Kraken," apparently in reference to the fishing practiced in the narrow strait between the large island and its largest cousin.

The lower and even colder hills to the east called the Twelve Duns are occupied by the Trow (see pp. 64-65), who even now admit visitors only begrudgingly and with excellent cause. They continue to spar infrequently with the game-if-foolhardy Berserks. Most of the Trow population exists in the hills and plains to the east (see *Avernus*, p. 16), split from the Twelve Duns contingent by the Deep (see p. 17) and the Dire Marsh (see p. 16). Since the inlet to the Deep rarely freezes completely over, Trow don't appear to swim, and the marshes pose special hazards for such massive creatures, it is not known if or how the Trow of Twelve Duns communicate with their eastern brethren.

The Great Devoid

The Great Devoid is the greatest monument to raw magical potential in the lands of Myth. Located in the heart of the mountains east of Muirthemne, it is a gigantic, bottomless chasm. Balor met what is believed to be his final destruction when his head was tossed into the Great Devoid. Presumably it is still falling.

An ancient race called the Callieach created the Great Devoid ages ago to end a war waged with the Trow – destroying themselves and many of the Trow with powerful magics once they had determined that their cause was lost.

The Dwarves often explore the Great Devoid, scaling its sheer sides to discover connections to ancient tunnels and catacombs under their mountains.

Some magical theorists believe the Great Devoid reaches a finite limit in some netherworld or alternate plane of existence, perhaps even serving as the conduit to the world of the Fetch (see pp. 40-41). The Dwarves, with the most intimate experience among living races, scoff at such speculation and avow that its pit just keeps going and going and going without end.

The Ermine

The larger of Myth's two massive forests, the Ermine boasts a canopy that stretches unbroken for 70 leagues by 40 leagues. Legend has it that if a man walked from one end to the other he might never see the sun. Not that many humans can

claim to have walked the Ermine's length and avoid being branded a liar (and a bad one, at that).

The Ermine hides and protects a possibly human head-cult, known as the bre'Unor (see pp. 36-37). These Dark, profane creatures lurk in waiting for prey of just about any sort, to add their craniums to their treasures.

Constantly skirmishing with these foul cultists are the fir'Bolg (see p. 71), a strangely humanlike race. They usually avoid humans, perhaps judging them all by the bre'Unor example.

Extensive amounts of timber are cut on the western and southern edges of Forest Heart. This has shrunk the forest over the centuries, so that the land for a few leagues prior to reaching the forest from these directions is a jumble of ancient, dried stumps. Parties of lumberjacks rarely forage more than an hour's hike into the woods, and more rarely still without armed guard.

Rumor has it that gryphons (see **GURPS Fantasy Bestiary**, p. 28) make their home in the northern Ermine where it ascends the slopes of the Cloudspine.

Forest Heart

Though smaller than the Ermine, this forest still stretches roughly 40 leagues square, and if anything is even more dense and overgrown than its northern relation.

The Forest Giants call this woods home, and legend has it that their huge oaken forms are merely offshoots of massive mystical trees thriving in Forest Heart's center. No other intelligent race shares their lands, for not even the Trow dared assault the Forest Giants on their home ground. The Ghôls – far less powerful but far more cheeky than the Trow – occasionally steal into the southeastern regions, presumably in search of food.

The Wild River runs alongside Forest Heart's western edge. It cannot be navigated and defies fording. No bridges survived Soulblighter's advance, but the resettlers of Tarhan Downs have begun building new ones with the intent of harvesting wood. Historically, the Forest Giants have made this far more risky than similar operations in the Ermine.

The Mysteries of the Arbors

The deep woods harbor mystery and frightening things in Myth, but may also shroud wondrous surprises and treasures for those unafraid to seek them. Soulblighter himself located the Tain (see p. 85) within Forest Heart's boughs.

So little is known about the fir'Bolg that no one can say the Ermine doesn't hold vast fir'Bolg cities, perhaps incorporated into groves of immense trees. The fir'Bolg are known to craft incredible magic bows and quivers of various properties; what other magic they weave has eluded human eyes.

The bre'Unor also defy intimate knowledge, but are never seen to wield the expensive equipment taken into the Ermine by crusaders who seek to destroy them yet never return. Where this equipment ends up is unknown.

The Forest Giants don't appear to create much, but Forest Heart lies relatively close to regions of immense magical power. Who knows what entities dared the giants' ire to use their home as a convenient hideaway from prying eyes?

Those entering the forests should prepare for the worst. The forests themselves are considerable barriers, with concealed ravines and impenetrable underbrush awaiting the unwary traveler. Many stretches require a party guide to make a Survival (Woodlands) roll each day to avoid the worst pitfalls, with the day's travel limited to miles equal to the amount by which he made his roll. Should some ancient map be unearthed, Orienteering would still be at -5 for the short sightlines and maddeningly similar terrain features.

Beyond the land itself, any exploring party runs about a 5% chance (5 or less on 3d) of being ambushed in any given 24 hours – twice that (6 or less) if using campfires by night. If *every* party member can make a Stealth roll once during the morning's hike and once during the afternoon's hike, ambushes occur on a 4 or less, 5 or less if using campfires.

The ambushers may be fir'Bolg or Forest Giants for parties that offend them. Bre'Unor will attack anything they believe they can beat. Ghôls and Myrkridia are unafraid to prowl either woods. Predatory wildlife also stalks both forests; in particular, the wolves of the Ermine often range far afield.

Rhi'anon

The mighty Trow created the most impressive cities in all of Myth's history, though all now lie in ruins, even their capital, Rhi'anon.

The Trow sites weren't actually cities in the human sense, but rather massive temple complexes forged in iron and stone at a scale to fit the 18-foot-tall worshipers. Records of the era describe an unbelievable aesthetic, monument stacked upon monument, all dedicated to the glory of Nyx.

Directing mighty magics, the human Connacht (see p. 20) melted these superb complexes into the ice of the Twelve Duns and Avernus. Scavenged metal from these sites has been highly prized by weapon smiths, though it is now almost impossible to obtain.

In human lore, only the ruins of Si'anwon remain, sunk beneath the waters of the Deep in the meteor strike that created that body of water long before Connacht passed his judgment. The 19th canto of the *Regnum Annis* attributes to a Fallen Lord (see *The Watcher* on pp. 101-102) most of human knowledge concerning the Trow: He descended to the flooded, rusting halls of Si'anwon and under the sea there took no breath for nine days, searching the ruined palaces and temples of the Trow for the runic dream of unlife.

Since being freed from Connacht's imprisonment, the Trow have resettled the site of Rhi'ornon, in the Twelve Duns on the shore of the Deep. Balor used the site of Rhi'anon as his base in the Great War, and it suffered a terrible explosion at the end of that campaign.

Rumor has it that Trow rebuilding has begun at Rhi'anon. Since they first built their cities, the Trow have sworn not to handle iron. Whether this rebuilding would signify that they have given up that oath has been the subject of many a scholarly debate.

Anyone who could obtain reliable information on the current Trow intentions and policy would earn great favor from Alric's administration.

GOWER

Gower is a poor human kingdom, more renowned for the simple feat of survival than for any ambition. Between the Mauls to the North, the mysterious Dark lands to the north and east, Ghôl raids from the south, the hazards of the Dire Marsh to the west, and the standoffish Trow to the northwest, the citizens of Gower spend most of their time facing one hazard or another.

This constant skirmishing turns many men of Gower into quiet but competent warriors, wishing only to be left alone but well-versed in the arts of war. The greatest human warrior in history usually is credited as arising from an eastern Gower village.

Gower's inhabitants live in simple villages or hamlets. They farm, raise cattle, grow orchards, and get by as best they can. This far east, the weather can be less predictable than in the western lands, with long droughts or deluges not uncommon. Even nature appears to take a more aggressive stance with the enduring people of this kingdom.

In periods of defense, the populace of surrounding villages retires to the local lord's castle or stronghold. Often these boast nothing more stout than short, wooden walls – but Gower tradition doesn't rely on strong walls nearly as much as strong sword arms.

The kingdom has traditionally maintained cordial if distant relations with Cath Bruig, only becoming affixed to that empire when its own son, Connacht, opened a new age of Cath Bruig glory as emperor. Currently it is its own kingdom, and with the buffer of the Dire Marshes between them it regards Alric as little less suspicious than the various other hazards surrounding the state.

The Dire Marsh

This vast expanse of marshland poses a variety of hazards such as mosquitoes, leeches, disease . . . and undead. Many of these became stuck in the mire when Balor's and Soulblighter's armies crossed the marshes in their advances. Immune to drowning and disease, there they remain. Living travelers to or from Gower may prefer braving the Ghôls to the southeast, instead.

AVERNUS

This land is home to the ancient Trow (see pp. 64-65). They take a dim view of anyone so foolish as to cross the Dire Marsh or the poisonous ice river Gjol. The land grows vastly colder to the north, where the mountainous hills are covered in ice year-round. It is punctuated by frequent fog and great regions of slag iron – the once-proud Trow temple-complexes. The rivers around Rhi'anon (see sidebar, p. 16) ran red with blood during the Great War, but it's believed Balor's practices created this effect rather than natural causes.

Traveling along the northern bank of the Gjol will minimize the chance of actually encountering the Trow. Travel further north is not advised for those without good reason for audience with the giants.

The Blind Steppes

Fog shrouds this vast wasteland for 19 days of every 20. It is home to the Mauls (see pp. 48-49), who practice a tribal existence, hunting meat and eagerly awaiting an excuse to foray into warmer climes. Rumor has it that huge, predatory creatures ("Slightly larger and ever more slightly dumber than the Mauls themselves," comment a few wags.) prowl the steppes.

Few humans have reason to visit this inhospitable region.

The Deep

After the death of the gods but before the Age of Man, a part of the sun fell to earth and began to chew its way toward the world's heart. Wyrd waited two days and then hurled the northern ocean into its burrow, extinguishing the ember and blanketing the world in steam for nine years.

– from the lore of Myth

The Deep is a large inlet of the northern ocean into which the Dire Marsh drains. Trow-inhabited hills or the marsh command its shores. Every few winters it grows cold enough to ice over the narrow channel between Avernus and the Twelve Duns.

Humans seeking out the Trow often choose to travel by ship to the Deep. Since the Trow appear to practice no seamanship nor swimming, this allows a convenient exit should the exchange turn against the frail humans . . .

THE DROWNED KINGDOM

One of the greatest mysteries of Myth is the Drowned Kingdom. More than 2,000 years ago Yer-Ks was a vigorous human state, famous for its powerful sorcerers, mighty knights, and fearless seafaring. For reasons unknown a cataclysm occurred – the sea rushed in and flooded the once-great nation.

Vast ruins now slumber beneath the waves of the northern ocean. To date, those mages with the magic to reach them have shied away from the kingdom's dark legend. Whispered tales say that Yer-Ks obtained a power that threatened the Trow – and the powerful Trow used a fragment of Callieach (see p. 14) magic in retribution. Other versions attribute the same motive to the dark gods themselves.

Fisherman and sailors swear that the waters over Yer-Ks are always rougher than those to north, west, or east.

Deep Mire

This salty marsh is home to the Skrael, an amphibious race long subject to the kingdom of Yer-Ks. The Skrael inherited its "lands" when they sank into the ocean. They have since given up living in the ocean (though they still patrol the region of Yer-Ks), and make their villages in Deep Mire. They are roughly human-sized, with a long snakelike tail rather than legs, and green scaly skin.

Fortified by their belief in reincarnation (see sidebar, p. 9), the Skrael fight well on their home turf, using slings as their primary missile weapons. They fought with the Light during Balor's invasion. It is believed that they would defend Yer-Ks as their own property as well. Diarmuid's *Vieah Skrael* (Life Among the Skrael) provides most of what is known of this race.

The Acit El ("gold age") calendar, also called the New Calendar, was conceived in the Cath Bruig empire during the reign of Clovis of the Bruig, to celebrate the completion of the royal palace at Llancarfan and the creation of the imperial seat at the same location (see p. 19).

Ironically, it was not widely used until Llancarfan – renamed Muirthemne – was sacked, burned, and finally flooded during a massive barbarian raid 500 years later. The calendar was used as a tool to reinforce the considerably weakened imperial authority. The old calendar is discussed in the sidebar on p. 74.

Dates proceeding from the founding of Cath Bruig are designated with an A.E., for Acit El. Dates preceding the founding are designated with the initials H.C. No one remembers what these initials stand for.

The Myth year and months are equivalent to our own.

CAMPAIGNING IN OTHER AGES

GURPS Myth assumes that campaigns will be set just after the events of *Myth II: Soulblighter*, but GMs should consider exploring the extensive prehistory of Myth.

A campaign centered on Connacht's struggle with the Dark would feature events just as epic as those in Alric's turn, without being handcuffed by the detailed history set forth in *Myth: The Fallen Lords*. The battles fought by Tierces are even more open to campaigning, since nothing more is known than that he eventually won!

Campaigns set in previous ages also offer the opportunity to introduce new "old" races, either those mentioned in recorded history, such as the Oghres, or GM creations.

Alternately, a careful reading of the accounts of the Great War and Soulblighter's campaign reveals that much fighting took place "off stage" of the events portrayed in *Myth* and *Myth II*. GMs wanting to stage an epic battle between Light and Dark should be able to find fresh battlefields within the recent milieu.

Times of Old

The following history dates events by the Acit El calendar (see sidebar). The current year is 2542 A.E.

Scholars of Myth recognize four great ages. The first extends back several millennia into shadowy prehistory, to the very creation of the land of Myth. The last three recognize the 1,000-year cycles of Light and Dark ascendant. Since Balor, a fifth age has begun, but it is too soon for the academic community to have settled upon a name for it. Its very nature must first be determined.

THE 1,000-YEAR CYCLE

Though only three – four if one includes the one just beginning – great cycles are recorded, this is primarily a limitation of literacy. Only small pockets of humanity possessed writing – much less accurate calendars and recordkeeping – before the Age of Reason. What records do exist suggest that the great cycle extends much further back into the Golden Age of the Trow.

The Trow themselves could no doubt shed more light on the subject, but they have not yet chosen to speak of it.

INEXACT SCIENCE

On a similar note, the cycle itself does not seem to hold to a split-second precision. For instance, in the last changing of the epochs, Balor's initial invasion coincided closely, by most accounts, to exactly 1,000 years after the last comet foretold Connacht's great triumphs. Yet the comet heralding the new age – and the eruption of Tharsis which traditionally seconds it – did not appear till five decades later!

Many scholars shrug this off as evidence that the gods don't partake in clockwork timing. Others blame inaccuracies in human timekeeping and calendar reforms.

A small third group says that the unarguable and unprecedented delay between the arrival of Balor and the comet brings to doubt whether he really *was* the Leveller. Learned audiences usually greet this theory with laughter.

The Golden/Axe Age

The Trow refer to all of prehistory as the Golden Age, which it was for them, while humanity refers to it as the Axe Age, which it was for them.

The Trow claim that Nyx shaped them from clay at the dawn of time (see sidebar, p. 8). They say they watched the rest of the world born countless eons ago. A variety of races crawled from the sea, burrowed out of the soil, fell from the sky. These died or thrived, a handful reaching the ability to challenge the ageless Trow – at which point they were crushed.

Rise of the Trow

The greatest of these prehistoric races were the Callieach, called by some Sovereigns of the Time Before, mighty magic-users who came into conflict with the Trow. They realized the hopelessness of their cause in a battle that the Trow commemorated with their marker of the Red Seal. The Callieach served up a Pyrrhic victory – harnessing massive magics to destroy themselves and many of the Trow in creating the Great Devoid (see p. 14).

During the aeon of peace that followed their defeat of the Callieach, the Trow returned to building their massive temple-cities, monuments to Nyx in all her splendor. Their Golden Age was at its height.

The Age of Reason

Human scholars also call this the Golden Age of Man, although the Trow look upon humanity at this period as still a simple beast. Their inability to grasp humanity's early potential is perhaps the most important factor in shaping events to come – for the Trow never make the effort to extinguish or enslave this seemingly ineffectual race.

This millennium extends from 3,111 to 2,112 years ago.

The first human hero to emerge from the fog of prehistory was Tireces, who arose to challenge the first recorded Leveller – as all the champions of the Dark have been surnamed. Little is recorded of this battle waged in 570 H.C., except that (perhaps for the first time) the Light was able to harness sorcery to immobilize the Leveller.

The dark lord was beheaded and burned at the stake.

In 562 H.C. Tireces founded the city of Llancarfan before he faded from view.

In the year 1 A.E. Clovis founded the Cath Bruig empire. He renamed the capital, Llancarfan, as Muirthemne – though the massive imperial palace retains the Llancarfan name to the current day. At this time the Trow ranged across the known lands of Myth, but they ignored most of their "possessions." The human empire sought to consolidate these vast pockets of inattention – careful to never confront the Trow and content to take what was left.

Decline of the Trow

An older humanoid race, the Oghres, began to taunt the Trow about 180 A.E., calling them nothing more than a race of consorts to Nyx. The Trow had to realize the truth of this challenge.

Their pride pricked, the Trow responded by enslaving those races of any use to them, eating many of the rest. The Oghres resisted fiercely, but the Trow developed ironworking. With their new weapons they soon realized their inevitable victory, and the Trow began adorning their cities with their new metal, unaware that their civilization had begun its decline.

For the remainder of this age, the Cath Bruig empire carefully expanded from Muirthemne, while human knowledge of iron and magic expanded as well. The human empire formed almost an overlay of Trow dominions, ruling in all matters mundane while the Trow attended to the few things that held their interest.

The Trow slowly degenerated into slavemasters, relying on the effort of those they dominated rather than their own considerable brawn. They became even more introspective as they directed their Oghre subjects in backbreaking constructions that put even the older Trow temples to shame. They hardly noticed the expansion of humanity.

The Wind Age

This millennium extends from 2,111 to 1,112 years ago. Its name elicits shivers in most human listeners, given it represents everything the Light fights to avoid.

In 431 A.E. a comet heralded the return of the Leveller. This time he called himself Moagim. His terrible ambition knew no bounds. History has lost the name of whatever hero opposed him, but doubtless the man met a terrible fate.

Moagim, though, met worse. Even as he secured Dark's victory, Moagim himself was captured, then drawn and quartered on the plains before Ileum. Tireless horses were sent dragging his remains to the four corners of the world. This set the uneasy precedent that a Dark lord's personal fate need not mirror the fate of his cause.

In his war effort Moagim organized the Myrkridia, who had been haphazardly terrorizing humanity since prehistory. After Moagim's tutelage, the Myrkridia were too numerous to count and as war-savvy as their limited intelligence allowed. These dreadful creatures ruled the night across the length of the land – and would continue to do so for centuries to come.

The Oghre Rebellion

As humanity struggled with these nightmares, in 1435 A.E. the Oghres rebelled. For four years they waged war with the Trow, till the elder race extinguished them in the monthlong Battle of the Valley of the Red Seal, waged in the same area as the climactic confrontation with the Callieach. The Trow looked over their work and dropped their weapons in disgust at their own actions, leaving iron to the younger races.

The Age of Light

This millennium extends from 1,111 years ago to 112 years ago. In some references it is also called the Wolf Age.

In 1431 A.E. a comet filled the western sky of a world still under siege by Myrkridia. Connacht emerged from the east – from a village on the eastern edge of Gower some say, from beyond that say others.

Gathering together desperate bands of human warriors, Connacht waged war on the Myrkridia, defeating their assem-

bled hordes and imprisoning them in the Tain (see p. 85), a prison without walls that he commissioned from the spider-Smiths of Muirthemne (see p. 13).

The reputation that Connacht gained from this deed swelled his forces and influence. Striking quickly, he turned his attention to the weakened Trow – still at low ebb from the casualties and self-loathing that the Oghre rebellion caused.

History suggests that this age's Leveller chose this moment to invade the west, confident that such mighty foes as the Myrkridia and Trow would weaken even the greatest of heroes. In the face of these overwhelming odds, Connacht continued to show a talent for enlisting mighty magical aid. He defeated and entombed the Trow, and had their iron temple-cities melted into the ice of Avernus and the Twelve Duns.

The Leveller of this age – some scholars name him Moagim reborn, but others claim this is an error in copying and recopying ancient sources – stood no chance. Connacht turned the remaining Dark forces and personally slew the Leveller. He had the Leveller's body destroyed by fire, his ashes mixed with salt, and the remains buried under the legendary Mountains of Kor in the Untamed Lands.

One significant casualty of this battle was the emperor of Cath Bruig, who fell at the head of his Heron Guards. By popular acclaim, Connacht – now surnamed the Wolf, lending the age an alternate title as the Wolf Age – ascended the throne.

By then the cyclical nature of the ages had become all too obvious – and certain facts whispered of a cyclical nature to the Levellers and the heroes who oppose them, as well. Connacht's greatest quest began about 1433, as he set out to destroy the cycle of Light and Dark itself.

He dispatched his lieutenant Damas to seek out items of power – the five Eblis Stones, Trabist's Mirror, the Total Codex, and more. Damas – far less the governor than Connacht but far better the adventurer – destroyed what he could and secreted the rest.

Connacht's reign closed in 1462 A.E. His end is not chronicled, though legend has it that he feared he had not done enough to end the cycle, and wandered into a self-imposed exile.

Balor Plots

The chronicles pick up the tale of the latest Dark lord much earlier than those of his predecessors. By 2181 A.E. Balor – the latest Leveller – thrived in the east, recruiting and creating his evil hordes. Balor enticed the Myrmidons (see pp. 52-53) – once proud human warriors – into volunteering for the grisly undeadhood that drives them mad to this day.

From 2311 to 2331 the Twenty Years' War of succession was waged in the Province around Covenant. The Province emerged with its own king, semi-independent of the empire.

The Leveller summoned the Fetch (see pp. 40-41) from another dimension about 2422, bargaining with these vile priestesses in an accord still not fully understood.

His forces slowly assembled, undead and alive alike, and in 2431 A.E. Balor began moving west with his six Fallen Lords (see pp. 99-102), among them such terrifying figures as Shiver, the Deceiver, the Watcher, and Soulblighter.

The New Age

This age begins 111 years ago, ending the Age of Light or Wolf Age. Some scholars have taken to calling it the Sword Age – given the new heights of ferocity reached in this latest Great War – but the name is too new and too little used to be considered *fait accompli*.

EARLY CONQUESTS

In 2431 A.E. Balor and his vast armies announced their presence in grand style, putting Muirthemne to the torch in an immense mystical blaze that created the Barrier (see p. 14). The 24-century-old empire of Cath Bruig collapsed.

Despondent over their loss of emperor and honor, the Heron Guards of the emperor of Cath Bruig sought the way of the Journeyman (see pp. 73-74) as penance. They further developed their healing arts.

Attacking as Balor's left flank, the Ghôls overwhelmed the Dwarven cities of Myrgard and Stoneheim in the same year. The Dwarves became refugees, fleeing west with none of their arms other than the strange alchemical formulas locked in their heads.

Seizing the opportunity left by the Light's preoccupations, the pirates of Leix looted and burned parts of Tyr in 2458. Returning from campaigns in the east, the Avatara Maeldun simply stated, "Show me the way to Leix." He quickly exacted retribution.

THE GREAT WAR

In 2463 the Province led a very late coalition of Light forces into a more organized resistance to Balor's invasion. The series of separately fought campaigns finally became a Great War between a united Light and Balor's Dark armies.

Bolstered by a contingent of Forest Giants, the Light's Legion held back Dark forces attempting to cross Bagrada in 2465 and 2466, and a massive attempt on Seven Gates in 2467. The next year the Forest Giants failed to appear, and the Dark crossed Seven Gates, though all too aware of how much damage the giants had inflicted and determined to counter any future appearance.

Advancing rapidly westward, the Dark razed Covenant in 2468 – Soulblighter left a 26-mile-wide swath of corpses around the city. The battle shattered the spine of the Province's armies. Tyr suffered a Dark sacking in 2471 A.E.

Stunned and broken by Balor's ferocious onslaught, the Light scrambled to reorganize its resistance. The Nine – a circle of powerful sorcerers also known as the Avatara – took over command of the Light in 2473 A.E.

By 2476, the fir'Bolg realized they must join decimated humanity and the Dwarves. Ou'Kahn, the great king of the fir'Bolg, and Caliban, king of the Province, arranged a truce.

The Onslaught Falters

In August of 2480, Shiver and her army reached Madrigal, capital and greatest city of Province.

In the following days, the Nine found The Head (see p. 84), all that remained of an entity claiming to be an ancient enemy of Balor. It told the Avatara Rabican of Shiver's weakness – vanity. In a spectacular dream duel during the first night of the four-day siege of Madrigal, Rabican defeated Shiver, making her the first Fallen Lord to fall.

The Head sent the Avatara in search of the Total Codex in Covenant's ruins, and Alric himself on an urgent mission to the east. The Watcher followed closely on the tail of the team sent to find the Codex. A legionnaire who opened the Codex read of a man unborn who would unleash the Myrkridia and revisit their horrors on the world.

By November, the army of Light was holding Seven Gates and Bagrada, attempting to keep the Deceiver from adding his army to the Watcher's in the Province. This required shattering a World Knot (see p. 85) on the west face of Cloudspine.

At Bagrada the Fallen Lords surprised the Light with a potent, new ally – the Trow, freed from their centuries of captivity.

Anchored by Rabican's forces at Seven Gates, the Light held the passes till the snows closed them. Concern rose as Alric failed to return with his eastern army.

Treachery and Deceit

The Light learned that Alric had been captured and his forces decimated. Five heroes were sent via balloon to rescue Alric. The failure of Alric's mission caused the Nine to wonder why the Head sent Alric east – and upon rescue Alric himself said he felt betrayed.

The Final Thrust

Alric led his forces to the Dire Marsh, reaching it in mid-June. He told his men that Madrigal, Willow, and Tandem would be lost with or without them. Instead, he planned to strike at Balor's fortress on the site of Rhi'anon. Balor deployed the Watcher before and Soulblighter behind Alric, but the Legion eluded their Dark armies. Alric fashioned magical arrows from the Watcher's own arm that proved instrumental in slaying him.

By July 21 a great comet grew in the east and Madrigal had fallen. The last 2,200 warriors of Light confronted the approximately 500,000 Dark troops around Rhi'anon as a diversion for Alric, who slipped into Rhi'anon and used a World Knot to convey a small, handpicked contingent.

Alric instructed his troops to hoist a Myrkridian battle standard taken from the Tain, confident that the shadow of Connacht within Balor would be enraged by this, and the Leveller would come out to personally deal with the affront.

The ploy worked. Balor confronted Alric, who wielded an Eblis Stone (see p. 83) to immobilize Balor just long enough for his troops to cut off his head.

Alric explained that Balor had been killed before, but only to come back stronger each time. The head had to be thrown into the Great Devoid to end the horror.

He sent a party via the World Knot to the Great Devoid. Soulblighter attempted to thwart the mission, slaying the Dwarf assigned the task just after he threw Balor's head over the rim. Soulblighter fled. A huge explosion consumed the Dark contingent at Rhi'anon.

The Legion turned its attention to the area around Silvermines, where the Deceiver had been searching for his rival the Watcher's lost arm (see p. 102) since summer. They raided and seized the arm.

On Nov. 30 Tharsus erupted, turning the high-mountain winter into summer. The Watcher encircled Rabican's forces and slew the archmage and his army with mighty magics that the Light mages were powerless to counter. Seven Gates was a raging river, but the pass was to open as soon as the waters subsided. Meanwhile, the Deceiver had been turning Light troops to his own cause in his pursuit of the Watcher's arm.

On Dec. 7 the Watcher entered Seven Gates but found the Deceiver's army opposing him! The Watcher barely survived their last clash; this time the Deceiver had to flee and was presumed lost.

In May of 2481 the Legion escorted the archmages Cu Roi and Murgen to Forest Heart in an effort to re-enlist the Forest Giants. At the same time, Soulblighter entered the massive woods from the southeast in search of the Tain (see p. 85). He captured the wizards and their Legion within it.

Within the Tain, the Legion found grisly Myrkridian monuments. Murgen led a handful of men past the Tain's many traps to its exit, determining to destroy it to free the rest of the Legion. He did so, but along with Cu Roi died in the effort. Soulblighter fled with a fragment of the shattered artifact.

At Cloudspine, the Dark overcame the passes. Maeldun lost Bagrada and suffered wounds that eventually killed him. In his flight, the Deceiver attempted to cross at the Stair of Grief but was attacked by Light forces.

Back west, the remaining members of the Nine confronted the Head with its treachery, only to discover that it had recruited Light troops to its cause. A sort of civil war erupted, and two Avatara died before the matter was settled in favor of the Nine – now but the Three. Meanwhile, Dwarven commandos managed to retake Myrgard.

Interlude

After the Great War, Alric took up the throne he once abandoned in Madrigal and began rebuilding the Province. The Trow retreated to the north and reached an uneasy truce with humans. The fir'Bolg returned home and swore never to fight outside their borders again – but humans took up the bow in the process of improving their overall military program.

The Warlocks (see p. 75), ancient allies of the Deceiver and Fallen Lord collaborators from the Scholomance, heard the rumors of the Deceiver's fate and sought him out. The Dwarves developed mortars to address "the Ghôl problem," their hatred for their ancient enemy more fierce than ever.

Soulblighter Plots

Soulblighter did not stay idle during these years. About 2517 he recruited the stranded Fetch, by promising them a way home. He passed on the secret of reanimating corpses to human mages in his train to create the Ghasts (see pp. 44-45) and replace the incredible casualties suffered by Balor's undead armies. By 2527 Soulblighter recruited human swordsmen and archers for his cause.

Within a few more years, Soulblighter was ready.

Soulblighter's Return

In August of 2540 A.E., Legion patrols discovered undead activity northwest of Forest Heart. By September the undead had overrun the region, and the name of their lord was uncovered – Soulblighter. King Alric – the last of the Nine – was warned in Madrigal.

Alric sent the Seventh Legion to Scales to destroy Soulblighter's forces before they grew. He realized Soulblighter was searching for the Summoner, the man foretold by the Total

Codex, he who would unleash the Myrkridia. Alric sent troops to retrieve the Codex and outrace Soulblighter to the Summoner.

In late September and early October Soulblighter's armies raced across the Province, taking Scales, Covenant, and Tyr yet again. A survivor of Tyr told of a disfigured and enraged woman seeking vengeance on Alric – it appeared that Shiver had made an even more impressive return than Soulblighter, considering that she was dead at last notice.

Alric sent the remains of his army to Tandem. To their horror, he and the rearguard discovered that Soulblighter had found the Summoner – the Myrkridia were being released and led the Dark forces into Madrigal.

The Deceiver

In November, Alric defended White Falls, the key to Tandem. He also attempted to find the Deceiver, seeking to enlist the disgruntled Fallen Lord. A handpicked group of legionnaires stole through the Ermine to the Stair of Grief to rendezvous with a Journeyman who knew of the Deceiver's fate.

They arrived in late December. The Journeyman explained that the Deceiver was frozen beneath the Dramus River, kept alive only by his magics. The troops had to hold the Stair of Grief from a winter crossing by Dark forces as the Journeyman obtained the Deceiver's scepter. Afterward, they set out in search of the Deceiver himself, and in January of 2541 encountered the Warlocks, who also sought the fallen Fallen Lord. The Light forces led their Dark pursuers into confrontation with the Warlocks, slipping away, reviving, and enlisting the Deceiver in the confusion.

Back in the west, Shiver's monthlong assault on White Falls was broken and her army destroyed – but she returned a scant week later with an army of Myrkridia and prevailed.

Alric's Grand Plan

Revived, the Deceiver led the Light troops to the Twelve Duns, where he ultimately enlisted the Trow for one year's service to Light. By the end of February the legionnaires and their new Trow allies rejoined the rest of the Legion at Muirthemne, which Alric ordered the Legion to capture before his arrival in a week. The Light forces overcame the defending troops led by the Shade called Herod.

Alric arrived and revealed his intention – to recover the legendary Ibis Crown (see p. 84) and restore the empire of Cath Bruig to its former glory with himself on the throne. Alric sent the Deceiver and his escort to Forest Heart in April to search for a fragment of the shattered Tain – within it they could seek out the Summoner and cut off Soulblighter's access to the Myrkridia still trapped within it.

At Alric's coronation, the Journeymen threw down their coats and swore fealty to him, taking up their duties as Heron Guards (see pp. 73-74) once again. Hours later, Myrkridia overran Muirthemne and the Heron Guard seized their chance at redemption.

The Deceiver's party entered the Tain and destroyed the Summoner. The Deceiver then led them to Soulblighter's camp for a surprise attack that ended in capture, the Deceiver himself held in the huge grip of some elemental-like beast. By this time, Shiver had crushed all resistance in the west and was returning east, perhaps to assist Soulblighter in retaking Muirthemne.

The Death of Crows

The captured group of legionnaires escaped, and in a skirmish with Soulblighter the Deceiver managed to catch and kill one of the crows that made up the Fallen Lord's were-form.

Alric led 3,000 men from Muirthemne to meet Soulblighter near Silvermines, but Shiver intercepted them in the valley of the dammed Ire River. Alric – and perhaps Shiver as well – avoided Soulblighter's trap. Alric dispatched the Deceiver and a small crew of veterans to track down and kill Shiver. Outflanking Soul-

blighter, Alric's main force pinned the Fallen Lord at the foot of Tharsis.

Unable to escape because of the wound inflicted by the Deceiver, Soulblighter fled into the very Eye of Tharsis. The Legion pursued him inside on April 27, 2541, seeking to destroy him before he could destroy Tharsis and shatter the Cloudspine, taking all the lands of Myth with him.

In an epic confrontation, Alric bested Soulblighter.

AFTERMATH

A year after Soulblighter's demise, the rebuilding of the civilized lands has begun once again, perhaps the more swiftly for all the experience gained in the last few decades of evil hordes razing and rampaging.

Alric spends most of his time in Muirthemne, but leaves some question whether he will rule from that ancient city or Madrigal (see sidebar, p. 12). The assumption is that Muirthemne will serve as his future capital.

Remnants of Balor's and Soulblighter's forces still wander the civilized lands, hunted down by decent folk and the Legion as they appear. The Dwarves still face a major challenge in casting the Ghôls from their ancient citadel of Stoneheim – but nothing else on their agenda carries a fraction of the same importance. Meanwhile, the Trow have retreated in aloof silence, their year of servitude to the Light expired and their intentions as cryptic as stone.

And the scholars . . . the scholars whisper among themselves of the nature of things, of how Soulblighter represented an aberration in the cycle of Light and Dark. But was Soulblighter cause, or effect? For did not a greater miscarriage occur when Balor's head plummeted into the Great Devoid, setting off a backlash that consumed most of the evil in the land and defied the natural cycle of things? If Tierces triumphant returned as Moagim, victor of and in death, and if Balor the last Leveller was Connacht, greatest hero of all, how does the Dark's stunning setback in the Great War fit in the even greater cycle?

The scholars whisper, search the faded lines in their musty volumes, and cast anxious eyes toward their archmage emperor . . .

2. Taking on Mythical Proportions

**The world of Myth is a hard place, filled
with creatures of extraordinary ability.**

Mixing It Up

GURPS assumes that campaigns start out with PCs of equal if varying ability. While egalitarian, this doesn't well represent the average Myth party, which might include a 150-point Warrior, 175-point Bowman, 250-point Journeyman, 300-point Warlock, and 500-point Trow.

GMs should consider mixed starting-point levels for a Myth campaign. This can be approached in several ways.

Experienced roleplayers may simply be comfortable with characters of widely differing point totals. If so, the GM may want to set a minimum of 200 points, but allow those wanting to play more-powerful archetypes the cost of their racial and/or character templates plus 30 points or so.

Other roleplayers – perhaps just as experienced – will want something in return for playing little fish in a big pond. The GM might simply raise the campaign power level to meet his players' highest need, then allow those playing low-point characters to spend excess points on powerful magic items per p. CI17.

Alternately, the GM can allow an "experience deficit" for those wanting to play powerful creatures. The players can take "negative" experience to pay for the difference between their template costs and the campaign starting level. For instance, the GM of a 275-point heroic campaign might allow a player whose character just can't fit under 350 points to take -75 points in experience to start the campaign.

Experience earned during the campaign goes toward paying this deficit before the player can spend it. The GM might allow some small fraction (around 25%) to be spent during play with the remainder paying the deficit.

This system's primary weakness is that large experience deficits will outlive many campaigns. To keep experience relevant, a GM could apply *earned* experience as a marker for overall "competence" in reputations and NPC relations. For instance, NPC mage-sages casting Aura on a 150-point swordsman with 47 earned experience points would find him more worthy of respect than the 400-point archmage who's only earned 34 points toward his -250 deficit. Each is judged according to his abilities.

Creating a Character

The following chapter describes the *GURPS* mechanics specific to the *Myth* setting. Character and racial templates are found in the following chapter.

Setting Basics

The world of Myth is TL3, except the Dwarves, who harness limited TL4 technology. Magic is common, functioning as in *GURPS Magic* with a few differences (see Chapter 5, *Magic in Myth*). The lands of Myth primarily feature normal mana. High mana is relatively common at sites of great mystical legacy. Very high mana is not unknown. Most likely stretches of the Barrier (see p. 14) and Avernus (see pp. 16-17) possess low or no mana, as may other locales.

Starting Points

Myth campaigns can fit into a range of cinematic starting-point totals, depending on whether the adventures feature swordsmen just trying to survive each day – or archmages and Trow tussling on even terms. See Chapter 6, *Campaigning in Myth*, for more ideas on campaign style. Ordinary heroes should be played at 200 starting

points. The cream of the Legion fit into a 250- or 275-point campaign. Powerful mages such as the Warlocks require a 300- to 350-point campaign. Archmage campaigns should start at 400 to 500 points. Legendary heroes, Trow, and Giant Myrkridia require at least a 500-point campaign.

For those familiar with *Myth*'s character cost for multiplayer games, the point conversion follows:

Character Point Conversions

Myth	GURPS	Myth	GURPS	Myth	GURPS	Myth	GURPS
1	100	5	225	11	325	18-19	425
2	150	6	250	12-13	350	20-21	450
3	175	7-8	275	14-15	375	22-23	475
4	200	9-10	300	16-17	400	24	500

Determine the *Myth* multiplayer cost at which you would like to play. Add 25 to 50 points (for PC customization) to determine starting-campaign points.

Female Characters

Though both *Myth* games feature male character-animations almost exclusively, the world of Myth is generally equal opportunity. Women often fill non-combat roles in human society, particularly given the military efforts and casualties of recent years. The Legion takes female volunteers, who are often hard to distinguish from males behind the chain and shield. Unless a character or racial template in Chapter 3 discusses gender identity, assume it's a non-issue.

Advantages, Disadvantages, and Skills

Some advantages, disadvantages, and skills feature special circumstances in the Myth setting. The setting requires some new examples, as well.

Existing Advantages

Many of these elaborations deal with mechanics needed to design the powerful wizards and archmages that dominate the setting. See p. 87 for further discussion of these.

Extra Fatigue 2 points/level (Spellcasting Only)

Normally spellcasters can't purchase more than a few levels of Extra Fatigue (see p. CI24). Myth waives this restriction. Furthermore, even human mages may purchase Extra Fatigue with the -33% limitation that it can be used only for magic or psionics. This limited fatigue costs only 2 points per +1.

Also see the *Extra Fatigue (One Spell Only)* limitation below.

Extra Fatigue 1 point/level (One Spell Only)

Myth mages can purchase Extra Fatigue with the -67% limitation "can only be used on *x* spell," where *x* is a single spell specified when the Extra Fatigue is purchased. The spellcaster may still use any all-purpose or magery-only fatigue to cast the spell as well, either separately or in tandem with the One Spell Only Fatigue.

A spellcaster might end up with the fatigue from his own ST, regular Extra Fatigue, Extra Fatigue (Magery only), and several pools of Extra Fatigue (One spell only). If so, he recovers any fatigue spent from ST first as usual, then the pools alternate recovering one point at a time.

A few Myth spellcasters have a powerful spell that they can only use a handful of times in a given combat, unless they come across special sources of energy. Extra Fatigue (One spell only) emulates that.

High Pain Threshold see p. B20

Some undead creatures in Myth don't qualify as having this advantage. These undead will flinch and stagger after taking damage as much as most humans do. Most likely these undead don't *technically* feel the pain from a blow; regardless, damage does disorient them.

The Myth setting is more flexible about other advantages and disadvantages traditionally held by the undead, as well.

Magery and Power Investiture

The Myth setting employs the Extended Magery rules introduced in ***GURPS Wizards***. Mages may purchase levels of Magery beyond 3. Magery 4 costs 50 points, Magery 5 costs 65, Magery 6 costs 85, Magery 7 costs 105, and additional levels cost another 25 points each; this follows the attribute-cost progression. Magery 4+ is added to spells, Thaumatology skill, and the IQ roll to sense magic, just like Magery 1-3. Each level of Magery beyond Magery 3 *also* lets the mage exceed the usual limits of a spell by one level of effect if he spends additional energy.

For instance, Magery 7 (4 "extra" levels) lets one cast a PD 9 Shield for 18 energy, a 7d Fireball for 7 energy (takes 7 seconds), and a Major Healing spell that heals 16 points for 8 energy.

Power Investiture (p. CI42) may be purchased at any level for 10 points per level, following the other rules above.

Magic Resistance 1 point/level (vs. spells resisted by attribute only)

Myth characters may take Magic Resistance with the -50% limitation "vs. spells resisted by (attribute) only." This allows fine-tuning resistance by ST, DX, IQ, or HT. An advantage to doing so is that the negative effects of Magic Resistance on beneficial spells only apply if the beneficial spell directly deals with the same attribute. For example, a character with Magic Resistance vs. IQ-resisted spells only would suffer its effect if he wanted someone to cast Soul-Rider (normally resisted by IQ) on him or if he wanted to receive a Wisdom spell (not resisted, but IQ-related). Most other spells would ignore his specialized Magic Resistance. This limitation can be unbalancing in many campaigns. In the megamagic Myth setting, it can improve the odds a bit.

Pestilence 5 points/disease

Many Myth undead inflict disease with their attacks. Since carrying these doesn't bother them, it's an advantage – living carriers should take Social Disease or Terminally Ill (p. CI84) instead. Each disease is a separate advantage – see pp. CII167-174 for inspiration – with equivalents to bubonic plague, leprosy, smallpox, and typhoid fever all common in Myth.

After battling a Pestilence carrier, roll vs. HT for *each* disease carried. Apply -3 if they wounded you, +1 if they simply touched you, or +2 otherwise. On any failed roll, you're infected. Out of combat, use the standard contagion rules on p. B133. Disease-resistant advantages protect normally.

Terror 30 points +10 points/-1 to Fright Check

This advantage – unveiled on p. UN60 – can be taken by certain races, and is discussed on p. 51. A few Fallen Lords may possess this ability as well.

in Myth. Therefore, this effect amounts to a -0-point racial feature for undead creatures.

The dormant bodies of undead creatures may be burned or hacked apart normally in no-mana zones. Damage beyond 0 HT will prevent the undead from reawakening once mana is restored, just as it would destroy them in a region with mana.

New Myth creatures may take Dependency to mana normally.

Poor Vision
-2 points/level

Some Myth races don't see well, but not so severely as in the Bad Sight disadvantage. Instead, they purchase the reverse of Acute Vision per the existing guidelines for reverse Alertness on p. CI13. This is recorded as a disadvantage.

Existing Disadvantages

These special circumstances apply to *GURPS* disadvantages. For related information, see *Raising the Undead* on p. 35.

Berserk see p. B31

GMs should be lenient in allowing players of Berserks (see pp. 70-71) to leverage this disadvantage. In Myth, the Berserk troops don't go around erupting into homicidal rages at the drop of a hat – they only do so when it counts. A Berserk PC who keeps trying to switch his Berserk rage on and off as convenient shouldn't be penalized for poor roleplaying. Despite that, a failed Will roll is a failed Will roll . . .

Dependency (Mana) see p. B31

Many recent *GURPS* books give this Disadvantage to undead or other magical creatures. *GURPS Myth* does not. Assume that Myth undead simply "deactivate" if caught in a no-mana region, but will return to life (such as it is) should they be relocated to an area with mana.

Undead without physical bodies (such as the Shadows known as the Mahir) will simply vanish without a trace in a no-mana zone, leaving nothing behind to be moved to a region with mana – *but* if the no-mana region in which they disappeared should be made magical (via Restore Mana, a nearby Mana Enhancer, etc.), then the undead entity *will* be restored.

Undead with physical bodies will decompose normally while in a no-mana zone, but then many do so in mana-filled regions as well.

This period of mana-deprived suspended animation will do no other sort of harm to the undead, and no-mana zones are rare

New Advantages

Myth is "high fantasy," with powerful wizards tossing about dragon-shriveling fireballs all day without raising a sweat. The following allows Myth mages to match that performance while using the *GURPS Magic* rules. GMs should consider game balance before introducing it into more conventional settings.

Fatigue Recovery varies

This advantage increases the rate at which spellcasting fatigue is recovered. It represents increased ability to tap the surrounding mana. In a non-magical campaign, Fit or Very Fit should be purchased instead. Fatigue Recovery does not speed up recuperation from fighting, running, etc.

Fatigue Recovery is purchased just as if increasing an attribute with a -50% limitation; i.e., 5 points for +1, 10 for +2, 15 for +3, 23 for +4, 30 for +5, 40 for +6, 50 for +7, and 12.5 (round up) per additional level.

The following chart shows the time required to recover a point of fatigue with Fatigue Recovery. Add +1 for Recover Strength-15+ or +2 for Recover Strength 20+.

Level	Time	Level	Time	Level	Time
0	10 minutes	4	30 seconds	8	2 seconds
1	5 minutes	5	15 seconds	9	1 second
2	2 minutes	6	8 seconds	10	2/second
3	1 minute	7	4 seconds	+1	×2/second

High to low mana will not modify these rates, though low mana will impose a -5 to effective Recover Strength skill. Very high mana renders Fatigue Recovery irrelevant, and no mana renders it useless by drying up its source of power.

This advantage has no impact on enchantment times. The GM may rule that spellcasters with a huge Fatigue Recovery will often "tap out" their local mana, requiring that they relocate or lose the benefits of Fatigue Recovery. Another option is to limit levels in Fatigue Recovery to the wizard's levels of Magery or fewer.

ΠΕW SPELLS

Myth and its background introduce a variety of powerful spells to *GURPS* magic.

Charge Mandrake   Enchantment

The mandrake root has long held a special place in the folklore of magic. In Myth, the root can be used for its mundane if risky medicinal properties (see ***GURPS Fantasy Bestiary***, p. 99, ignoring the magical effects described there except for the difficulties in digging it up), but is more often turned into a sort of unrechargeable Powerstone, much like the Manastone described on p. G42 but usable only for Healing spells.

An average root can store 7 points of energy; a large one might hold 10 or a small one 4. This maximum may be reached via several enchantments if need be, or a root may be "partially" charged. Once charged to any level, a root crumbles to dust when its energy is completely used up. Charged mandrake roots don't interfere with Powerstone recharging in any way.

Energy cost to cast: 2 per point of energy placed in the mandrake root. Multiple points of energy may be enchanted into a root with one casting!

Prerequisites: Enchant, Minor Healing, and Powerstone.

Cloudkill   Regular

This Air spell creates a sparkling golden cloud around the target, which may Dodge but not Block or Parry. Metal armor adds no PD to the Dodge. If the target fails to defend, the Cloudkill bombards him with thousands of tiny lightning bolts.

The bolts fire in rapid succession in perhaps a score of locations; either thousands of them do harm or none of them do. Roll 1d+1 for damage, subtracting DR normally for an electrical attack (i.e., metal armor counts as only DR 1). Then multiply any damage that gets through by 5!

The caster must touch the subject.

Duration: 1 second. Cannot be maintained.

Cost: 10.

Prerequisites: Spark Cloud.

Confusion (VH)   Regular; Resisted by IQ

This Mind Control spell causes the subject to lose all track of what he is or should be doing. The subject will stop whatever he was doing, stand still, and notice *nothing* going on around him. Even physical injury or successfully resisting another spell will only give the subject another resistance roll vs. the Confusion spell, with a maximum of one additional resistance

roll per turn no matter how many times the subject is attacked! A low-IQ subject may stand by helplessly while hacked to pieces.

Duration: 10 seconds.

Cost: 6.

Time to Cast: 4 seconds.

Prerequisites: Daze and Mental Stun.

Mass Confusion (VH)   Area; Resisted by IQ

As above, but can be cast over an area.

Duration: 10 seconds.

Base Cost: 5; minimum radius 2 hexes (costs 10).

Time to Cast: 1 second for each energy point spent.

Prerequisites: Confusion and IQ 13+.

Dispersal Dream (VH)   Missile; Resisted by HT

This spell can annihilate entire legions in a single casting, spreading its tendrils of damage for as far as men stand within pike's reach of men.

The caster attacks a single target normally. If struck, the target *and everyone within 5 hexes of him* suffer the attack. The victims may not defend, but do each get a HT roll to resist. No sort of DR protects from the damage. On a failed resistance roll, each victim undergoes an internal explosion, suffering dice of damage according to the level at which the spell was thrown.

If the Dispersal Dream reduces a victim's HT to -1, an Unliving victim explodes spectacularly. A living victim will be stunned and collapse regardless of High Pain Threshold or similar advantages, and will explode if a HT roll to avoid death is failed normally.

In addition, if the spell's damage takes the initial target's HT to -1 *and* the HT of any other victim to -1, the spell "disperses" to the location of the secondary victim. If more than one bystander was damaged to -1 HT, it jumps to the nearest one; choose randomly among equidistant victims.

On the spellcaster's next turn, the Dispersal Dream detonates again, centered on the new location and once again damaging anyone who fails to resist within 5 hexes. It will keep bouncing and detonating each round until it fails to damage a bystander to HT -1!

Those previously damaged by the spell are immune to any secondary detonations, even if they become the epicenter of a subsequent detonation. The spell only damages any individual once per casting, but a bystander who successfully resisted one detonation would have to resist subsequent detonations within 5 hexes of him normally until he takes damage.

The spellcaster only spends fatigue for the initial casting of the spell; its subsequent detonations cost him nothing and are completely outside his control. He himself can take damage normally if the spell disperses back in his direction!

The Dispersal Dream may not be cast on inanimate objects, nor does it damage them in its area of effect.

This powerful spell combines elements of the Fire and Body Control colleges, and counts as belonging to each. It has SS 13, Acc 0, 1/2D 20, and Max 40; the caster uses the Spell Throwing (Curse Missile) skill.

This spell is a dream spell (see pp. 95-96), therefore secret in nature and known only to a few archmages living and undead. Obviously, it presents game-balance risks: Cast in a packed stadium, a single Dispersal Dream could claim more than 100,000 victims.

Cost: 3 to 18; the Dispersal Dream does 1d damage for every 3 energy put into it.

Time to Cast: 1 to 6 seconds.

Prerequisites: Magery 6, Burning Death, Curse Missile, Deathtouch, Link.

Explosive Lightning   Missile

Creates a very powerful bolt with the same relationship to the Lightning spell that Explosive Fireball has to the Fireball spell.

Cost: 2 to 6; does 1d-1 damage for each 2 energy spent, plus does damage in adjacent hexes, subtracting 1d-1 per hex distant from target hex.

Time to Cast: 1 to 3 seconds.

Prerequisites: Lightning.

Item: Staff or wand – bolt is fired from end of item. Cost to create: 1,200 energy, $1,500 for platinum decorations. Usable only by a mage.

Mass Zombie (variants) (VH)
Area

This spell from p. UN41 doesn't exist in its pure form, nor does the original Zombie spell (see p. M73) – see *Zombie (variants)* on p. 31 for more information.

A Mass Zombie variant in Myth will create the appropriate type of undead creature from all qualifying corpses in the area of effect. The corpses must be lying at their place of death or in their burial site, or the spell won't affect them. Corpses in graves up to 4 yards deep will claw their way to the surface to join their master.

Undead created by this spell become the loyal servants of their master. They may only be given orders *en masse*; individuals may not perform unique tasks. If this spell is cast ceremonially, the leader of the circle is the master. (The others in the circle will be viewed as "lieutenants," and their orders obeyed, but the master's commands take precedence.) Optionally, control of the undead created in a casting may be divided up equally among circle members.

In an average graveyard or battlefield, this spell will raise (R×R)/2 undead, rounding down, where R is the spell radius. This number could halve in a noble graveyard full of stately crypts or double at a mass grave.

Duration: The undead remain animated until destroyed.

Base Cost: 7. Minimum radius 2 hexes.

Time to Cast: number of minutes equal to radius.

Prerequisites: The appropriate Zombie variant, and at least two levels of Strong Will or Charisma.

Ring of Fire   Area

This Fire spell creates a circle of flame related to but even more intense than essential flame. The circle must be centered on the caster, who is immune to his own spell. As hot as the flames are, they do most of their damage by superheating the air in the area of effect. Anyone in the area for part of a turn takes 2d-2 damage, 2d if they spend the whole turn in it. Armor – other than sealed ultratech armor or natural DR – does not protect!

Though the spell appears as a ring of burning hexes at the outer edge of its area, damage is inflicted uniformly throughout the area of effect.

The caster may move normally after casting Ring of Fire.

Duration: 7 seconds. Cannot be maintained.

Base Cost: 5 (minimum 2 hexes, cost 10).

Time to Cast: 5 seconds.

Prerequisites: Create Fire, Essential Flame, Heat.

Skull Strike   Missile

This Necromantic spell conjures the image of an ancient skull in the caster's hand. He then hurls it using the Spell Throwing (Ice Sphere/Stone Missile) specialty with SS 13, Acc +1, 1/2 Dam 35, Max 70.

The spell is handled like a Stone Missile in most respects.

Cost: From 1 to 3; the missile does 1d damage for each energy point spent.

Time to Cast: 1 for each point of energy used.

Prerequisites: Skull-Spirit.

Exploding Skull Strike   Missile

This spell has the same relationship to Skull Strike as Exploding Fireball has to Fireball. The user conjures a bundle of skull images, which spread their damage by scattering as they fly toward the target or target point.

Cost: 2 to 6; does 1d damage for each 2 energy spent, plus does damage in adjacent hexes, subtracting 1d per hex distant from target hex.

Time to Cast: 1 to 3 seconds.

Prerequisites: Skull Strike.

Steal Toughness (VH)   Regular

This Necromantic spell transfers the subject's Toughness to the caster. The caster gains +1 or +2 DR while the subject loses the same amount.

The caster cannot steal natural DR, only levels of the Toughness advantage. (However, if the caster steals the DR *permanently*, record it on his character sheet as natural DR at 3 points per level, to allow for accumulating DR 3+.) The victim must be an intelligent, living being.

The caster *must* touch the subject and hold onto him for the entire casting time; neither can do anything while the spell is being cast.

Duration: 1 day; at the end of that time, both caster and subject regain their normal DR.

Cost: 10 to steal Toughness 1 or 25 to steal Toughness 2. For double cost casting is *permanent*.

Time to Cast: 1 minute.

Prerequisites: Magery 3, Armor, and Steal Health.

Zombie (variants) Regular

Standard *GURPS* zombies do not exist in Myth, but a variety of other undead do. Many of these are created by necromancers, and each type requires its own spell (unlike with Zombie, where a single spell creates one of several undead depending on the raw materials).

The Chapter 3 profiles describe the various spells required to create the undead. Assume that the standard prerequisites, casting times, and other particulars for the Zombie or Mass Zombie spell apply unless otherwise noted.

These spells are closely related among themselves (and to the Zombie spell in a crossover campaign), but do not provide any defaults to one another. They must be purchased separately.

CREATING NEW SPELLS

Individual Fallen Lords and archmages in Myth display other powerful spells that defy description as existing *GURPS* magic, and Myth mages believe that as many as 49 "dreams" (ultrapowerful spells) existed at one time, though some may be gone and others unremembered by any living soul (see pp. 95-96). GMs or players may want to recreate these spells, or create new spells inspired by effects they've created while dabbling in *Myth*'s editing program, *Fear*.

Most Myth spells can be interpreted as a "variant" of an existing *GURPS* spell and built with the existing spell as its framework, especially when one recalls that many Myth spell-casters have Magery 4+ to explain the very powerful impact of their magic. This sort of reasoning formed the Explosive Lightning spell as an Air college variant of the Fire college's Explosive Fireball; the Fetch depend on very high Power Investiture to cast it as potently as they do.

The dream spells should be more unique – and more powerful. These are *supposed* to be far better than an average spell. To compensate, they should require at least Magery 5. (Remember to increase the conventional limits to effects. For instance, the Dispersal Dream on pp. 29-30 would normally have a 1d to 3d range, but has a 1d to 6d range given it requires Magery 6. Magery 7 would allow 7d casting, etc.) These should also require an extensive number of prerequisites, to portray the encyclopedic knowledge of magic required to grasp their essence.

GMs must approve any player-created spells, of course. See Chapter 5, *Magic in Myth*, for more information.

Status

Most of the lands of Myth are medieval in their social structure, with slightly improved conditions. Most Humans are peasant farmers, free men of Status 0 who own a right to farm their piece of land. (By letter of the law, a noble owns the land, and can force the peasant off of it should he fall behind in his taxes. In practice, the emperor frowns upon misuse of this power.)

The Cath Bruig empire forbids slavery, but slaves are found under Dark regimes and in distant portions of Gower. In the empire, Dark races often find themselves convicted as criminals and put to work under circumstances where the line between convict and slave blurs . . .

Status Table

Status	Titles
8	Dark Lord, Emperor of Cath Bruig
7	King, Ephor, Head of Church†
6	Archmage, Fallen Lord, Regent, Duke, Archbishop†
5	Baron, Count, Bishop†
4	Landed Lord, Very Powerful Mage
3	Lesser Lord, Powerful Mage
2	Mayor, Merchant Prince, Knight, Military Rank 6-8*
1	Merchant, Squire, Priest†, Military Rank 3-5*
0	Legionnaire, Heron Guard, Freeman
-1	Bondsman, Servant
-2	Criminal (not currently wanted)**; "Good" Barbarian
-3	Street Beggar, Barbarian**
-4	Serf, Slave, Undead Minion**, Wanted Outlaw**

* Military Rank provides "default" Status as per p. B22, but will not *further* increase already existing Status. A duke commanding an army keeps Status 6, not Status 8, the same as his counterparts still at home.

† Purchased with Clerical Investment, per p. CI22.

** Usually these represent Social Stigmas rather than Status. Each -5 points of most Social Stigmas subtracts -1 from reaction rolls. A high-Status person who also has a Social Stigma (for instance, a duke who also is a wanted outlaw) will *not* be reacted to at the penalty shown on this table for their Social Stigma (-4 in this example), but at a combination of their Status and Social Stigma reaction modifiers (6-4, or at +2 in this case, given a Status 0 audience and no other reaction modifiers). Those with -1 or lower Status and a Social Stigma just take the *lower* reaction penalty.

Jobs and Wealth

Given the damage caused by two colossal wars, the average inhabitant of Myth does not possess average **GURPS** wealth. Most peasants will be Struggling, or even Poor, hastening to repair the damage caused by marauding undead (and empty-bellied legionnaires). Some young Legion members are Struggling as well.

In times of peace, the average peasant might be of average wealth and boast a lifestyle with not inconsiderable creature comforts, especially in the rich farmlands of the Province. Nobles and merchants might amass vast fortunes in coin, lands, and even magic-item inventories.

Starting Cash

Characters of average wealth start out with the standard $1,000. GMs may rule that some percentage of it may not be spent on adventuring gear.

The various lands of Myth use a variety of precious-metal coins for money. The Cath Bruig standard denominations are a $1 copper farthing at 50 coins to the pound, a $4 silver penny at 250 to the pound, and a $100 golden imperial at 200 to the pound.

Inflation and rapid shifts in valuation are common. Street-level commerce more commonly involves barter than exchanging currency.

Cost of Living

Myth characters pay the standard fantasy/medieval monthly cost of living found on p. B191.

JOB TABLE

Job (requirements), Monthly Income	Success Roll	Critical Failure
Poor Jobs		
Beggar* (must appear pitiable, Panhandling 10+), $50	PR	-2i/-3i, 4d
Fireball Fodder (Weapon skill 10+), $125	Tactics	4d/8d, LJ
Forest Predator* (Combat skill 12+, Survival (Woodlands) 10+), $80	Worst PR	4d/6d
Forest Scavenger* (Weapon skill and Scrounging 12+, Stealth 10+), $100	Worst PR	3d/5d, -2i
Lowly Servant (no attribute below 7), $100	Savoir-Faire (Servant)	LJ/LJ, fed to dogs
Street Thief* (3+ Thief skills at 13+ or 1 at 16+), $100	Best PR-2	3d/3d, arrested
Struggling Jobs		
Actor* (Bard or Acting 13+), $120	Best PR	-3i/-5i, 2d
Horde Trooper (Weapon skill 15+), $150	Tactics+1	3d/7d, LJ
Peasant* (Agronomy 10+), $120	PR	-2i/-3i, 3d
Sailor† (Seamanship 12+), $100	DX	2d/4d, LJ
Tavern Bouncer (ST 13+, Intimidation and Brawling 12+), $150	Brawling	3d, LJ/6d, LJ
Average Jobs		
Bodyguard (ST 13+, Weapon skill 15+), $25×IQ	ST	-1i, LJ/-1i, LJ, 4d
Brigand* (ST 13+, Broadsword 12+), $250	Tactics+1	3d/6d, arrested
Cat Burglar* (Stealth and Lockpicking 15+), $300	Worst PR-3	3d/5d, arrested
Combat Wizard (40+ points in combat spells), $350	Tactics+3	1d/7d, LJ
Dwarven Legionnaire (Throwing 12+, explosives), $300	Tactics	2d/8d
Heron Guard† (Katana 16+, Will 14+), $70	Will	3d/6d
Journeyman* (Theology 11+, Will 15+), $200	Will	2d/4d
Legion Bowman† (Bow 16+), $100	Tactics+2	2d/7d
Legionnaire† (Sword skill 15+, HT 12+), $100	Tactics+2	3d/6d
Trow Citizen† (Trow in good standing with community), $100	IQ	3d/8d, exiled
Comfortable Jobs		
Court Wizard (100+ points in spells, Status 1+, Politics 15+), $70×Politics	PR	-2i. 3d/-3i, 5d, LJ
Elite Bodyguard (250+ points in combat-related attributes, skills, etc.), $30×IQ	IQ	-2i, LJ/-2i, LJ, 5d
Elite Trooper† (300+ points in combat-related attributes, skills, etc.), $375	Best Combat skill-5	3d/7d, LJ
Merchant* (Merchant 15+), $(Investment/100)×Skill	PR	-2i/-6i
Military Officer† (Leadership and Weapon 13+, Military Rank 3+), $100×Rank	Tactics	3d/7d, lost command
Minor Noble or Official (Status 2+ and Administration 12+), $45 × Status×Skill	PR	-3i/-5i, LJ
Necromancer* (100+ points in necromantic spells), $700	Best spell-4	-5i/torn to pieces
Spy* (60+ levels in Thief/Spy skills), $30×Best PR	Best PR	4d/4d, arrested
Wealthy Jobs		
Court archmage* (Magery 6+, 200+ points in spells), $120×Magery×Status	IQ-1	4d/eaten by demon
Noble (Status 4+, Administration 13+, land), Skill×0.1% of real-estate value	PR-2	-5i/tried for treason

Key to Table

* Freelance job.

† Room and board paid. These amount to two-thirds of cost of living.

Note on Incorporating Other Job Tables

Several other *GURPS* books have featured fantasy job tables, which may be incorporated into the career choices in a Myth campaign. GMs should note, however, that the above Myth job table doesn't compensate most professions as well as they are compensated elsewhere. This is meant to reflect the low priority that the setting gives to wealth, and to reinforce its "hand-to-mouth" atmosphere. Those incorporating other job tables probably will want to adjust the incomes on one or the other to prevent large differences in compensation for similar jobs.

3. Denizens of Myth

A wide variety of nightmarish creatures face off against the various human and Dwarven heroes in Myth.

Myth features a variety of living and undead races, from the mighty Trow to the lowly Thrall. As wide a variety of Human professions exist as well, from nigh-omnipotent Archmage to dirt-and-blood-encrusted Warriors.

Racial Templates

The following pages describe the most common races from *Myth* in *GURPS* terms. A racial template (a set of attribute, advantage, disadvantage, and skill modifiers, as well as a list of innate skills and spells, all of which are further described on pp. CI173-179) forms the core of each description.

Following each template is a "standard" member of the race, embellished with common modifications to the racial template. Usually these modifications are nothing more than additional skills and spells. This standard writeup reflects the performance of that race in the *Myth* computer games. It rarely includes more than the attributes and skills portrayed in the game; i.e., little has been added to "flesh out" the standard characters other than spell prerequisites.

Veteran *GURPS* players will notice that many of these characters are "inefficient," in that points spent one place might be better spent another. This represents both a legacy of the conversion process (as described in Chapter 7, *E-Roleplaying*) and a tool for PC creation. Applying a minimal number of additional character points to the standard characters can create PCs with substantially improved performance.

For convenience, the racial templates and standard characters both use the skill-description format used for character templates and described on p. 68.

Final Touches

The *Myth* computer games primarily deal with combat, and though their storylines illustrate various races and characters using non-combat skills, this venue of character creation is decidedly undeveloped. The GM should feel free to add background skills to the racial template and/or standard character writeup to reflect aspects of a race that don't immediately manifest themselves in battle. Some small instances of this have been completed where they provide an immediate personality hook – for instance, Dwarves have been given their traditional motive of Greedy for both their technological zeal and their seemingly callous lack of discretion in combat – but a great deal more potential exists in many of the races, particularly the mysterious and all-but-all-knowing Trow.

Each racial writeup includes a brief summary of the race's cultural outlook and society. This might provide inspiration for the GM in these efforts.

Players should be encouraged to develop new skills and abilities in their characters when using racial templates; this will provide hooks for developing that race's identity in a given *GURPS Myth* campaign. At the same time, they shouldn't be discouraged from spending some of their excess points on improving combat performance: *GURPS Myth* is still primarily about combat, after all, and survival will depend upon holding an edge over one's contemporaries.

GURPS' mindless undead tend to be as agile and combat-effective as living fighters, while carrying roughly a dozen disadvantages that reduce their point cost to a negative total. *Myth*'s mindless undead tend to be more the shambling sort, a little slower than the living, with higher comparative costs that much more accurately reflect their combat potential (if not their *roleplaying* potential) as compared to a living opponent.

In order to more-or-less cleanly convert *Myth* characters to *GURPS*, the undead had to become less combat effective yet more costly than standard in *GURPS*.

Primarily, this called for dropping a number of standard undead disadvantages. Mindless undead can improve their performance in Myth, so they do not have the Cannot Learn disadvantage. The computer games do not address Dependency (Mana), but it's been dropped in this setting; for further elaboration, see p. 28.

For the most part, mental disadvantages such as Low Empathy, No Sense of Humor, and Obdurate are considered to reflect behavior already encompassed by combining Slave Mentality with an "evil" set of operating instructions and low IQ. These are not added to a template with Slave Mentality unless the undead creature exhibits extreme behavior of the sort.

The other major design element was to give them low DX and very high skill investments in their primary weapons. This simultaneously reflects their low threat response in *Myth*, increases their point cost somewhat in compensating for the low DX, and portrays the natural result of having a sleepless, low-maintenance slave practice his craft 24 hours a day seven days a week.

GMs should feel free to adjust these templates to become more compatible with established *GURPS* undead and improve character-point efficiency, especially if not planning on conversions to the *Myth* platform as described in Chapter 7, *E-Roleplaying*. Those planning conversions should be aware that even minor changes will significantly improve the performance of these races upon translation back to *Myth*.

THE BRE'UNOR

Mystery surrounds these Dark cultists who plague the fir'Bolg and humanity alike from their havens in The Ermine. Even their origins remain in doubt. Humans claim the bre'Unor are renegade fir'Bolg, while fir'Bolg claim they are renegade humans. If anyone has put them to the fertility test, they have not confessed to it. The bre'Unor may well be neither human nor fir'Bolg, but yet a third distinct race sharing the same general features.

Another theory claims the bre'Unor are partially undead humans, suspended precisely on the line between life and unlife. Those veterans who've stuck a sword in one generally scoff at this notion.

Society

The bre'Unor live aboriginal lives hidden away in their forest home and punctuated by the violent religion that they practice.

As best as civilized scholars can determine, the bre'Unor believe that their air-spirit deity, b'Y'laggo, draws strength from the dying breaths of their victims. Eventually, the bre'Unor believe, b'Y'laggo will grow strong enough to scatter all of their enemies. The bre'Unor collect their victims' heads for use as offerings.

No one has ever come across an established bre'Unor settlement. Habitat sites that have been unearthed were located in the deepest recesses of The Ermine, and would qualify as little more than crude campsites by most standards. Elaborate altars of carved bone command many of them, and represent the one refined object found in bre'Unor possessions. The shrines usually portray a demonic figure (presumably b'Y'laggo) interrelating with several bre'Unor and their victims in obscene and/or gory detail. Examples retrieved from The Ermine often draw large prices as art objects, despite the palpable presence of evil in their nature.

The fir'Bolg swear they've never seen evidence that the bre'Unor use fire, and that the savagery the bre'Unor inflict on their prey makes a great waste of edible meat. Those proposing that the bre'Unor are semi-undead point to this as evidence to support their view, while most simply believe the cultists live on a diet of raw flesh, and likely engage in eating other sentients.

Any female or young bre'Unor also have eluded outside eyes – one of the prime facts supporting the theory that the cultists are actually human or fir'Bolg renegades.

The bre'Unor practice no technology to speak of.

The cultists have been heard to speak their own language. Most observers assume they know no civilized tongues, since they're never heard to speak them, but others insist they understand other languages, choosing not to speak them so that experienced opposition such as the fir'Bolg are lulled into speaking openly even though a bre'Unor could be stalking them from behind the next tree.

The fir'Bolg and those humans living near The Ermine usually encounter the bre'Unor in small groups. These rarely exceed 20 in number, though in war several such groups have been known to converge. Within the deep forest, lone bre'Unor are more commonly encountered.

Legend has it that the bre'Unor possess the ability to command wolves.

BRE'UNOR NAMES

The name bre'Unor itself isn't the cultists' own word, but the term by which the fir'Bolg call them. The bre'Unor appear to refer to themselves collectively by a variety of names, which aren't yet fully understood.

Some personal names that they've been heard to call themselves would translate as: Ur-Kaol, Ton-Phal, Jav-Tara, Vir-Hajas, Ten-Dihn, Yer-Tith, Nolan-Gor, Tal-Had, Tal-Hajas, Phal-Dara, Tars-Nolan, Tar-Phal, Tith-Gor, Jav-Hajak, Ur-Thuvin, Nur-Ash, Jat-Nolan, Ras-Dihn, Tal-Mors, Tar-Tith, Ten-Kaol, Gor-Tars, Tith-Hajak, Tak-Tara, Nur-Kaol, Mors-Jat, Kajas-Ur, Tal-Nolan, Vir-Kajas, Ton-Jat, Nolan-Vir, Gor-Ash, Ras-Phal, Tak-Jat, Tak-Thuvin, Ton-Hajak, Hajak-Tak, Dihn-Nur, Kajas-Gor, Tith-Tar, Kaol-Tara, Phal-Thuvin, Vir-Mors, Ras-Tars, Tak-Hajak, Jat-Tal, and Nolan-Ur.

Plan of Battle

The bre'Unor religious fervor becomes an unmatched bloodthirstiness and alliance to the Dark in worldly dealings. They seek out combat for no other reason than that it provides opportunity to kill, and they apparently support a Dark dominion simply because it would provide even more opportunity.

Despite their ferocity, the bre'Unor are cunning in battle, careful to minimize their own losses. They favor skirmishing tactics, striking from ambush and flitting away before their victims can respond. During the periods in which the Dark has been driven from western lands, the bre'Unor have contented themselves with skirmishing with the fir'Bolg and the occasional raid into human villages or farms. They seem wary of patrolling far from their forest home without a Dark army in escort.

Standard bre'Unor   200 points

A bre'Unor appears to be a normal human male, with height and weight standard for his ST. The only difference is the skull of some unidentified beast that each wears upon his head; it does *not* come off. Most scholars believe the skull is magically melded to the skin of the bre'Unor's head in some dark initiation rite.

Attributes: ST 14 [45], DX 13 [30], IQ 11 [10], HT 12/13 [20].
Advantages: Acute Vision +3 [6]; Combat Reflexes [15]; DR +2 (Covers only skull and face, but not jaw, -75%) [2]; Extra Hit Point +1 [5]; PD +3 (As per DR, -75%) [19]; and Toughness +1 [10].
Knacks: Beast Summoning (Wolf)-15 [8] and Mammal Control (Wolf)-15 [12].
Disadvantages: Bloodlust [-10]; Intolerance (fir'Bolg) [-5]; Primitive -2 TL1 [-10]; Social Stigma (Bloodthirsty cultists) [-20]; Vow (Bone weapons only) [-10]; and Wealth (Struggling) [-10].
Primary Skills: Axe/Mace (P/A) DX+3 [16]-16; Axe Throwing (P/E) DX+3 [8]-16; and Tactics (M/H) IQ+1 [6]-12.
Secondary Skills: Armoury/TL1 (M/A) IQ+2 [6]-13; Boneworking (treat as Woodworking) (P/A) DX+2 [8]-15; Brawling (P/E) DX [1]-13; Camouflage (ME but based on Survival-2) IQ+4 [2]-15; Gesture (M/E) IQ [1]-11; Knife (P/E) DX-1 [1/2]-12; Naturalist (M/H) IQ-1 [2]-10; Running (P/H – HT) HT-3 [1/2]-9; Stealth (P/A) DX+2 [8]-15; Survival (Woodlands) (M/A) IQ+5 [12]-16; Theology (M/H) IQ [4]-11; and Tracking (M/A) IQ+2 [6]-16*.
* Bonus of +3 for Acute Vision already applied.
Languages: bre'Unor (M/A) IQ [2]-11 and one native (M/A) IQ [0]-11.
Customization Notes: Many bre'Unor will have lower Wealth, but a significant portion will retain loot from former victims that technically makes them affluent. Regardless, their choice of arms and no armor appears to be a religious Vow. If the bre'Unor are renegade humans or fir'Bolg, a bre'Unor PC likely will exceed the campaign's disadvantage cap. The GM should consider waiving the cap in this instance. Bre'Unor as renegades allows adding just about any imaginable skill as experience gained prior to joining the cult.

Equipment

The bre'Unor wear no armor other than the greatskulls permanently adorning their heads. In battle they wield the jawbones of large carnivores that they have killed, carefully selected for durability and sharpened to a razor edge on every suitable surface. These are treated as cheap axes doing -1 damage (2d+1 cutting in the above example) and shattering twice as often in combat (if a 1-in-6 chance is called for, they break on 2-in-6, and so on). A bre'Unor typically carries five or six jawbones into battle.

AFTER several days of noticing lone wolves urgently scouting about, the PCs traveling near or through the Ermine receive a startling visitor – a single bre'Unor, unarmed and injured. If allowed to keep breathing, he indicates through crude gestures that he wants the PCs to follow him with great haste. When the opportunity presents itself, he'll communicate that he wants to leave the bre'Unor cult and enter civilization. He offers humanity's first real opportunity to see into the inner workings of the cult. Of course, every bre'Unor in the area is fervently hunting their renegade – and now the PCs as well . . .

THE PCs enter a remote village near the Ermine only to discover the bre'Unor have just left – and taken away all the young girls, alive and unharmed at last sight. The villagers despair to think of the bre'Unor intentions, but most of their able-bodied men already lie dead or dying from the raid. A band of determined mothers has begun arming themselves as the PCs arrive . . .

BRE'UNOR PCS

A bre'Unor really has few redeeming qualities unless the campaign is centered on Dark characters. In a Dark campaign, they probably should be one of the more *pragmatic* characters. Unlike most of their contemporaries, the bre'Unor don't slay for fun, out of a sense of rage, or to mindlessly comply with orders. They slay to gather heads for their religious rites, and they're fully aware that getting killed will play havoc with their quota.

Something to keep in mind is that the average bre'Unor isn't so much a warrior as a hunter. They'd much rather stalk than frontally assault.

In a campaign where bre'Unor are renegade humans or fir'Bolg, a fascinating PC might be built based upon the character's experiences before initiation – especially as they relate to his current status as a loathed cultist. A former cleric turned bre'Unor might have difficulty keeping up the grisly standards of his new fraternity.

Dwarven Technology

The Dwarves are the sole culture to have advanced to TL4 in Myth. They are, in fact, dabbling at TL5, as befits a race of gadgeteers.

Dwarven advancements have made only a small impact on the world of Myth at large. Dwarves do make TL4 firearms, though being Nearsighted they have almost no use for long-range weapons of their own.

They export a small number of firearms to allied Human concerns, but interest in muskets has not nearly met Dwarven expectations. Part of this stems from a few regrettable, drunken incidents in Human testing of the new weapons, but mostly it reflects a world in which wizards routinely wield fireballs and lightning capable of ruining a black-powder-laden soldier's day. Dwarven cannons have been greeted a bit more enthusiastically.

Humans have shown more interest in the Dwarven research into lighter-than-air flight. The Dwarves are perfecting hot-air and hydrogen balloons, with intent to aerially bombard Stoneheim's defenders (see sidebar, p. 14).

Steam-driven Da Vinciesque tanks and similar fare are certainly within Dwarven potential.

Dwarven Names

Examples include: Bui, Brami, Hrani, Barri, Durin, Alfrigg, Dvalin, Berling, Grerr, Solblindi, Uni, Iri, Bari, Var, Vegdrasil, Ori, Delling, Ivaldi, Brokk, Eitri, Baugi, Tind, Haddings, Soli, Nori, Jar, Jari, Vnarin, Ari, Eri, Telling, Felling, Gilling, Duri, Trakk, Ivoldi, Norling, Solling, Varling, Jvalin, Badi, Tadi, Abi, Ebi, and Sak.

Dwarf

Foremost among non-Human defenders of the Light, these little mechanics bring powerful weapons – and a disturbing disregard for collateral damage – to the fight for truth, justice, and the peaceful pursuit of obscene profits.

Society

Before the wars, the Dwarves inhabited the mountains around Myrgard and Stoneheim, ruled by their twin ephors (seen by Humans as city-state kings). Their social structure, little understood by Humans, more resembled that of a guild than a nobility. The Ghôls claimed footholds only in the north.

The Dwarves busied themselves with mining and technological innovation. Always hungry for material wealth, they understood that their inventions would ultimately increase their worth far beyond what an ordinary pick can gouge out of the earth. Lately, they've grown fascinated with their technology for its own sake as well. Devices delight them, though not so much as wealth.

Since the wars, many Dwarves have re-established themselves around Myrgard. Others have decided to settle in the Human west to which they fled as refugees. West or east, they all want Stoneheim back *badly*. It's too great an investment to write off.

Dwarf Racial Template   122 points

Dwarves average 2′ shorter than a human of the same ST, but weigh 30 more pounds. Males are all bearded. Their hair tends to turn gray early in their lives, perhaps as a result of spending too much time around high explosives. They can take a *lot* of punishment . . . but tend to receive it in their usual place in the Light's vanguard.

Dwarves born without the racial nearsightedness get groomed for the relatively new mortar troops; nimble individuals with magical aptitude often become Pathfinders.

Attribute Modifiers: ST +3 [30], IQ +1 [10], HT +2 [20].

Advantages: Extended Lifespan +1 [5]; Extra Encumbrance [5]; Extra Hit Points +7 [35]; Gadgeteer [25]; High Technology +1 [20]; and Literacy [10].

Disadvantages: Bad Sight (Nearsighted) [-25]; Callous [-6]; Greed [-15]; Intolerance (Ghôls) [-5]; and Reduced Move -1 [-5].

Quirks, Features, and Taboo Traits: Cannot learn Climbing skill [-0].

Skills: +3 to all Craft skills [18].

Standard Dwarf Fighter   250 points

ST: 13 [0]   **IQ:** 12 [10]   **Fatigue:** 13

DX: 15 [60]   **HT:** 13/20 [10]   **Senses:** 12

Speed: 7   **Move:** 6   **Will:** 12

Advantages: Dwarf Racial Template [122].

Disadvantages: per Dwarf Racial Template.

Skills: Armoury/TL4 (M/A) IQ+4 [4]-16*; Axe/Mace (P/A) DX-1 [4]-14**; Blacksmith/TL4 (M/A) IQ+3 [2]-15*; Engineer/TL4 (Bombs and Traps) (M/H) IQ [4]-12; Engineer/TL4 (Mining) (M/H) IQ+3 [10]-15; Mechanic/TL4 (Common magical devices) (M/A) IQ+3 [2]-15*; Parachuting (P/E) DX [1]-15; Piloting/TL5 (Lighter-than-air) (P/A) DX-1 [1]-14; Prospecting (M/A) IQ+1 [4]-13; Tactics (M/H) IQ-2 [1]-10; Thaumatology (M/VH) IQ-2 [2]-10; Throwing (P/H) DX+1 [8]-16; and Traps/TL4 (M/A) IQ+1 [4]-13.

* Bonus of +3 from racial template already applied.

** Penalty of -2 for Nearsightedness already applied.

Languages: Bruig (M/A) IQ-1 [1]-11 and Dwarven (M/A) IQ [0]-12.

Equipment: Backpack containing 40 Dwarven cocktails and 4 satchel charges.

Standard Mortar Dwarf
275 points

ST: 13 [0] **IQ:** 12 [10] **Fatigue:** 13
DX: 14 [45] **HT:** 14/21 [20] **Senses:** 12
Speed: 7 **Move:** 6 **Will:** 12

Advantages: Racial Template *minus* Bad Sight [147].
Disadvantages: per Dwarf Racial Template.
Skills: Armoury/TL4 (M/A) IQ+4 [4]-16*; Axe/Mace (P/A) DX [2]-14; Blacksmith/TL4 (M/A) IQ+3 [2]-15*; Engineer/TL4 (Bombs and Traps) (M/H) IQ [4]-12; Engineer/TL4 (Mining) (M/H) IQ+3 [10]-15; Gunner/TL4 (Mortar) (P/A) DX+3 [4]-17†; Mechanic/TL4 (Common magical devices) (M/A) IQ+3 [2]-15*; Parachuting (P/E) DX+1 [2]-15; Piloting/TL5 (Lighter-than-air) (P/A) DX [2]-14; Prospecting (M/A) IQ+1 [4]-13; Tactics (M/H) IQ [4]-12; Throwing (P/H) DX+1 [8]-15; and Traps/TL4 (M/A) IQ+1 [4]-13.
* Bonus of +3 from racial template already applied.
† Bonus of +2 for IQ already applied.
Languages: Bruig (M/A) IQ-1 [1]-11 and Dwarven (M/A) IQ [0]-12.
Equipment: Dwarven mortar with 6 rounds of ammunition, and pot helm.

Pathfinder
275 points

The Pathfinders are an ultra-secret elite military group within Dwarven society. Other Myth races don't even realize they exist, and part of their Extremely Hazardous Duty includes keeping things that way even if it requires self-sacrifice.

ST: 13 [0] **IQ:** 13 [20] **Fatigue:** 13
DX: 13 [30] **HT:** 14/21 [20] **Senses:** 13
Speed: 6.75 **Move:** 7 **Will:** 13

Advantages: Dwarf Racial Template [122] and Telepathy Power 14 (-50% limitation, can't read thoughts; see below) [35].
Disadvantages: per Dwarf Racial Template and Extremely Hazardous Duty [-20].
Skills: Armoury/TL4 (M/A) IQ+2 [1]-15*; Axe/Mace (P/A) DX-2 [2]-11**; Blacksmith/TL4 (M/A) IQ+1 [1/2]-14*; Engineer/TL4 (Bombs and Traps) (M/H) IQ-2 [1]-11; Engineer/TL4 (Mining) (M/H) IQ+1 [6]-14; Fast-Draw (Dwarven cocktail) (P/E) DX [1]-13; Mechanic/TL4 (Common magical devices) (M/A) IQ+2 [1]-15*; Parachuting (P/E) DX [1]-13; Prospecting (M/A) IQ [2]-13; Running (P/H – HT) HT-3 [1/2]-11; Stealth (P/A) DX+1 [4]-14; Tactics (M/H) IQ-1 [2]-12; Thaumatology (M/VH) IQ-3 [1]-10; Throwing (P/H) DX+3 [24]-16; and Traps/TL4 (M/A) IQ [2]-13.
* Bonus of +3 from racial template already applied.
** Penalty of -2 for Nearsightedness already applied.
Languages: Bruig (M/A) IQ-1 [1]-12 and Dwarven (M/A) IQ [0]-13.
Psionic Skills: Illusion (+50% group effect, -50% invisibility only; see p. P21) (M/H) IQ+1 [6]-14; Telereceive (M/H) IQ+1 [6]-14; and Telesend (M/H) IQ+1 [6]-14.
Equipment: Backpack containing 40 Dwarven cocktails and 4 satchel charges.
Customization Notes: Pathfinders aren't true mind-readers. They can read and transmit only general emotions and sensory input. This greatly limits Telereceive and Telesend, and would do the same to Telescan. They can't learn Mindswitch, Mindwipe, Suggest, or Telecontrol. All other skills (see pp. P20-26) would work normally. The GM may rule which skills beyond those listed are available.

Equipment

Dwarves typically wear no armor, trading its utility for increased ammo. (A few diehards with ringing ears believe they should dust off the old plate and battleaxes . . .)
See p. 80 for statistics on Dwarven weapons.

THE Dwarves have decided that the time has come to retake Stoneheim! Every patriotic Dwarf will be called into the fray, as will select Legion units (the empire owes the Dwarves its support) and mercenaries of any sort willing to skewer a Ghôl. The massive mobilization will be heartening, but unfortunately the Ghôls have detected the efforts and the mountains around Stoneheim are just crawling with them . . .

AN inventive Dwarf has discovered an improved explosive compound for their Dwarven cocktails! He needs help in transporting a sample to the nearest Dwarven city for evaluation and full-scale production. Simple enough, except the Dwarven inventor intends to keep experimenting while on the road, and the new formula isn't entirely stable . . .

DWARVEN PCS

Dwarves make fine PCs, able to keep up with mages in body counts, prone to be a bit full of themselves, and driven by the profit motive.

A Dwarf can be played for black comic relief, constantly imperiling his companions nearly as much as the opposition and shrugging it off with a casual "My bad." Even played straight, all Dwarves think *differently.* They're traditionally Greedy, but have moved on to TL4 concepts such as "risk vs. reward" and "return on investment." Since lives matter less than bottom lines, they're willing to risk a comrade or two to imperil a Ghôl or 10. TL3 Humans don't always get it.

Fetch Names

The annals of the Great War and Soulblighter's return record no personal names for these beings. Some claim the Fetch keep these secret so as to avoid giving Human sorcerers great power over them. Others observe this makes little sense in light of all the evidence that suggests the Fetch *want* to go home.

Fetch PCs

The Fetch wield great power, and are far more easily handled as NPCs than PCs. Still, in a high-powered campaign with less-than-noble teammates, a Fetch might be made to fit in. Her utterly corrupt reputation would make her the enemy of just about every sentient she encountered, but if that's the player's preference, so be it.

Theoretically, the PC Fetch could be reformed, or at least on that path, seeking to work peacefully with forces of Light to find a way home. This should be roleplayed as an immense internal conflict for the Fetch – their baseline behavior isn't anywhere close to socially acceptable. The GM would be justified in taking away some or all of her powers to work magic. This is, after all, clerical magic, and if the Fetch can still draw upon their superior being's or beings' power in a new dimension, then logically said creature(s) can observe their servants' actions in the same dimension.

Summoning Fetch

Presumably a relatively straightforward version of Planar Summons (see p. M74) will fetch a Fetch. This should cost far more than the standard 20 energy, in light of their intense magical nature and powers. The spell is not commonly known, and may well have died with Balor.

For whatever reason, Fetch are not so simply banished back to their home dimension. The GM should rule whether Banish (p. M75) does not affect them at all or can work if cast at incredible skill levels. The conventional wisdom among Myth scholars suggests that unearthing the original Planar Summons spell would give vital clues toward reversing its work.

The Fetch

Summoning the Fetch from another dimension ranked as the most unprecedented move by Balor in his millennial bid for dominion over Myth. War historians differ on whether Balor himself wielded the magics that made this possible, or whether Dark mages in his service did the work at his bidding, but the spell has been lost since the Dark lord's death.

For the last few decades the Fetch have been doomed to roam the lands of Myth, hostile strangers in an equally hostile strange land. They took up Soulblighter's cause in the forlorn hope that he would honor Balor's pledge to forge their path home, but since his death, they have returned to an exile status.

Society

Little is known of Fetch culture in their home dimension, and since they don't tend to congregate, little Fetch culture exists in Myth. All the summoned Fetch were priestesses, but likely other castes of these creatures also exist.

The Fetch universally react to all native life with hostility, simmering with anger over being stranded in this world they find so distasteful. If not under the command of a great lord, they've been known to attack Dark forces as willingly as Light.

Flaunting their power, the Fetch wear the skins of their (usually Human) victims as a sort of grisly bodystocking. Recent legend has it that they have a practical reason for this. The chronicles of the Journeyman Thirteen Bloody Crocodile record, "The Fetch wear the skins of men out of necessity, for if the eye of Wyrd were to fall on them not so adorned He would recognize their alienness and smite them." Most scholars believe the Fetch could procure less objectionable materials if they did not intend to display these horrid skins as malicious trophies.

More details on the Fetch background would greatly interest many archmages and the empire.

Plan of Battle

The Fetch serve as living artillery on the battlefield, wielding an inexhaustible supply of high-powered lightning bolts capable of eradicating legions. Opponents find them fairly fragile and easily dispatched when they can get close to them, however. If operating within some Dark lord's contingent, the Fetch usually will enjoy a screen of shock troops such as Thrall to keep foes at bolt's distance. When encountered in unsupported groups, the Fetch will attempt to attack from several flanks. Solo Fetch simply attempt to destroy as many opponents as they can as quickly as possible.

Fetch Racial Template   105 points

The Fetch are gaunt humanoids of human weight for their ST but averaging 6″ taller. Their physical features are unknown – they always appear completely wrapped in Human or similar skin – but apparently include the horns which aren't a standard feature of their outerwear.

Fetch complete their wardrobe with a long skirt that conceals the small steps of their rapid but mincing walk; from a distance they appear to glide as if levitating. They actually are remarkably unagile, negotiating terrain no better than a Dwarf.

Pentagrams and similar magic should affect the Fetch normally, but no enterprising mage has survived to report research on the topic.

Attribute Modifiers: ST +1 [10], DX -1 [-10], IQ +4 [45], HT +1 [10].
Advantages: Bioelectric Shock [10]; Doesn't Eat or Drink [10]; Doesn't Sleep [20]; Horns (Butting) [5]; Increased Speed +1 [25]; and Unaging [15].
Disadvantages: Reduced Hit Points -1 [-5] and Weakness (Direct sunlight on skin, 1d per 5 minutes) [-30].
Quirks, Features, and Taboo Traits: Cannot learn Climbing skill [-0].

Standard Fetch   250 points

ST: 11 [0]   **IQ:** 14 [0]   **Fatigue:** 11
DX: 9 [0]   **HT:** 11/10 [0] **Senses:** 14
Speed: 6   **Move:** 6   **Will:** 14

Advantages: Clerical Investment [5]; DR +4 (vs. electricity only) [4]; Fetch Racial Template [105]; Luck [15]; Mana Enhancer (+2, self only) [50] and Power Investiture +7 [70].
Disadvantages: Bad Temper [-10]; Oblivious [-3]; Odious Racial Habit (Wears human skin) [-15]; Sadism [-15]; and Social Stigma (Dark race) [-20].
Skills: Intimidation (M/A) IQ-1 [1]-13; Spell Throwing (Lightning) (P/E) DX+7 [40]-16; Thaumatology (M/VH) IQ-2 [2]-12; and Theology (M/H) IQ+1 [6]-15.
Spells: Clouds-19 [1]; Create Air-19 [1]; Create Water-19 [1]; Destroy Air-19 [1]; Destroy Water-19 [1]; Explosive Lightning-20 [2]; Lightning-19 [1]; Purify Air-19 [1]; Purify Water-19 [1]; Rain-19 [1]; Seek Water-19 [1]; and Shape Air-19 [1].
Languages: Bruig (M/A) IQ [2]-14 and native tongue (M/A) IQ [0]-14.
Equipment: Their human skins (which give them PD 1, DR 1 in combat as essentially light leather armor) and skirts appear to constitute the Fetch's worldly assets. Despite this meager inventory, they don't qualify as having a Wealth-related disadvantage. If they wanted to they could earn *very* good money as mercenaries for unscrupulous employers.
Customization Notes: Additional spells would be appropriate, though the GM must approve any additions. More worldly skills could accrue as the Fetch learn more about their new habitat. Should the Fetch appear horrid beneath their leathers – and they probably do – the appropriate Appearance should be added to their racial template, lowering its cost.

FETCH ADVENTURE SEEDS

THE most competent mage among the PCs receives a most unusual visitor – a powerful Fetch. The otherworldly sorceress believes she has discovered a method for returning to her own dimension. The process involves magics beyond her own expertise, however. If the mage balks at aiding something of such immense evil, the Fetch will calmly point out that any possibility of sending her home is a chance to do *good*. If the mage buys into this argument and completes the Fetch's magical research for her, the Fetch will stop on the threshold to her own dimension and gleefully point out to the mage that now he'll never know whether she'll ever return with reinforcements and her own agenda . . .

WANDERING far from civilized lands, the PCs stumble into the lair of a powerful Dark archmage – and the nearby gathering of a large group of Fetch preparing to attack him! It seems the archmage has been dabbling in interdimensional summonings, and is preparing to call into being something that even the Fetch fear . . .

Forest Giants are huge, intelligent tree-beings who make their home in Forest Heart (see p. 15). Also known as Ents, they have played pivotal roles as reluctant Light warriors. Their appearance in a battle often proves decisive, but no commander should count on them to appear till he can place gauntleted hand on wooden thigh.

Society

"When asked of the source of their animosity toward the Trow, all were silent. After a time the eldest among them looked down and seemed to weep, 'It was they who poisoned the soul of iron.'"

– from the lore of Myth

Forest Giants appear to number no more than a few score throughout all of Forest Heart, and to practice nearly as much reclusiveness among themselves as with other races. Since all known Forest Giants seem to be full-grown males, some scholars suspect that a variety of females and "saplings" may remain hidden deep in the woods.

Despite the males' tendency to remain physically isolated, they seem to stay current on events and congregate on need without any visible signs of communication. Forest Heart travelers swear that sometimes the leaves rustle despite the absence of any breeze.

Ents simply avoid Humans unless offended, and don't display their dislike of Dwarves as long as the diminutive ones stay in the mountains above the tree line, but they really do not care for the Trow. They are cryptic about this ancient enmity, but apparently it stems from the Trow inventing technology. Forest Giants have resisted progress in several venues, shattering dams and collapsing mines too close to their homelands.

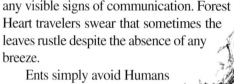

FOREST GIANT NAMES

The Forest Giants choose descriptive names, and these can change over the course of a Giant's life as they become outmoded. This rarely causes confusion within the race. Since so few Forest Giants exist, most know each other too intimately to lose track simply from a name change. Some instances include: Grayleaves, Graybark, Oldbark, Deeproots, Longbranches, Hardwood, Wisebark, Oldgrowth, Highbranches, Ironwood, Stoneroots, Millionleaves, Yellowleaves, Stonebranches, Evergreen, Wintergreen, Greatwood, Ironroot, and Morningwood.

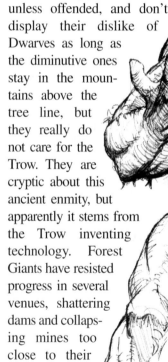

FOREST GIANT PCs

The Forest Giants make perfectly good PCs in a high-powered campaign. GMs should note: Forest Giants wield more power in hand-to-hand combat than any other Myth race, even the Trow. With a prudent player refining a Forest Giant PC's capabilities, the character could become overwhelming.

A PC Forest Giant probably will be an extremely outgoing example of his race, and might even qualify for the Xenophilia disadvantage to reflect this.

Forest Giants can be mages. Naturally, a high percentage of them are specialists in the Plant college, whether through choice or from the limitations of One-College Magery. The Light and Darkness, elemental, and Healing colleges are other areas Forest Giant mages have been seen to master.

Plan of Battle

Forest Giants will serve Light when their reluctance to mingle can be overcome – and eagerly assault those who carelessly hunt or harvest timber in Forest Heart's interior. In a fight, they come straight on, but show an interesting knack for entering and leaving a battle without notice.

Forest Giant Racial Template   441 points

Forest Giants resemble trees shaped like men. They have leaves and brown bark for skin. They stand three times as high and weigh 18 times as much as an equivalent human before the racial ST increase.

Forest Giants must spend time in *rich* soil and absorb several gallons of water each day. Essentially this takes as much of their time as eating meals would. While rich soil is cheaper and more convenient than fauna's food, it can't be found at all in deserts, many plains, etc., which greatly limits the Ents' range. Their life-support needs average the same inconvenience as those of more traditional lifeforms.

Their last 34 points of ST are purchased with the Natural limitation from p. CI8. Ents move slowly for their size, but can summon incredible ST on demand.

Attribute Modifiers: ST +6/40 [139] and HT +5 [60].

Advantages: Alertness +1 [5]; DR +7 (Only DR +2 vs. fire, lightning, and explosions, a -15% limitation on the additional DR +5) [19]; Extra Arm Length +2 [40]; Extra Hit Points +18 [90]; Injury Tolerance (No blood, No brain, No neck, and No vitals) [20]; Longevity [5]; PD +2 [50]; Plant Empathy [5]; Secret Communication [20]; and Unusual Background (To purchase Power Blow) [20].

Disadvantages: Inconvenient Size [-10]; Intolerance (Trow) [-5]; Reclusive [-10]; Reduced Move -1 [-5]; Reputation (Grumpy, unreliable) [-10]; and Shyness [-10].

Skills: Power Blow (M/H) IQ+5 [14]-15. When in a forest (a -20% limitation), Ents receive +1 to Tracking, +2 to Stealth, and +3 to Camouflage [4].

Standard Forest Giant   500 points

ST: 16/50 [0]   **IQ:** 10 [0]   **Fatigue:** 16
DX: 10 [0]   **HT:** 15/33 [0]   **Senses:** 11
Speed: 6.25   **Move:** 5   **Will:** 10

Advantages and Disadvantages: Forest Giant Template [442].

Skills: Area Knowledge (Forest Heart) (M/E) IQ+2 [4]-12; Brawling (P/E) DX+6 [32]-16; Camouflage (M/E) IQ+5 [4]-15*; Power Blow (M/H) IQ+9 [8]-19; Stealth (P/A) DX+3 [4]-13*; Tactics (M/H) IQ [4]-10; and Tracking (M/A) IQ+2 [2]-12*.

* Racial and Alertness bonuses already applied.

Languages: Bruig (M/A) IQ-1 [1]-9 and Entish (M/A) IQ [0]-10.

Customization Notes: Many Ents are plant mages of considerable prowess. Older Forest Giants have no upper limit on size; though very rare, they would possess incredible ST. Coupling it with further mastery of their Power Blow would create devastating attacks.

FOREST GIANT ADVENTURE SEEDS

PILLARS of smoke alert the PCs to a huge forest fire in Forest Heart! Combating the blaze will earn the respect and gratitude of the Forest Giants in the region, who for all their might are fairly powerless against this common threat . . .

WHILE hunting for some treasure in the deeps of Forest Heart, the PCs do something to deeply offend a single Ent. He's too canny to confront them face-to-face in a fight that he would lose, but will follow them as they travel through the woods, setting traps, misdirecting them, and generally making their lives miserable. Anyone foolish enough to wander away from the main party will regret it . . .

LOGGING has become big business on the western edge of Forest Heart, thanks to the demands of rebuilding Strand and villages in its vicinities. So far the Forest Giants have tolerated this activity in light of their recent Human alliances, but they've become restive as more and more timber disappears. The PCs are placed in a position to negotiate concerning this increasing tension. They must seek out and speak to the Ents, and find a way to ease their concerns that respects Human resource needs as well. If they fail, they'll need to figure out how to defend the loggers from the Ent attacks that will soon come . . .

Ghast PCs

Mindless creatures, undead or otherwise, usually make poor PCs. A ghast doesn't really think or have a personality; it simply follows its master's commands. Removing the Slave Mentality and Reprogrammable Duty disadvantages would create a self-willed Ghast, which may be horrified by its undead condition. This could represent an entirely new variety of undead, or the GM could invent some process which provides self-will to any mindless undead that undergo it.

Ghast Adventure Seeds

A slain ally reappears in the PCs' lives as a common Ghast. The PCs may want to seek vengeance on whoever transformed their friend into fiend, and to see that his mortal remains receive proper burial. On the latter point, bystanders will be less picky, and simply want to hack and burn . . .

CITY fathers discover an army of Ghasts centered on the cemetery has burrowed a vast underground labyrinth beneath their town. They hire the PCs to clean out the tunnels, and to find out why they were dug and who's behind the plot . . .

Ghasts

"The unholy throng stumbled through the woods . . . their wretched claws searching . . . mouthing words noiselessly . . . drawn to the village they had called home not so long ago . . ."

– from the lore of Myth

Ghasts represent one of the more basic varieties of undead found in Myth. They do not appear in combat as often as their numbers would suggest, because their masters find them more useful later in their undeath . . .

Necromancers create Ghasts using a variant of the Zombie spell (see *Creating Ghasts* sidebar on p. 45). This turns a fairly fresh – though rotting – corpse into a servant of the caster, who may then transfer its loyalty to anyone he chooses.

The reanimated corpse will retain *none* of the skills it had in life, and only the shadow of its former memories; its mind starts out a clean slate save for a basic grasp of its former native language. A loved one's face, its name called out, or the sight of its onetime home may cause a Ghast to hesitate and grasp at the faded recollections of the person it once was, but mindless duty will soon take over again.

Ghasts can be trained, though not always easily, and their mindless nature leaves certain skills beyond their grasp. New Ghasts are usually set to nonstop melee among themselves in order to gain a high proficiency in the Brawling skill. This otherwise efficient form of education can cause some undeaths, leaving a necromancer eight or nine combat-ready Ghasts where he reanimated 10 inept ones.

Society

Mindless undead don't have a culture, but they certainly impact that of their "source" race. Dark lords overrunning Light lands usually regard all Light casualties, prisoners, and inhabitants of occupied territories as their *own* potential cannon fodder. Only the number of necromancers in a Dark lord's train limits the rate at which prisoners or slain foes become new undead recruits. Raiding parties have often carted off the entire populace of a village (or just the adult males in a large town). Their neighbors may see them return days later as a new company of undead.

Since Humans abhor looking into the unlit eyes of friends and loved ones in the opposing ranks, the populace in general tries to take great care with its dead. The Legion tends to the dead on a battlefield promptly, and will even take further losses to hold the ground on which it took casualties. Villagers lay out cemeteries in easily defended sites, and prudent ones post sentries in times of war.

Some pragmatists call for funeral rites to embrace cremation, but most major religions avoid the practice. Their texts show that in days of old, even more foul undead could be created from the ashes of the cremated. These spells might still exist in some not-quite-forgotten Dark library.

Plan of Battle

Those commanding Ghasts generally keep them away from front-line duties, where a determined Legion company could hack them apart. They will often use Ghasts in interior operations – rounding up hapless villagers to transform into more Ghasts, watching over prisoners, etc.

In combat, Ghasts almost invariably hold orders to All-Out Attack, throwing their minimal ability to defend themselves aside in favor of overwhelming the opposition through sheer ferocity.

Ghast Racial Template 92 points

Their putrescent nature gives Ghasts two special qualities. The first is that wounds from their long, hardened fingernails or their bite *burn* wickedly, given the variety of foul fluids they convey. Immediate nausea and more serious discomfort often accompany a wound from a Ghast, and it will usually infect.

Second, a Ghast eventually transforms into a Wight as it rots (see *Creating Ghasts* sidebar).

Attribute Modifiers: ST +8 [90], DX -1 [-10], IQ -2 [-15], HT +3 [30].
Advantages: Doesn't Breathe [20]; Doesn't Eat/Drink [10]; Doesn't Sleep [20]; Extra Hit Points +9 [45]; High Pain Threshold [10]; Immunity to Disease [10]; Immunity to Poison [15]; Injury Tolerance (No blood) [5]; Night Vision [10]; Pestilence (varies) [5]; Temperature Tolerance +5 [5]; Unfazeable [15]; and Venom +5 (Irritant, but delivered via blood with clawing hand attacks) [75].
Disadvantages: Appearance (Hideous) [-20]; Bad Smell [-10]; Mute [-25]; Reprogrammable Duty [-25]; Slave Mentality [-40]; Social Stigma (Dead) [-20]; Sterile [-3]; Unhealing [-30]; Unliving [-50]; and Wealth (Dead Broke) [-25].
Quirks, Features, and Taboo Traits: Affected by Control Zombie, Pentagram, and Turn Zombie [0]; Cannot swim [0]; No mental skills [0]; and Will decay into Wight [0].

Standard Ghast 100 points

ST: 18 [0] **IQ:** 8 [0] **Fatigue:** 18
DX: 9 [0] **HT:** 13/22 [0] **Senses:** 8
Speed: 5 **Move:** 5 **Will:** 2

Advantages: Ghast Racial Template [92].
Disadvantages: per Ghast Racial Template.
Skills: Brawling (P/E) DX+3 [8]-12.
Languages: Bruig (M/A) IQ [0]-8.
Equipment: Ghasts generally have none, other than the clothes rotting off their backs.

Customization Notes: Ghasts' attributes will vary according-
ing to the quality of the person whose corpse they are. Ghasts *can* be taught any physical skill, and are in some very limited respect good learners since they'll practice 24 hours a day and never presume they "know better."

CREATING GHASTS

Ghasts are created by mages using a variation of the Zombie spell (see p. M73 and p. 31). The Ghast spell costs more because Ghasts are more powerful than standard Zombies (though not more powerful than a Zombie created from the corpse of a very skilled warrior).

The Ghast spell costs 39 energy to cast, per the rules on p. UN89. GMs may want to reduce the price to reflect that Myth necromancers will not fully benefit from "competent corpses" and must provide their new minions some minimal training before they become truly useful.

The base cost of a Mass Ghast casting is 38 points.

Another difference between the standard Zombie spell and the Ghast version is the choice of corpses. Those eligible to become Ghasts must be in fairly good shape, intact but not dried out or embalmed. Skeletons will not do (though they provide the raw building material for Soulless) and dried or preserved corpses provide fodder for Thralls instead.

Since they do rot, Ghasts eventually transform into Wights (pp. 66-67). This transformation can take as long as two years in a Ghast transformed just after death, to a month for a Ghast seriously decomposed at the time of reanimation.

Ghôl Names

Ghôl parents don't name their young, who get the privilege for themselves should they defy the odds and enter adolescence.

The young Ghôl, not unjustifiably, takes a great deal of pride in this accomplishment, and chooses a name to reflect it, as the following examples illustrate: Crusher, Masher, Breaker, Snapper, Smasher, Killer, Grinder, Gnasher, Screamer, Splitter, Eviscerator, Destroyer, Crasher, Dasher, Wounder, Ruiner, Tamer, Gentler, Butcher, Slaughterer, Extinguisher, Pulper, Flattener, Squasher, Squisher, Pounder, Bruiser, Hasher, Pulverizer, Harasser, Tormentor, Shrieker, Squealer, Screecher, Howler, Severer, Mangler, Eradicator, Lascerator, Disabler, Crippler, Lamer, Mutilator, Thrasher, Cruncher, and Knacker.

Ghôl PCs

A Ghôl PC could be a lot of fun, given a broadminded set of companions. Ghôls aren't inherently evil, and a PC Ghôl exhibiting a certain amount of restraint isn't out of the question, but no Ghôl would ever qualify as polite company.

Even if a PC Ghôl forgoes the Odious Racial Habit of eating other sentients, he *will* suffer the Reputation for the behavior among all who don't personally know him, taking a -3 to reaction rolls. The GM probably should allow a PC Ghôl to swap out the Reputation (which will usually be -15 points unless the Ghôl and his dietary prudence are well-known) for the Odious Racial Habit in the racial template; i.e., the Reputation would not count against any limit on personal disadvantages.

The racial Uneducated disadvantage should only be bought off with GM oversight. Though individual Ghôls can be *very* clever, they're much more prone to exhibit high intelligence in application of Tactics or Scrounging than Theology or Engineer. The race has never been known to produce a mage.

No matter how good a Ghôl's individual conduct may be, the vast majority of Dwarves will not tolerate his company. A PC party with both Ghôls and Dwarves will need some inventive extenuating circumstances or character concepts to avoid internal bloodshed.

Ghôls

Less evil than stupendously unrestrained, Ghôls roam the lands of Myth raiding and sniping and scratching out a hand-to-mouth existence in which, often as not, the hand recently belonged to someone in the Ghôl's way.

Society

Until recent decades, the vast majority of Ghôls could not envision seeking a better life than the day-to-day pillaging that most still practice. That changed when they took up Balor's banner and exploited the opportunity that he presented to drive the long-hated Dwarves from their historic twin capitals. Although the Dwarves have since retaken one city, within the other the Ghôls are attempting to improve their standard of living. This might even introduce civilizing influences if they can withstand the Dwarven onslaught that they know will soon come.

The Ghôls want to hold Stoneheim as fervently as the Dwarves want to regain it. They celebrate its capture with feasts at each full moon, re-enacting its spoliation so as to never forget their triumph. To defend it, these eaters of other sentients have set the goal of "devouring the Dwarves from existence." Human Brigands have also taught them to use the Dwarven weapons that remained after the siege.

Plan of Battle

Ghôls make canny light infantry. They will thoroughly scout an opponent prior to coming to blows, skirting his flanks and fleeing if need be. They prefer to carefully close in under cover, then rush any missile troops first. Killing them improves the odds considerably, since if things don't go well Ghôls can usually outrun melee troops.

Their long arms give Ghôls great throwing ability, which they use in combat, picking up anything they might find to hurl at a foe. Their ability to digest anything extends to touching it; they can even handle pieces of Wight and hurl them without ill effect.

Ghôl Racial Template   60 points

The Ghôls are semi-humanoids who run on all fours but fight standing on their hind legs. They weigh as much as a human of the same ST, but stand 4″ shorter when upright and 2′ shorter when on all fours. Their skin is usually a shade of gray, from bone white to charcoal, or a shade of brown. A prominent muzzle full of teeth commands their faces.

Though their long arms are extremely nimble, the Ghôls are surprisingly clumsy at moving in other than a straight line.

Attribute Modifiers: ST +1 [10], DX -2 [-15], IQ -1 [-10], HT +3 [30].
Advantages: Acute Hearing +2 [4]; Cast Iron Stomach [15]; DR +1 [3]; Disease-Resistant [5]; Early Maturation +1 [5]; Extra Arm Length +1 [20]; High Pain Threshold [10]; Magic Resistance +4 (vs. spells resisted by ST only, -50%) [4]; Modified Arm DX +6 [48]; Sharp Teeth [5]; and Temperature Tolerance +3 [3].
Disadvantages: Appearance (Hideous) [-20]; Odious Racial Habit (Eats other sentients) [-15]; Primitive -1 (TL2) [-5]; Semi-Upright [-5]; Social Stigma (Dark race) [-20]; Uneducated [-5]; and Wealth (Poor) [-15].
Skills: +3 to Throwing [8].

Standard Ghôl   150 points

ST: 12 [10]   **IQ:** 9 [0]   **Fatigue:** 12
DX: 9 [10]   **HT:** 15 [20]   **Senses:** 9 (Hearing 11)
Speed: 6   **Move:** 7   **Will:** 9

Advantages: Ghôl Racial Template [60].
Disadvantages: per Ghôl Racial Template.
Skills: Axe/Mace (P/A) DX+6 [2]-15*; Brawling (P/E) DX+6 [1]-15*; Climbing (P/A) DX+1 [4]-10; Gunner/TL4 (Cannon) DX [2]-9; Running (P/H – HT) HT [4]-15; Scrounging (M/E) IQ+1 [2]-10; Shadowing (M/A) IQ+5 [12]-14; Stealth (P/A) DX+1 [4]-10; Survival (Plains) (M/A) IQ [2]-9; Tactics (M/H) IQ+2 [8]-11; and Throwing (P/H) DX+10 [8]-19*.
* Includes bonus for Modified Arm DX +6 and/or racial skill bonus.
Languages: Bruig (M/A) IQ-1 [1]-8 and Ghôl (M/A) IQ [0]-9.
Equipment: Ghôls don't bother with clothing. They usually carry a long, crude sickle (treat as an axe in combat, at +1 to damage for their extra-long arms) and wear a gunny sack slung over one shoulder in which they carry victuals, random items to be thrown, etc.

THE PCs come across a pitiful Ghôl baby in the wilderness, apparently forgotten by a rapidly moving mother. What to do with it should present a challenge; after all, it *is* just a baby, if one festooned with sharp teeth . . .

SEVERAL burglaries have baffled local authorities. The burglar enters second-story rooms with barred doors, and windows that can't be reached except from the roof by someone with an 8-foot armspan . . .

A pack of Ghôls assaults the PCs, who overcome several before the remainder flee. Should the PCs rummage among the fallen, they'll find that one carries some rations with him – a few finger bones with scraps of meat still on them wrapped in an old piece of parchment. Examining the parchment and making a Research, History, or Thaumatology roll will reveal that it's torn from an ancient magical tome of great power, long believed lost somewhere in the general vicinity. Should any of the fallen Ghôls remain alive, nursing him back to health might allow opportunity to negotiate for more information, though the PCs will have to figure out what would tempt a Ghôl enough to betray his own brethren . . .

Maul Names

Mauls use single, multisyllable names that convey a surprising amount of family history. A Maul usually can determine the tribe and father of another Maul from his name. Some examples include: Bandoona, Arcooh, Naracoorte, Tantanoola, Warbla, Wigunda, Wooltana, Yamnti, Ithapi, Wakarla, Koomooloobooka, Koomalboogurra, Bildoolja, Noolook, and Myora.

Maul PCs

Mauls make an excellent race for characters of the big, strong, and odoriferous type. A PC Maul who expects to mingle with Human society would need to buy off the racial Bad Temper, or risk a lynch mob every time he lost control of his behavior. He probably should also buy off the Hidebound disadvantage, or else he would be incapable of so radically changing his conduct from the racial standard!

Even a Maul with a kind nature and iron self-discipline would be regarded with a great deal of suspicion; as with most Dark races, it would take a very unusual character concept to buy off the racial Social Stigma.

The nimblest Maul isn't too nimble, nor the brightest too bright. PC Mauls shouldn't exceed DX 11 or IQ 12. No one has ever recorded an encounter with a Maul mage.

A concept that fits into society fairly smoothly is the Maul bodyguard. Even Light mages and high nobles have been known to employ the massive creatures in this role. A PC Maul could take another PC or an NPC as a Patron whom he serves in this role.

Maul

Massive humanoids resembling a cross between a boar and a tavern bouncer, Mauls often form the juggernaut core of a Dark army. As with the Ghôls, their nature isn't purely evil, but they do tend to take the direct approach and play to their own strengths, and their own strengths involve pounding those who oppose them into mush.

Society

Mauls maintain a nomadic tribal society in their far northern homelands (see p. 17). The average tribe counts about 200 adults and twice as many children. Surprisingly for such a violent race, they carefully nurse their young to adulthood, but childhood mortality is high for reasons not entirely known to civilized scholars.

Roughly every 13 months, several tribes will converge to trade mates. Young males without mates often join another tribe at this opportunity as well.

Without more intelligent oversight, the Mauls rarely engage in interracial aggression more sophisticated than a single tribe raiding into human lands for a month or so. They very much covet a more hospitable home than they now claim, but under normal circumstances the Mauls are just smart enough to know that they're not smart enough to take those lands from humans backed by sorcery. They also possess enough sense to avoid stirring up their other neighbors, the Trow.

Soulblighter convinced the Mauls that his invasion would provide their chance to seize better lands, and his advance spread small pockets of Mauls across the continent. For the most part, these now try to make their way back northward to the relative safety of their traditional home. Rumors have it that a few are trying to settle remote regions, though likely the empire would send the Legion to force any such colonists out.

Plan of Battle

Maul tactics consist of moving straight forward, obliterating anything in their path.

A Maul tends to pick a favorite weapon early in life, then use it for hunting, personal defense, warfare, and some forms of social interaction during just about every waking minute thereafter. Most choose a spiked club, heavy-ended and crude, which should be treated as a cheap mace in combat. A few others have been seen to carry a two-handed version, to be treated as a cheap maul wielded with Two-Handed Axe/Mace instead of the usual Axe/Mace expertise.

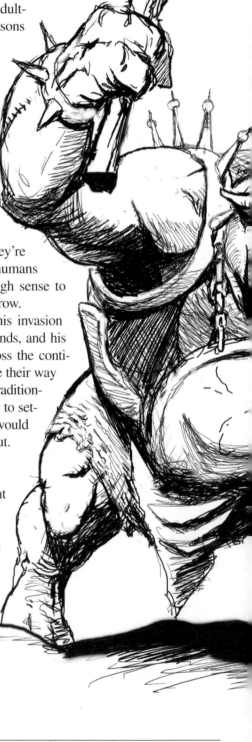

Maul Racial Template   118 points

Mauls are very stout piglike creatures with roughly human proportions. To determine a Maul's height and weight, look up how tall he would be before the racial ST modifier, then add 15″; weight will be five times Human weight before the racial ST modifier.

A Maul's purple-pinkish skin is covered in coarse hair. Their boar faces feature a pair of tusks that curve to the sides. These can't be used as a weapon, but do protect the face from injury. Their beady yellow eyes, imbedded in a massive brow, give them notoriously poor sight.

Mauls prefer a carnivorous diet – they adore snake – and will gladly eat seven times as much as a Human when they can, but they can go extended periods without eating any greater quantities than a Human.

Mauls purchase the last 9 points of their ST with the -40% natural limitation from p. CI8.

Attribute Modifiers: ST +3/+12 [90], DX -2 [-15], IQ -1 [-10], HT +3 [30].

Advantages: Acute Hearing +4 [8]; DR +3 [9]; DR +4 (Face only, -60%) [5]; Early Maturation +1 [5]; Extra Hit Points +2 [10]; High Pain Threshold [10]; Injury Tolerance (No Neck) [5]; PD +1 [25]; Recovery [10]; Sharp Teeth [5]; Strong Will +2 [8]; and Temperature Tolerance +5 [5].

Disadvantages: Appearance (Hideous) [-20]; Bad Temper [-10]; Hidebound [-5]; Magic Susceptibility (vs. spells resisted by ST only, -50%) -10 [-15]; Poor Vision -4 [-8]; Primitive -1 (TL2) [-5]; Social Stigma (Dark race) [-20]; Uneducated [-5]; and Wealth (Struggling) [-10].

Skills: Axe/Mace (P/A) DX+3 [16]-11.

Standard Maul   200 points

ST: 16/25 [30]	**IQ:** 9 [0]	**Fatigue:** 16
DX: 8 [0]	**HT:** 13/15 [0]	**Senses:** 5/9/13
Speed: 5.25	**Move:** 6	**Will:** 11

Advantages: Maul Racial Template [118].

Disadvantages: per Maul Racial Template.

Skills: Axe/Mace (P/A) DX+7 [32]-15; Brawling (P/E) DX+3 [8]-11; Intimidation (M/A but based on ST-5 default) IQ+3 [2]-12; Running (P/H – HT) HT-2 [1]-11; Stealth (P/A) DX-1 [1]-7; Survival (Plains) (M/A) IQ+2 [6]-11; and Tactics (M/H) IQ-2 [1]-7.

Languages: Bruig (M/A) IQ-1 [1]-8 and Maulish (M/A) IQ [0]-9.

Equipment: As mentioned, Mauls usually favor a one-handed spiked club. They wear an assortment of armor, usually heavy leather, though generally just over their torso and very rarely enough to encumber them. They often augment this with a scavenged medium shield worn over their vitals. Treat this area as protected by PD3, DR5 armor (plus the Maul's native DR).

As with the Ghôls, the Maul nature poses a question in Myth: Are they fundamentally evil creatures or simply misunderstood races that can only find allies in the Dark?

The underlying assumption in the Ghôl and Maul writeups is that they are prone toward violence and other vile behavior because they lack many civilizing influences and are shunned by the civilizations that do exist. This antisocial behavior is reinforced by their associations with the Dark, but it isn't irreversible. This perspective allows for "Mauls gone good" PC concepts and a wider variety of dramatic potential. What if the average Maul returns good treatment with all the adoration that a dog would show? What if the Ghôls improve their ways in Myrgard just before the Dwarves assault?

The alternate assumption that either or both races defy any effort at reformation works, too. It trades the above dramatic possibilities for the confidence that cleaving their skulls always represents the right thing to do.

MAUL ADVENTURE SEEDS

A large war group or tribe of Mauls captures the PCs. Its leader sets them to an urgent task – teaching him to read. Though not unintelligent, he isn't going to pick up on it quickly, and will blame his teachers. He likes to backhand Humans who displease him, to see how far they'll fly . . .

LOCAL nobles have been told of a small band of Mauls in their area, and they are making sport of their capture, with fierce hunting dogs and scores of archers and nets and torches. The sounds of these massive hunts have filled the woods for weeks. Another one can be heard in the distance as a mud-splattered and wounded Maul stumbles upon the PCs, asking for sanctuary . . .

AN old and feeble wizard hires the party to capture a Maul for him. He specifies that he wants a young, strong, healthy male. He will ignore any questions as to his intents . . .

History doesn't record any individual names for the Myrkridia, not even the rather intelligent Large ones. Scholars do not yet know why this is so, for the Myrkridia *do* understand language.

Some theorize that the individual is nothing but part of a pack in the Myrkridian world view, and thus doesn't warrant his own name.

MYRKRIDIAN PCS

The Myrkridia would be difficult to rationalize as PC material except in the darkest, most anarchic campaign. Unlike some other Dark races, their nature runs toward pure evil down to its very core. Their lack of self-control also presents a major social obstacle.

MYRKRIDIAN ADVENTURE SEEDS

EXPLORING in an ancient and remote locale, the PCs stumble across the ruins of a long-dead Myrkridian civilization! A temple at the ruin's center houses a small, intensely magical statue of some sort of Myrkridian fertility goddess. Should it be molested, a bloodcurdling howling will sound from the hills all around the ruins. The explorers should anticipate company on short notice . . .

THE city in which the PCs currently live is suffering the attentions of a serial killer. Stalking only at night, the killer has mauled to death several women leaving only grisly remains that suggest a Myrkridia. The attacker might indeed be one of the monsters or someone emulating their style . . .

A Large Myrkridia stalks the dreams of one of the PCs! Treat this as the Nightmare spell (see p. M73). The victim apparently has caught the attentions of a powerful Myrkridian mage, whose intentions can only be guessed at . . .

50

MYRKRIDIA

" . . . the world lived in the long shadow of the Myrkridia – a race of flesh-eaters too horrible to describe . . . creatures able to keep the land stricken with fear for hundreds of years."

– *from the lore of Myth*

Of all the Dark races, none holds a terrifying grip on Human memory like the Myrkridia. Savage creatures of berserk ferocity, the Myrkridia have terrorized humanity since its earliest days. In the Wind Age their efforts redoubled, and for 1,000 years humankind made what progress it could by day only to see it savaged by night.

A little over 1,000 years ago the great human hero Connacht made his reputation by defying all odds and defeating the Myrkridia. For reasons lost in time, he did not slay the horrors, but instead trapped them in the Tain (see p. 85), a magical artifact.

There the Myrkridia wandered, suspended in time and perhaps becoming even more mad than before, till Soulblighter freed them with the help of the Summoner. Once again loose upon the world, though few in number, the Myrkridia seem hellbent on making up for lost time.

Society

The primitive Myrkridia ran in simple packs, building nothing other than the horrid skull platforms they instinctively constructed from the severed heads of their victims. Moagim taught them the fundamentals of battlefield behavior, rallying to war standards and the like, and after his death they retained the standards if not the slightest idea how to fabricate one.

Within the pack they act as mercilessly as without. Any sign of weakness gets a Myrkridia eaten by his fellows.

About 1 in every 100 Myrkridia born becomes a Large Myrkridia. These rule their pack when present. All mages, Large Myrkridia will often wander off by themselves, to meet with others of their special kind and orally trade knowledge of spellcasting.

Myrkridia talk among themselves, and seem to know what Humans are saying, but rarely speak to other races.

Myrkridia Racial Template 180 points

Myrkridia stand 6″ taller and weigh 30 more pounds than a human of the same ST.

Attribute Modifiers: ST +5 [60], DX +4 [45], IQ -1 [-10], HT +3 [30].

Advantages: Acute Hearing +3 [6]; Breath Holding +3 [6]; Claws (Long talons) [55]; Combat Reflexes [15]; DR +2 [6]; Discriminatory Smell [15]; Early Maturation +1 [5]; Extra Hit Points +1 [5]; Fur [29]; High Pain Threshold [10]; Night Vision [10]; Sharp Teeth [5]; Strong Will +2 [8]; and Terror [30].

Disadvantages: Appearance (Hideous) [-20]; Berserk [-15]; Bloodlust [-10]; Mute [-25]; Odious Racial Habit (Eats other sentients) [-15]; Primitive -3 (TL0) [-15]; Social Stigma (Dark race) [-20]; Uneducated [-5]; and Wealth (Dead Broke) [-25].

Standard Myrkridia 200 points

ST: 15 [0]   **IQ:** 9 [0]   **Fatigue:** 15
DX: 14 [0]   **HT:** 13/14 [0]   **Senses:** 9 (Hearing 12)
Speed: 6.75   **Move:** 8   **Will:** 11

Advantages and Disadvantages: Myrkridia Racial Template [180].

Skills: Brawling (P/E) DX+1 [2]-15; Jumping (P/E) DX+2 [4]-16; Running (P/H – HT) HT-2 [1]-11; Stealth (P/A) DX [2]-14; Survival (Woodlands) (M/A) IQ+2 [6]-11; and Tactics (M/H) IQ [4]-9.

Languages: Bruig (M/A) IQ-1 [1]-8 and Myrkridian (M/A) IQ [0]-9.

Large Myrkridia Racial Template 422 points

A Large Myrkridia stands 3′ taller and weighs 2.5 times as much as a human of the same ST before the racial +9. They usually All-Out Attack in melee combat.

Attribute Modifiers: ST +9 [100], DX -1 [-10], HT +6 [80].

Advantages: Breath Holding +3 [6]; Claws (Long talons) [55]; Combat Reflexes [15]; DR +4 [12]; Discriminatory Smell [15]; Extra Arm Length +1 [20]; Fur [29]; Fatigue Recovery +6 [40]; Magery +7 [105]; Night Vision [10]; PD +4 [100]; Sharp Teeth [5]; and Strong Will +3 [12].

Disadvantages: Appearance (Horrific) [-30]; Berserk [-15]; Bloodlust [-10]; Inconvenient Size [-10]; Mute [-25]; Odious Racial Habit (Eats other sentients) [-15]; Poor Vision (-4 to Vision rolls) [-8]; Primitive -3 (TL0) [-15]; Social Stigma (Dark race) [-20]; and Wealth (Dead Broke) [-25].

Skills: +2 to Spell-Throwing (Ice Sphere/Stone Missile) [1].

Quirks, Features, and Taboo Traits: Illiterate mages, restricted per p. M103.

Standard Large Myrkridia 500 points

ST: 19 [0]   **IQ:** 10 [0]   **Fatigue:** 19
DX: 9 [0]   **HT:** 16 [0]   **Senses:** 10
Speed: 6.25   **Move:** 8   **Will:** 13

Advantages and Disadvantages: Large Myrkridia Racial Template [422].

Skills: Brawling (P/E) DX+3 [8]-12; Running (P/H – HT) HT+1 [8]-17; Spell Throwing (Ice Sphere/Stone Missile) (P/E) DX+4 [4]-13; Survival (Woodlands) (M/A) IQ+1 [4]-11; and Tactics (M/H) IQ [4]-10.

Languages: Bruig (M/A) IQ-1 [1]-9 and Myrkridian (M/A) IQ [0]-10.

Spells: Death Vision-15 [1]; Exploding Skull Strike-17 [4]; Find Weakness-15 [1]; Ignite Fire-15 [1]; Lend Health-15 [1]; Lend Strength-15 [1]; Minor Healing-15 [1]; Purify Air-15 [1]; Magic Resistance-25 [20]; Recover Strength-20 [10]; Seek Earth-15 [1]; Seek Water-15 [1]; Sense Spirit-15 [1]; Skull Spirit-15 [1]; Skull Strike-15 [1]; Steal Health-15 [1]; Steal Strength-15 [1]; and Test Food-15 [1].

Equipment: Ornamental belt of skulls. These bear a striking resemblance to the special effect of their Exploding Skull Strike spell, but do not serve as ammunition for it in any capacity.

TERROR in MYTH

Myth's atmosphere mixes high fantasy and horror, as the brave mortals of the Legion stand fast before the fearsome Myrkridia and vast undead hordes. Fear should be palpable and constant in a Myth campaign true to its source material, and even hardened legionnaires will sometimes find themselves dripping in cold sweat. This sidebar summarizes the guidelines for Fright Checks.

Creatures with Horrific appearance always prompt a Fright Check in onlookers. (Among standard Myth characters, only the Large Myrkridia has Horrific features.) Creatures of Monstrous or Hideous appearance also require a Fright Check if the check would have modifiers of -1 or worse.

Modifiers

Other than those found on p. B93, modifiers to the victims' Fright Checks include -1 for an established "Dark race" (i.e., one with the appropriate Social Stigma), +1 per appearance after first within 24 hours, -1 for five frightening creatures, -2 for 10, -3 for 20, -4 for 50, and -5 for 100 or more. The presence of a powerful Dark lord or the equivalent would subtract an additional -2.

The Terror Advantage

Some creatures can require a Fright Check only when they desire to do so, as can the standard Myrkridia when they cavort and howl or just stare evilly and growl. This requires all onlookers to make a Fright Check immediately, and again if they reappear after an absence of at least one hour. This Fright Check takes the standard modifiers listed above.

Terror costs 30 points plus 10 points per -1 to the "base" Fright Check.

Myrmidon

Centuries ago, all the might of the Dark stood powerless before the Light's Myrmidons, warriors of vast skill . . . and vaster pride.

Unable to beat them, the Dark lord Balor enticed them to join him. He offered them immortality in exchange for their services. It seems unlikely that the Myrmidons – who spent the eve of battle with a mirror rather than a bedroll – understood all the terms of the pact they had struck.

Also known as the Kithless, the Myrmidons are free-willed undead, still terrible in battle, but now just as terrible to behold.

Society

The Myrmidons may have once been northern tribesmen, perhaps even related to the Berserks, though suggesting as much to a Berserk will ignite a brawl. They wore their hair long and painted their bodies, just as the Berserks still do.

Today, they appear to resent their loathsome existence; certainly they show only utter hostility to the still-living, and have been known to flock to particularly handsome targets in battle.

Myrmidons do congregate in groups of up to several score, but no living soul has been able to get close enough to observe them without soon having to retreat or slay them. Their habits when not attacking the living are little known.

Plan of Battle

When they have superiority in numbers, Myrmidons attack relentlessly with zeal. A single, outmanned Myrmidon *can* show more restraint – though they don't always do so – and retreat temporarily till the odds improve. Eventually, though, they'll assault. It's the only activity that seems to fill the holes left by their souls.

Myrmidon Racial Template   80 points

Myrmidons are decaying human corpses held together by their bandages and fierce will to rend the living. They have the same height as a living man of the same ST before racial modifications and weigh 30 pounds less.

Attribute Modifiers: ST +4 [45], DX -1 [-10], IQ -1 [-10], HT +1 [10].

Advantages: Ambidexterity [10]; Combat Reflexes [15]; DR +2 [6]; Doesn't Breathe [20]; Doesn't Eat/Drink [10]; Doesn't Sleep [20]; Extra Hit Points +12 [60]; High Pain Threshold [10]; Immunity to Disease [10]; Immunity to Poison [15]; Injury Tolerance (No blood) [5]; Strong Will +2 [8]; Temperature Tolerance +6 [6]; and Unaging [15].

Disadvantages: Appearance (Hideous) [-20]; Eunuch [-5]; Fanaticism (Kill!) [-15]; Low Empathy [-15]; Mute [-25]; Sadism [-15]; Social Stigma (Dead) [-20]; and Unliving [-50].

Quirks, Features, and Taboo Traits: Affected by Pentagram [0].

Standard Myrmidon   150 points

ST: 14 [0]   **IQ:** 9 [0]   **Fatigue:** 14
DX: 9 [0]   **HT:** 11/23 [0]   **Senses:** 9
Speed: 5   **Move:** 5   **Will:** 11

Advantages: Myrmidon Racial Template [80].
Disadvantages: per Myrmidon Racial Template.
Skills: Shortsword (P/A) DX+9 [64]-18 and Tactics (M/H) IQ+1 [6]-10.
Languages: Bruig (M/A) IQ [0]-9.
Equipment: Myrmidons carry a pair of *gridaksma* blades, built from a human femur with a steel scythe blade attached to each end. They keep these lovingly sharp. The change in handles makes the weapons into essentially two-bladed shortswords, regardless of where the business ends originally came from. They carry no other equipment. They seem to eschew armor even when available (yet another hint at Berserk ties . . .) and have no use for wealth other than that inherent in their weapons.

Customization Notes:

In the 300+ years since they last drew breath, most Myrmidons have gone insane in their rage, retaining only the two skills that they constantly practice – though they have honed their Shortsword skill to frightening levels given that constant practice with it! Other Myrmidons – perhaps made of sterner stuff to begin with – have retained other skills. They have no  restrictions on learning skills of any kind. No Myrmidon mage has ever been recorded, but such a creature isn't out of the question. Myrmidons who left life with very high attributes would probably have higher attributes in unlife, though few display exceptional DX (their bodies are dry and stiff) or IQ (madness has left none of them completely untouched). Either attribute exceeding 12 would be rare.

MYRMIDON NAMES

Myrmidons reflect their rage in their names. Examples include Warrage, Lifestifle, Ironfate, Bloodfate, Soulfate, Lifedoom, Hearttear, Skinpeel, Doomrage, Deathcaress, Gorecaress, Frothinghunger, Bonepowder, Bonesplinter, Bonehunger, Boneflame, Bonehammer, Boneslaughter, Bonerage, Hearthammer, Heartflame, Hearthunger, Fleshbite, Fleshthirst, Fleshhunger, Fleshrage, Fleshdoom, Fleshtear, and Ironheart.

MYRMIDON PCs

A Myrmidon can't really be a Myrmidon without displaying constant fury. They probably best serve as NPCs only, except in a Dark campaign.

MYRMIDON ADVENTURE SEEDS

S EVERAL Myrmidons assault the PCs out of the blue. The next night they return in full force – even the ones that were slain or destroyed! The PCs must discover the reason for the attacks, and the magic that rejuvenates their foes . . .

R AMPAGING Myrmidons cart off a noble's daughter. Her beauty leaves even these undead smitten, it seems. The PCs must retrieve her. The Myrmidons vastly outnumber them. They must find something to *trade* for the daughter . . .

CREATING MYRMIDONS

The process for creating Myrmidons undoubtedly relates to the other undead-raising spells in Myth, but probably is far more complex given that it creates a *free-willed* creature.

Regardless, it disappeared with Balor. Any necromancer worthy of the name would be eager to discover the spell, and it's probably written down in some dusty library at the end of a long and perilous journey to the East.

Examples include Herod, Nym, Sycorax, Gullveig, and Cailleac Bheur.

SHADE PCs

Shades are fundamentally evil and powerful creatures. They might suit as a PC race in a high-powered campaign leaning toward Dark races, but usually are best reserved as NPCs.

SHADE ADVENTURE SEEDS

RECENTLY unearthed documents in Muirthemne suggest that the powerful artifact known as Fortuna's Folly lies in the ruins of Strand. The PCs are sent to investigate, but discover that a powerful Shade called Tarentus Dar and his underlings also are pursuing the magic item. The Shade will make a cunning and dangerous adversary as the two parties race to and through Strand . . .

A Shade captures the PCs and imprisons them in a mystical artifact similar to the Tain (see p. 85) in concept if not necessarily in style. To free themselves, the adventurers will have to work their way through a variety of strange landscapes and creatures, in an environment where the standard laws of physics and magery need not always apply. Non-hostile encounters should include other prisoners who testify to how incredibly long they've been trapped and how hopeless it is to try to escape . . .

SHADES

"Turquine so mistreated his subjects that even his personal guard abandoned him . . . he agreed to endure the indescribable tortures of the Fallen that he might have his revenge."

– from the lore of Myth

Perhaps the most powerful undead forces in Myth, Shades are mighty sorcerers who have exchanged a lifetime of hoarding power for an unlifetime of abusing it.

The process by which they undergo this transformation remains a mystery to the Light's archmages. Some archmages fear that even knowing *how* it's done would prove sufficient to immerse them in the Dark, so vile is the knowledge at its core. The most common belief is that most Shades, as powerful as they are, don't wield magic-weaving skills sufficient to transform themselves into the undead. They instead bargain with an even more powerful Dark agent for the conversion, which would explain why so many of these notoriously self-absorbed fiends serve a lower purpose.

Society

". . . those that Phelot deemed unsuitable for use as Thrall . . . were given to the Ghôls, who hacked their limbs and chewed their flesh . . . this is how he dealt with the people of Avon's Grove."

– from the lore of Myth

Two dominant motivations appear to drive most Shades. Shades appear to resent the living, especially those who take any joy in that condition. They also appear more eager than most Dark lords to seize and maintain real political power. Where a Soulblighter would overrun, consume all, and move on, a Shade would establish an iron rule, settle in, and begin inflicting *prolonged* misery. Likely the two motives interrelate.

Shades usually work solo, which befits their self-importance. They will surround themselves with their own contingents of mindless undead, Fetch, and similarly damned sorts, even when the Shade himself forms part of a greater Dark lord's train.

Though as powerful as a living archmage in combat-oriented magery, Shades seem disinclined to master the art of enchantment, rather preferring to coerce (or even hire) lesser mages to fulfill their enchantment needs. This represents the sole venue in which a living Human might negotiate with a Shade with any sort of leverage. Shades particularly desire "energon cubes" – square-cut, one-shot Powerstones also favored by many living archmages. These relatively inexpensive items allow them to tap awesome magical energies that their unliving forms can't supply.

Plan of Battle

Shades prefer to lead from the rear, screening themselves with their contingents of other troops. They usually attempt melee combat first, to preserve their inventory of unrechargeable energon cubes. When pressed, they *will* use their Dispersal Dream.

Shade Template   291 points

Shades appear to be withered, hairless corpses.

Attribute Modifiers: ST +3 [30], DX +1 [10], IQ +4 [45], HT +3 [30].

Advantages: DR +3 [9]; Doesn't Breathe [20]; Doesn't Eat/Drink [10]; Doesn't Sleep [20]; Extra Hit Points +4 [20]; High Pain Threshold [10]; Immunity to Disease [10]; Immunity to Poison [15]; Injury Tolerance (No blood) [5]; Literacy [10]; Magery 7 [105]; PD +3 [75]; Temperature Tolerance +10 [10]; Unaging [15]; and Wealthy [20].

Disadvantages: Appearance (Hideous) [-20]; Disturbing Voice [-10]; Dread (Running Water) [-20]; Fanaticism (Self) [-15]; Low Empathy [-15]; Megalomania [-10]; Sadism [-15]; Sterile [-3]; Social Stigma (Dead) [-20]; and Unliving [-50].

Quirks, Features, and Taboo Traits: Affected by Pentagram [0].

Standard Shade   400 points

ST: 13 [0]   **IQ:** 14 [0]   **Fatigue:** 13
DX: 11 [0]   **HT:** 13/17 [0]   **Senses:** 14
Speed: 6   **Move:** 6   **Will:** 14

Advantages and Disadvantages: Shade Package [291].

Skills: Administration (M/A) IQ [2]-14; Broadsword (P/A) DX+2 [8]-13; Intimidation (M/A) IQ [2]-14; Leadership (M/A) IQ [2]-14; Spell Throwing (Curse Missile) (P/E) DX+3 [8]-14; Tactics (M/H) IQ [4]-14; and Thaumatology (M/VH) IQ+5 [2]-19.

Languages: Bruig (M/A) IQ [0]-14.

Spells: Armor-20 [2]; Burning Death (VH)-18 [1]; Clumsiness-19 [1]; Continual Light-19 [1]; Create Air-19 [1]; Create Fire-19 [1]; Curse Missile-19 [1]; Darkness-21 [4]; Deathtouch-19 [1]; Decay-19 [1]; Delay-19 [1]; Dexterity-20 [2]; Dispersal Dream (VH)-20 [4]; Find Weakness-19 [1]; Heat-19 [1]; Ignite Fire-19 [1]; Itch-19 [1]; Lend Health-19 [1]; Lend Strength-19 [1]; Light-19 [1]; Link-19 [1]; Magic Resistance-20 [2]; Minor Healing-19 [1]; Pain-19 [1]; Paralyze Limb-19 [1]; Pestilence-19 [1]; Purify Air-19 [1]; Recover Strength-20 [2]; Rejoin-19 [1]; Repair-19 [1]; Resist Pain-19 [1]; Restore-19 [1]; Scryguard-19 [1]; Seek Earth-19 [1]; Seek Water-19 [1]; Shape Air-19 [1]; Shape Fire-19 [1]; Shield-25 [12]; Sickness-19 [1]; Spasm-19 [1]; Spell Shield-25 [12]; Steal Health-19 [1]; Steal Strength-19 [1]; Steal Toughness (VH)-18 [1]; Test Food-19 [1]; Walk on Air-20 [2]; Weaken-19 [1]; and Wither Limb-19 [1].

Equipment: Most Shades wear a long robe and wield a broadsword enchanted with Accuracy +2 and Puissance +2. They usually carry three or more 19-point non-rechargeable Manastones (see p. G42).

". . . an obsidian flame howled in a tongue he understood not, its words violent, clear, and distinct, tearing his breast and pulling him toward the dark thing which had risen from the shadows."

– from the lore of Myth

Shadow Names

The Mahir can't be said to have names in the conventional sense. What they do possess is a central *concept*, usually expressed in a handful of words. This concept gives them an individual identity, and can serve as a substitute for a proper name. Examples include: Deeper Shadow on a Waning Moon, Vile Oaths and Scorned Supplication, Quiet Whispers from Open Graves, Serene Death Stalking, Dreams of Lost Daylight, Denied Hope of the Wretched, Painful Memories of Lost Faith, Silent Student of Untaught Knowledge, Forever Cast in Deepest Night, Promises Broken to Greedy Ends, Final Sleep Without Rest, Bitter Legacy of Darker Deeds, Curse on a Final Breath, Silent Nightmare in the Twilight, and Hope Forever Lost to Fate.

Shadow PCs

Shadows, like traditional ghosts, tend to be bad people caught up in their own nature, but conceivably could be good or indifferent people pinioned to this plane by some great passion or injustice. This makes them suitable as a strange PC race should the GM allow.

Any Shadow's behavior should be completely centered upon its central concept, as discussed in *Shadow Names*, above. Whatever horrid deed or tragedy shaped the Shadow should be reflected in its Obsession, and that Obsession should occupy the Shadow at all times.

With GM permission, a player may buy down his Shadow's Obsession and explore what these creatures would do with a little free time.

The Obsession of many – though not all – Shadows confines them to a limited geographic area, just as with traditional ghosts. In the interests of playability, PC Shadows probably should avoid this limitation.

Shadows – also called the Mahir – are undead creatures born of obsession, much like traditional ghosts, but permanently suspended halfway between this world and the next.

No known conscious effort creates a Mahir. Once in a rare while they arise when someone dies in tragic or unjust manner, especially if that person was thwarted in some goal or routine. (The origins of Mahir probably will have less impact on a Myth campaign than those Mahir that already exist, but GMs can consult the *Rising From the Dead* sidebar on p. UN34 should the topic interest them.)

Unfortunately for those still living, most Shadows seem to form from evil intents, and take up the violence they practiced in life. Counterbalancing this is the tendency for their Obsession to confine them to one place, whether their place of death, the site of an artifact they covet, or somewhere else aligned with their one, true goal. This minimizes the odds of running afoul of one as long as one avoids dank crypts, ancient towers, and the like.

Society

Most Mahir avoid the living souls that they left behind, except to harm them. Mahir *can* speak, though they seldom do, in a dry, rustling, eerie whisper that seems to originate in the listener's head as much as from the region where the creature's lips should be. Everyone who hears this voice gets a mental impression of the Shadow's Obsession or reason for existence, often in the form of a sort of name (see *Shadow Names* sidebar). Their voices betraying their identity in this fashion may be why most Mahir prefer to remain mute.

Plan of Battle

Most Mahir rush to attack any living creature that violates the area they consider home. They're straightforward at most times: The Shadow will paralyze a victim at range, then close and attempt to slay him, usually by using a series of 1d Deathtouches to conserve energy. Their Deathtouch dries up and withers victims; the corpses of those slain will resemble mummies and crumble to the touch.

Shadows make extremely difficult opponents one on one. The Legion teaches its troops to attack only in numbers, since a Mahir can only paralyze one person before requiring an extended rest period to rebuild its energy. Fortunately for the overall success rate of this tactic, Shadows rarely use their superior speed to flee overwhelming odds, often attacking suicidally when their Obsession is triggered.

Shadow Racial Template   292 points

A Mahir appears as nothing more than a circular shadow, about 9′ across. When it moves it slides rapidly across the ground, leaving shadowy footprints as a clue to its real nature.

Upon approaching someone the Mahir's true form appears – a shadowy skeleton standing upright at the center of the circle. This is the body of the Shadow, which is attacked at the center of its 7-hex shadow-effect. Attacking the outer hexes does not have any effect.

Shadows are nearly impossible to distinguish when they hide in natural shadows. They move all but noiselessly.

Attribute Modifiers: ST +1 [10], DX +6 [80], IQ -1 [-10], HT -1 [-10].
Advantages: Combat Reflexes [15]; Doesn't Breathe [20]; Doesn't Eat/Drink [10]; Doesn't Sleep [20]; Enhanced Move 1 [10]; Extra Hit Points +6 [30]; High Pain Threshold [10]; Immunity to Disease [10]; Immunity to Poison [15]; Fatigue Recovery +5 [30]; Injury Tolerance (No blood) [5]; Invulnerability (All spells resisted by attribute, activation 11 or less for IQ-resisted spells, -10%) [90]; Magery (Body Control college only) 1 [10]; Night Vision [10]; Silence +4 [20]; Temperature Tolerance +10 [10]; Unaging [15]; and Unfazeable [15].
Disadvantages: Eunuch [-5]; *either* Obsession [-15] *or* alternately Compulsive Behavior [-15]; Shadow Form [-20]; Social Stigma (Dead) [-20]; Unhealing [-30]; Unliving [-50]; and Wealth (Dead Broke) [-25].
Quirks, Features, and Taboo Traits: Affected by Astral Block, Repel Spirits, and Turn Spirit [0]; Can be detected by sensitive individuals and animals [0]; Can be turned using True Faith [0]; Can't speak without revealing "name" [0]; Leaves "shadow footprints" that allow some chance to use Tracking or Shadowing against them [0].
Innate Spells: Deathtouch-15 [14] and Total Paralysis-20 (May be cast at range, +35%; Costs 4 extra energy for a net cost of 7, -20%) [28].

Standard Shadow   300 points

ST: 11 [0]   **IQ:** 9 [0]   **Fatigue:** 11
DX: 16 [0]   **HT:** 9/15 [0]   **Senses:** 9
Speed: 6.25   **Move:** 12   **Will:** 9

Advantages: Shadow Racial Template [292].
Disadvantages: per Shadow Racial Template.
Skills: Stealth (P/A) DX+2 [8]-18.
Languages: Bruig (M/A) IQ [0]-9.
Equipment: None. If the Mahir's Obsession revolves around an item, the Shadow likely will consider the item as "his," but has no way to pick it up or otherwise wield it.
Customization Notes: Shadows retain memories and skills from their lives, though apparently in a haphazard fashion. Any given Shadow might have some or all of the skills he possessed in life, enhanced attributes based upon exceptional scores in life, extended powers of spellcasting . . . or not. Some Shadows of formerly intelligent people appear to distill down to nothing more than the bare essence of their Obsession, wielding none of their skills from life and displaying little of their intellect. GMs can rule on how intact of a personality transfers from life to undeath; this phenomena can be used to offset the cost of a PC conversion into a Shadow, by stripping away skills, attribute increases, and advantages to help pay for the racial template.

A SHADOW has been terrorizing a baron's castle for weeks, to the point where his wife is in danger of miscarrying their first child. The frantic noble has tried a variety of remedies, and now entreats the PCs to stalk and slay the creature. This won't prove simple, for the Mahir only appears at night, when he's nearly impossible to spot, and slips through the twists and turns of the craggy old castle as if he was raised within its walls. After several nights of fruitless pursuit, the PCs should realize they'll have to offer the Shadow *bait*. The only problem is figuring out what it is the Shadow is after . . .

U PON slaying a Shadow, one of the PCs receives a vision of the great injustice that created it – some two decades ago the Shadow was a simple poet executed for the murder of the woman he loved, though innocent of the crime. The vision gives way to an overwhelming compulsion to solve the old crime and set the record straight. Should the PCs pursue this course, they'll discover that a powerful local authority actually committed the murder, and has no intention of just standing by as his old sins are unearthed. Overcoming this obstacle and seeing justice done likely will present no material reward – but the next morning the original PC will awaken to find a scrap of parchment on his pillow, with a single, simple verse of thanks penned upon it . . .

A PC who died under the right circumstances returns as an NPC Shadow! The newly undead creature fervently desires to correct the circumstances of its death, and wants the remaining PCs' help, but his preferred course will impose great peril on the living. The PCs must decide how much loyalty they owe to a companion in arms who no longer lives nor seems to care about their well-being, but obviously suffers an immortal anguish sufficient to return him to earthly existence . . .

Soulless

A form of mindless undead, the Soulless are also called "the Hollow Men." These common soldiers of the Dark nonchalantly defy the laws of physics and magery. They constantly harassed Legion forces in the wars just past.

Their lack of true substance allows them to levitate indefinitely, though it appears they must remain within a few feet of a solid object. For instance, a Soulless could ascend to a bit over the top of a tree, but could not maintain the same altitude without the tree's presence. Their vaporous form also keeps them from suffering the normal inconveniences of a skeletal form (see p. UN51), provides minimal protection from harm (+1 DR). It also has the quirk of allowing any attack to completely blow-through the Soulless, even though it damages him normally, and hit the character behind him!

Like other mindless undead in Myth, Soulless do not retain skills from their former life, though they do retain any higher or lower attributes (as modified by the racial template). Most necromancers immediately set their new Soulless to nonstop practice with their javelins.

Plan of Battle

Soulless attempt to find high, inaccessible locations and harass enemy units from them. Given their inexhaustible ammo, they will begin throwing their javelins at extreme range. Though well-trained in it, they avoid melee combat.

Soulless Racial Template   126 points

Soulless appear as semiethereal human half-skeletons, sometimes with bits of flesh still hanging from the bones. Their dangling spinal column never has leg or hip bones attached. They weigh nothing and rarely measure more than 3′ long.

Their back serves as a Cornucopia for wickedly barbed javelins. Several such javelins always protrude from it; this is simply a special effect. The Cornucopia produces just one javelin at a time, as per usual for the enchantment. Only a given Soulless may handle his own javelins. The Cornucopia is purchased as a Knack, ignoring the normal prohibition on Enchantment-college Knacks, but paying double the normal cost for the privilege.

As the javelins pass through the foul remains of the Soulless when pulled into action, they come away poisoned with various irritants and diseases. This causes wounds from them to burn particularly fiercely, though not so much as to register in game terms. These wounds will usually infect; legend has it that they never heal, but that's a (slight) exaggeration of the nastiness of the typical disease conveyed.

Even though the Soulless lack a very stable mode of flight, they do *not* take penalties to their combat rolls for attacking while in flight. Their javelin-use – as melee weapon or missile – is considered a "natural" attack for them, and any penalties caused by their flight are assumed in their low DX scores.

Attribute Modifiers: ST +3 [30], DX -1 [-10], IQ -1 [-10], HT +2 [20].
Advantages: DR +1 [3]; Doesn't Breathe [20]; Doesn't Eat/Drink [10]; Doesn't Sleep [20]; Flight (10-foot ceiling from nearest solid object, -20%, and only up to regular Move speed, -20%) [24]; Immunity to Disease [10]; Immunity to Poison [15]; Imperturbable [10]; Increased Speed +1 [25]; Injury Tolerance (No blood) [5]; Invulnerability (To all resisted spells) [100]; Knack (Cornucopia-15 producing javelins) [60]; Night Vision [10]; Pestilence (varies) [5]; Silence +2 [10]; Temperature Tolerance +10 [10]; and Unaging [15].
Disadvantages: Appearance (Hideous) [-20]; Eunuch [-5]; Hidebound [-5]; Lame (Cannot walk but usually countered by Flight advantage, -70%) [-10]; Mute [-25]; No Sense of Smell/Taste [-5]; Reprogrammable Duty [-25]; Slave Mentality [-40]; Social Stigma (Dead) [-20]; Unhealing [-30]; Unliving [-50]; and Wealth (Dead Broke) [-25].
Skills: +2 to Spear [2] and +3 to Spear-Throwing [2].
Quirks, Features, and Taboo Traits: Affected by Control Zombie, Pentagram, and Turn Zombie [0]; Cannot swim [0]; Javelins convey Pestilence at range [0]; No mental skills [0]; and Takes damage normally but attacks *completely* blow through in a manner defying mundane physics [0].

Standard Soulless   175 points

ST: 13 [0]   **IQ:** 9 [0]   **Fatigue:** 13
DX: 9 [0]   **HT:** 12 [0]   **Senses:** 9
Speed: 6.25   **Move:** 6   **Will:** 9

Advantages and Disadvantages: Soulless Template [126].
Skills: Flight (P/A) DX [0]-9; Spear (P/A) DX+7 [32]-16; Spear Throwing (P/E) DX+7 [16]-16; and Stealth (P/A) DX-1 [1]-8.
Languages: Bruig (M/A) IQ [0]-9.
Equipment: None other than their ever-present javelins.
Customization Notes: Several necromancers have attempted to fine-tune the spell for creating Soulless, to produce more graceful creatures that don't require intensive training to be competent with their weapons. So far this improvement has eluded them. Soulless can learn other physical skills, but rarely do so given the amount of training needed to master their basic abilities.

The Soulless form hovers between substantial and insubstantial properties in a way that defies most *GURPS* conventions. For the most part, they should be treated as substantial beings of average human weight when taking damage or knockback, fighting a headwind, etc. The known exception is their unusual blow-through detailed in the main text. GMs may decide they behave as non-solid objects in other circumstances as well. They *cannot* walk through walls or the like.

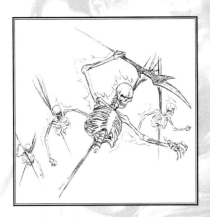

CREATING SOULLESS

Soulless are even more expensive to create than most Myth undead. The Soulless spell has a cost of 41 energy; the Mass Soulless spell has a base cost of 40! The Soulless spell requires the Enchantment spell Cornucopia as an additional prerequisite.

The necromancer must start out with a humanoid skeleton, though it can retain some gristle and bits. The hip and leg bones need be removed; this is a trivial process. A good spell to make use of these parts would be well-received in necromantic circles.

Despite the effort required to create them, Soulless are created nearly as often as Thralls and far more often than Ghasts. As expensive as they are, they survive combat well when properly deployed. The slight premium in energy cost paid to create one often pays off in longevity. A new Soulless needs about 14 months to learn the skill set in the standard writeup.

STYGIAN KNIGHT NAMES

Though as mindless as their undead contemporaries, Knights aren't usually sent into action in hordes. While most go unnamed, some necromancers make giving orders easier by christening them in a style that's consistent with weapon-naming; i.e., Dark Splinterer of Souls, Deathbringer, that sort of thing.

STYGIAN KNIGHT PCs

As with mindless undead, Knights make poor PCs, though the GM might consider allowing a Stygian Knight to somehow gain free will and making the character type open to players. This creature might resemble the Wraith from pp. UN86-87.

The PCs might have greater interest in a Stygian Knight *Ally*. Since both PC and Knight can inhabit the same suit of armor at once, a PC could share a Knight's armor and allow it to take over in combat, in the event that the PC is knocked un-conscious, etc.

Even when sharing space with some-one, a Knight can not speak to them!

STYGIAN KNIGHTS

The line between equipment and the eldritch blurs in these golemesque creatures who can cut terrible swaths through opposing ranks. The chronicles describe Stygian Knights as "empty shells of armor animated by mysterious sorceries" with "no true spark of life, and thus no fear of death." They serve their masters with complete, unthinking devotion.

The mages who create Stygian Knights must craft the armor themselves (see *Creating Stygian Knights* sidebar on p. 61), and usually choose to fit them with oversized but thin plate sporting a variety of spikes. This armor has a mundane PD4, DR5 and should be treated as half plate. Legend has it the enchanter must invest a piece of his soul in each Knight, but knowledgeable thaumatologists scoff at this notion. The legend might arise from a common result of rolling a critical failure on the enchantment, however.

Plan of Battle

Stygian Knights are usually encountered in small squadrons, and are normally assigned to defensive roles guarding some particularly valuable installation. Likely they represent too much investment to squander in offensive operations.

Strangely, their enchanters are seldom seen to "wear" their creations in combat (see *Stygian Knight PCs* sidebar), even though it's known that this can be done. Perhaps the enchanters know something that most people do not, such as that being slain within a Stygian Knight (or having one slain while wearing it) causes one's eternal soul to end up in unpleasant places.

Stygian Knight Template   166 points

A Stygian Knight resembles a golem made of plate armor. The armor usually boasts very large size (7' tall) and spikes, but thin metal (PD 4, DR 5).

Stygian Knights are not nearly as tough as they should be, and are particularly vulnerable to explosives. Many theories seek to explain this relative weakness, but none to satisfaction.

When disassembled into its component parts, a Stygian Knight becomes dormant (see the same effect for undead in no-mana zones on p. 28), though its parts still register as magical.

A Knight can be worn, though only if it's under orders to allow entrance or after a long struggle (the prospective wearer must win a contest of ST for each second that the given suit of armor normally takes to put on, losing two seconds' progress for each lost contest).

Stygian Knights are *exceedingly* dense, showing even less initiative than the mindless undead. They will stand by and watch their master's foes march past with him tied up and hoisted on their shoulders if not under direct orders to intervene. Treat them as akin to computers, requiring very explicit and carefully worded instructions to avoid confusion. Usually, a Knight under unclear orders will simply stop acting till given further instructions.

Attribute Modifiers: ST +8 [90], DX +3 [30], IQ -2 [-15], HT +1 [10].

Advantages: Doesn't Breathe [20]; Doesn't Eat/Drink [10]; Doesn't Sleep [20]; DR +5 [15]; High Pain Threshold [10]; Immunity to Disease [10]; Immunity to Poison [15]; Injury Tolerance (No blood, No brain, No impaling bonus, No Neck, and No Vitals) [40]; Magic Resistance +10 (Only spells resisted by IQ, -50%) [10]; PD +4 [100]; Short Spines [5]; Temperature Tolerance +11 [11]; Unaging [15]; and Unfazeable [15].

Disadvantages: Cannot Learn [-30]; Eunuch [-5]; Hidebound [-5]; Low Empathy [-15]; Mute [-25]; No Sense of Humor [-10]; Obdurate [-10]; Reprogrammable Duty [-25]; Slave Mentality [-40]; Social Stigma (Dead) [-20]; Unhealing [-30]; and Vulnerability (+3d from explosives) [-30].

Quirks, Features, and Taboo Traits: Affected by Control Zombie, Pentagram, and Turn Zombie [0]; Always insubstantial but wounds normally [0]; Cannot swim [0]; and No mental skills [0].

Standard Stygian Knight   175 points

ST: 18 [0]   **IQ:** 8 [0]   **Fatigue:** 18
DX: 13 [0]   **HT:** 11 [0]   **Senses:** 8
Speed: 6   **Move:** 7   **Will:** 8

Advantages: Stygian Knight Racial Template [166].
Disadvantages: per Stygian Knight Racial Template.
Skills: Axe/Mace (P/A) DX-2 [1/2]-11; Running (P/H – HT) HT-3 [1/2]-8; and Two-Handed Axe/Mace (P/A) DX+2 [8]-15.
Languages: Bruig (M/A) IQ [0]-8.
Equipment: Great axe (3d+3 cutting, no ready time).
Customization Notes: Mages have been known to craft Stygian Knights of better armor (plate or fine plate) further embellished with Puissance and Accuracy enchantments and of more traditional design. The alternate armor type *must* be a full, integral suit, at least prior to enchantment. Since the suit forms the Knight's body, it does pay for additional DR and PD, including that provided by enchantments. The enchantment used to create a Knight offers the enchanter opportunity to choose its primary and secondary weapon skills, so something other than Two-Handed Axe/Mace and Axe/Mace is an option.

THE PCs come into possession of a nice suit of plate armor under strange circumstances. (Maybe a merchant sells it cheap. Maybe it just shows up standing in their front room one morning.) It doesn't respond to any stimuli until someone puts it on, at which time the Stygian Knight will begin taking them back to its master! The Knight is under orders to trap warriors in this fashion. To take command of his own motions in any given second, the entrapped person will have to win a contest of ST with the Knight . . .

WHILE pursuing some great treasure, the PCs encounter a Stygian Knight whose long-dead master ordered it to guard the very same item. The treasure is located in some remote or dangerous place that the PCs can't access; i.e., underwater, in a chamber filled with poison gas, etc. They must get within conversation range of the Knight and fend off its attacks long enough to trick it into retrieving the item for them.

CREATING STYGIAN KNIGHTS

Stygian Knights are created with a variant of the Golem spell (see p. M44). This Stygian Knight spell works identically, except that rather than animating solid constructs, it can only animate devices already suitably articulated for movement. While whole suits of plate armor are the obvious example at hand, the spell could also be used on other primitive machinery – if anyone ever had any reason to animate a grain mill, this would be the spell to do it.

Being more limited in scope, the Stygian Knight spell is cheaper than Golem. Creating a Knight requires the mage to craft the armor himself. This uses at least $1,000 worth of materials (half the price of a finished suit of the armor in use), takes one week per $200 in materials, and requires successful Armoury and Shape Earth rolls. Energy cost to activate is 200.

THRALL

"Bahl'al spurred his army onward with a blistering wind. Three full days before his army arrived . . . the citizens of Tyr knew their doom lumbered nearer with each passing hour . . ."

– from the lore of Myth

Thralls usually form the core of Dark armies, just as Warriors do for the Light. They aren't flashy or individually powerful, but often overcome opposition with tenacity and numbers.

Society

See *Ghasts*, pp. 44-45, for how Thralls impact living society. Unlike Ghasts, Thralls can be created by plundering the "catacombs, crypts, and cemeteries of a thousand years" as one chronicler lamented, so Dark lords with sufficient necromantic resources often seem to boast an inexhaustible supply of them.

Plan of Battle

Thralls seek to overwhelm, pure and simple. Their masters deploy them in quantity, and usually order them to use All-Out Attacks to increase their effective skills. The ideal Thrall scenario has them filling all six hexes around a given foe, with 12 more Thrall in the immediately adjacent hexes attacking from the second rank! Their masters must expect to take casualties given opposition of any significance.

THRALL ADVENTURE SEEDS

E VIL necromancers have established a "Thrall factory" in the PCs' neck of the woods. The site is necromancy-aspected and near several large grave sites. The necromancers have access to the formidable energy required to cast the thrall variant of Mass Zombie, whether through huge personal reserves, Power- or Mana-stones, a mana basin (see p. MI12), or other resources. The PCs must hack their way through a literal stream of Thralls to shut the place down . . .

A NEW variety of Thrall appears on the battlefield, "armed" with the Independent Body Parts (see p. UN59) advantage! Hacking one of these to bits creates a variety of appendages still doing their best to attack Light forces or aid their intact comrades. Someone needs to hunt down and destroy the talented necromancer who developed this new Thrall, before the spell becomes commonplace . . .

Thrall Racial Template   62 points

Thralls appear as gray-skinned, leathery corpses. Sometimes their complexions have a greenish tint. Most of their hair has fallen out. Their dried tendons usually make them *very* clumsy and relatively slow-moving.

Attribute Modifiers: ST +6 [70], DX -3 [-20], IQ -2 [-15], HT +3 [30].

Advantages: Doesn't Breathe [20]; Doesn't Eat/Drink [10]; Doesn't Sleep [20]; Extra Hit Points +8 [40]; Immunity to Disease [10]; Immunity to Poison [15]; Imperturbable [10]; Injury Tolerance (No blood) [5]; Invulnerability (To spells resisted by IQ) [75]; Night Vision [10]; Temperature Tolerance +10 [10]; and Unaging [15].

Disadvantages: Appearance (Hideous) [-20]; Bad Smell [-10]; Hidebound [-5]; Mute [-25]; Reprogrammable Duty [-25]; Slave Mentality [-40]; Social Stigma (Dead) [-20]; Sterile [-3]; Unhealing [-30]; Unliving [-50]; and Wealth (Poor) [-15].

Quirks, Features, and Taboo Traits: Affected by Control Zombie, Pentagram, and Turn Zombie [0]; and No mental skills [0].

Standard Thrall   100 points

ST: 16 [0]   **IQ:** 8 [0]   **Fatigue:** 16
DX: 7 [0]   **HT:** 13/21 [0]   **Senses:** 8
Speed: 5   **Move:** 5   **Will:** 8

Advantages: Thrall Racial Template [62].

Disadvantages: per Thrall Racial Template.

Skills: Brawling (P/E) DX+2 [4]-9; Stealth (P/A) DX [2]-7; and Two-Handed Axe/Mace (P/A) DX+5 [32]-12.

Languages: Bruig (M/A) IQ [0]-8.

Equipment: Thralls usually wear armor made of leather and magically shaped bone. It protects with PD3, DR3, with full coverage of the feet, and one-half coverage of the torso, arms, and legs. (Roll 1d. Protects on a 1-3.) In addition, their arms bear light-leather (PD 1, DR 1) bracers with one-third coverage. (Roll 1d *only if* the previous roll failed. Protects on a 1-2.) Hands and heads are left unprotected. Their armor weighs 15 lbs. and costs $260. They almost universally carry great axes.

Customization Notes: See notes for *Ghasts* on p. 45.

THRALL NAMES

Thralls don't have proper names, nor do they usually have some sort of designation within their "unit." In most cases, whole hordes are waved into action en masse. Even if a Dark military leader wanted to attempt more precise maneuver and drill, the Thrall wouldn't be able to comprehend or learn what was asked of them.

THRALL PCs

See the *Ghast PCs* sidebar on p. 44. Thralls usually best serve as minor NPCs.

CREATING THRALLS

See *Zombie (variants)* on p. 31 and *Mass Zombie (variants)* on p. 30 for general information on creating undead in Myth. The Thrall spell costs 34 energy to cast; the Mass Thrall spell has a base cost of 33.

Thralls require preserved or dried bodies. They need not be intact or particularly *well*-preserved, but fresh corpses won't do.

As with all Myth undead, Thralls reanimate without any of the skills or memories they possessed in life, but can be taught physical skills. While most are trained in using two-handed axes (because these weapons are cheap and useful in non-combat applications as well), nothing other than tradition keeps a necromancer from fielding Thralls wielding flails, broadswords, or other weapons.

Usually, new Thralls are set immediately to work training in using their axes. Because encountered Thralls can vary wildly in age (though all in a given horde will tend to be the same age), their skill levels can vary considerably as well. A Thrall needs about 11 months to learn the skill set in the standard writeup.

TROW

"...when Soulblighter confronted the Trow, demanding their continued servitude, they replied 'Set iron to rest and choose you one from our number. Ask of his name and what he owes you.'"

– from the lore of Myth

These colossi have walked the lands of Myth since the beginning. Created by Nyx (see *Religion*, pp. 9-10), the Trow mix features of golems and an ordinary race. They wound normally, and can digest food though need not eat it, yet turn to stone when damaged to -HT × 10. They do not breed, which means each Trow lost is never replaced, and rumor has it that no more than a few score now exist. They certainly can think for themselves, yet sometimes approach events with a detached perspective that suggests a strong, alien sense of fate.

At most times they look down upon "normal" races, quick to point out human folly and unlikely to become fervent about any cause other than worshiping Nyx. The horror they once wrought (see p. 20) led them to forswear iron weapons – and in practice they avoid any weapon of any material – but a Trow will do massive violence with his bare feet and hands at minimal prompting.

Society

The Trow once ruled the lands of Myth, building city-sized temple complexes of surreal beauty in glorification of Nyx. A millennia ago, Connacht imprisoned them and destroyed their works (see p. 20). Released by Balor, they have been caught up in the wars till now, first on the side of Dark and then Light.

The direction that they will take with their freedom again and time on their hands is anybody's guess. They are assumed to be rebuilding their temples.

Trow Racial Template   444 points

The Trow are giant humanoids with gray skin. They all stand within inches of 18′ and weigh within 200 lbs. of 2,700 lbs. A Trow makes an immense amount of noise as he strides along. As described by one traveler, a Trow speaks in "a voice I felt as much as heard . . . his words slow and deliberate . . . each syllable the roaring of an ocean . . ."

The Trow aren't very agile in bending over; they can pick up items off the ground, but not lunge out and down to throw punches at human-sized foes. This requires them to kick at most adversaries, and limits their reach for all practical purposes (consider it +1 hex when dealing with something at least 10′ off the ground).

Their last 32 points of ST are purchased with the limitations "No jumping bonus" (-5%) and "Doesn't affect skill defaults" (-5%).

The Trow have a comfort zone between 25º and 140º – below 25º they begin slowing down from their Cold-Blooded disadvantage. Trow who reach Speed or DX 0 become immobile, still living but frozen solid. Berserks have been known to patrol the high mountains in storms to see if the weather caught any Trow by surprise, then hack them to pieces in safety.

Pieces of Trow fetch good prices as curios. A Trow skull (removed carefully before petrification) commands $2,000+.

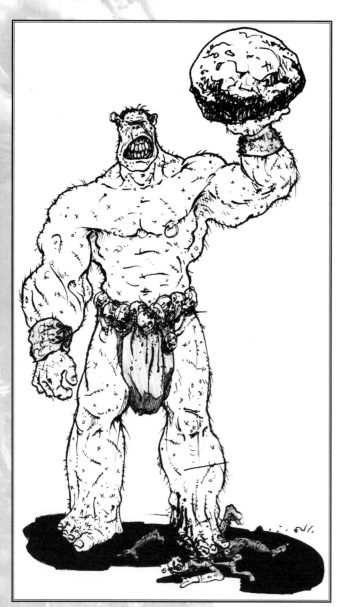

Attribute Modifiers: ST +8/40 [176], DX +3 [30], IQ +2 [20], HT +5 [60].

Advantages: DR +8 [24]; Doesn't Eat/Drink [10]; Extra Arm Length +1 [20]; Extra Hit Points +10 [50]; Increased Density +1 [5]; Injury Tolerance (No blood) [5]; Literacy [10]; PD +2 [50]; Status +1 [5]; Striker (May do swing damage with kicks) [25]; Temperature Tolerance +4 [4]; Unaging [15]; and Unfazeable [15].

Disadvantages: Bad Temper [-10]; Cold-Blooded [-5]; Disturbing Voice [-10]; Dying Race [-10]; Inconvenient Size [-10]; Reputation (Stomp) [-20]; Stubbornness [-5]; and Vow (Use no iron or weapons) [-10].

Quirks, Features, and Taboo Traits: Cannot learn Stealth skill [0]; Cannot punch human-sized opponents [0]; and Cannot swim [0].

Standard Trow   500 points

ST: 18/50 [0]   **IQ:** 12 [0]   **Fatigue:** 50
DX: 13 [0]   **HT:** 15/25 [0]   **Senses:** 12
Speed: 7   **Move:** 8   **Will:** 12

Advantages and Disadvantages: Trow Template [444].

Skills: Architecture/TL3 (M/A) IQ+3 [8]-15; Area Knowledge (Lands of Myth) (M/E) IQ+1 [2]-13; Artist (M/H) IQ [4]-12; Axe/Mace (P/A) DX [2]-13; Brawling (P/E) DX+3 [8]-16; Broadsword (P/A) DX [2]-13; Hidden Lore (Dawn of time) (M/A) IQ+1 [4]-13; History (M/H) IQ+4 [12]-16; Running (P/H – HT) HT [4]-15; Tactics (M/H) IQ [4]-12; Theology (M/H) IQ [4]-12; and Two-Handed Axe/Mace (P/A) DX-1 [1]-12.

Languages: Bruig (M/A) IQ-1 [1]-11 and Trow (M/A) IQ [0]-12.

Equipment: None. They wear a loincloth with a belt of human-sized skulls.

Customization Notes: A Trow who uses weapons must replace his Vow with the rest of his race as a full-time Enemy (a -110-point difference). The occasional tossed boulder will be overlooked, but even a single usage of iron implements will not be.

The Trow would make intriguing PCs in a high-powered campaign. The player and GM should be prepared to fill in many details of Trow history, since other players probably will ask questions and most Trow PCs should know the answers. A PC Trow probably shouldn't deviate too far from the racial template, other than by adding skills and (should surplus points exist) magical talents. The Trow are fairly homogenous.

TROW ADVENTURE SEEDS

THE Trow are converging en masse on Tharsis (see p. 11). Their motive remains a mystery. Do they intend to create some powerful new magic artifact? Do they intend to hold a religious ceremony of some sort? Do they intend to finish the job Soulblighter started, shattering the Cloudspine and destroying the lands of Myth . . .

THE PCs have opportunity to aid a Trow in great distress. In his gratitude he becomes something of an ally, a mixed blessing considering the attention he draws and his tendency to obliterate every annoyance in a second flat, before cooler heads can prevail . . .

Wight Names

Wights are referred to by a variety of unprintable names when they appear on a battlefield, but don't have individual names.

Wight PCs

Wights would only make PC material in a semi-humorous campaign. They take the concept of a "one-shot adventure" to a new level.

Wight Adventure Seeds

A N evil overlord has turned a Wight into a pathfinding device. The Wight will automatically begin walking back toward its master's lair if left unrestrained. The overlord intended this Wight to aid some of his allies in returning to safety from Light lands, but it's ended up in the PCs' hands. They can follow it back to the lair – if they can keep it in one piece and keep up with a tireless (though slow) traveler . . .

W ITHIN a densely populated area, the PCs come across a stockpile of Wight parts. They must discover who horded these grisly munitions, and why. They also need to destroy the stockpile, which will be harder than it appears at first glance. Manual removal will induce nausea and gagging even if sufficient protective clothing is used. Burning would spread irritants in the smoke. Some practical spellcasting might be in order . . .

Wight

"Once known as the Messengers of Culwyeh, a name now forgotten by all but the most devout pupils of Necromancy, these miserable creatures seek only release from their hellish existence."

– from the lore of Myth

These loathsome undead appear as bloated, ulcerous corpses, carrying a large knife and making no move to use it against their master's foes. Instead they shamble up to those opponents and use it on *themselves*, at which time the real horror begins.

Society

See *Ghasts*, pp. 44-45, for how Wights impact living society.

In addition, few Dark creatures evoke more horror than a Wight. They wield the psychological potency of a flamethrower, drawing attention all out of proportion even to their considerable potential. Otherwise disciplined troops often ignore other targets to join in killing a single Wight, doing enough damage to slay it seven times over while its non-Wight companions advance unmolested.

Plan of Battle

"Preceding the assault on Covenant . . . two score and nine Wights were herded into the Tiber an hour's march from the city, there to stand until they burst, rendering the water undrinkable."

– from the lore of Myth

Wights are weapons more than servants. Their masters attempt to insert them into large enemy units, to slay many of the troops and disrupt even more. Wights can also be used to poison water supplies, perform demolition, and more.

Their slow movement makes getting them to the target difficult. An exposed Wight will be attacked with missile weapons if possible, outrun if not. Despite their internal gases, Wights *can* submerge themselves and exist underwater indefinitely, so they often are placed in ambush at river crossings.

Wight Racial Template   163 points

Wights are *badly* decomposed Ghasts (see *Creating Wights* sidebar). Their bodies magically contain decomposition gases at incredible pressures. This gives them a bloated appearance, waddling gait – and explosive nature. Once a Wight reaches 0 HT (i.e., a hole has been opened into his interior cavities), he explodes in a massive torrent of foul gases and rotten bits. This explosion can outright kill bystanders, and will almost assuredly nauseate any survivors.

Wights really only exist to cease existing, preferably taking large numbers of the opposition with them in the transition. Their masters arm them with a large knife with which to slay themselves once among enemy troops; treat this as a blow to the vitals, All-Out Attacking (+4 to skill) a willing target (+4) for an effective Knife skill of 16 doing triple 1d+2 damage. If the first attempt doesn't do the trick, the Wight will simply keep trying; the second self-stabbing will suffice.

The obvious countermeasure is to fill a Wight with arrows long before he gets within his blast's range, setting off his explosion prematurely.

The Wight's attack does 7d uniformly over an area centered on himself with a radius of 12 hexes. It also acts as a sprayed level 5 irritant Venom (see p. CI71) over the same area. The attack is purchased with the damage properties (if not special effect) of a Sonic Blast (see p. CI73) for a base cost of 56 points with the enhancements "Linked" (+10%), "Area effect" (+50%), and "Increased area to 12 hexes" (+200%) and the limitations "One use *ever*" (-100%), "No range and must be centered on user" (-20%), and "Always and only triggered at 0 HT" (-100%) for a net 79 points. The Venom is purchased with the enhancements "Linked" (+10%), "Sprayed" (+100%), and "Increased area to 12 hexes" (+200%) and the same limitations as the Blast for a net 143 points. Don't apply a true Sonic Blast's armor-piercing effects, but do allow the damage to bypass unsealed, nonmagical armor like a real explosive would.

Wights *do* age, being so perilously close to overripe. Roll vs. HT+2 each month; on a failed roll the Wight spontaneously explodes. Note that a Wight with HT adjusted to 14+ must pay off the Terminally Ill disadvantage; Wights with HT 13 must reduce it to -50 points.

Pieces of an exploded Wight act as a level 3 irritant Venom when touched or flung on an unarmored portion of a victim. Ghôls handle these routinely, given their high HT and bonus to resist the effects stemming from their Cast Iron Stomach advantage. Most living races cannot, nor would care to do so if they could. The pieces also carry whatever Pestilence the Wight had. Assume 3d usable chunks scattered within 10 hexes of a Wight explosion.

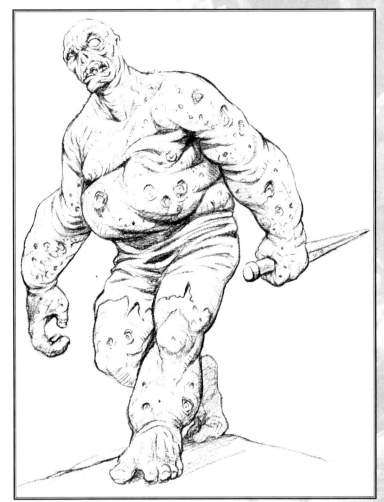

Attribute Modifiers: ST +8 [90], DX -2 [-15], IQ -2 [-15], HT +2 [20].

Advantages: Doesn't Breathe [20]; Doesn't Eat/Drink [10]; Doesn't Sleep [20]; Immunity to Disease [10]; Immunity to Poison [15]; Imperturbable [10]; Injury Tolerance (No blood) [5]; Invulnerability (To spells resisted by IQ) [75]; Night Vision [10]; Pestilence ×2 (both vary) [10]; Temperature Tolerance +8 [8]; and Wight Suicide Blast (see text) [222].

Disadvantages: Appearance (Monstrous) [-25]; Bad Smell [-10]; Eunuch [-5]; Hidebound [-5]; Mute [-25]; No Sense of Smell/Taste [-5]; Reprogrammable Duty [-25]; Slave Mentality [-40]; Social Stigma (Dead) [-20]; Terminally Ill [-75]; Unhealing [-30]; Unliving [-50]; and Wealth (Dead Broke) [-25].

Skills: Brawling (P/E) DX+3 [8]-11.

Quirks, Features, and Taboo Traits: Affected by Control Zombie, Pentagram, and Turn Zombie [0]; and No mental skills [0].

Standard Wight   175 points

ST: 18 [0]   **IQ:** 8 [0]   **Fatigue:** 18
DX: 8 [0]   **HT:** 12 [0]   **Senses:** 8
Speed: 5   **Move:** 5   **Will:** 8

Advantages and Disadvantages: Wight Racial Template [163].
Skills: Knife (P/E) DX+3 [8]-11 and Stealth (P/A) DX+1 [4]-9.
Languages: Bruig (M/A) IQ [0]-8.
Equipment: Large knife, usually cheap and/or rusty.
Customization Notes: A Wight's attributes vary according to the quality of the corpse used for the original Ghast. A Wight might have Reduced Hit Points, reflecting earlier damage and making it pose just as much threat to friend as foe. Wights learned Brawling as Ghasts; they must be taught their Knife and Stealth skills. They *average* carrying two diseases; some carry up to a dozen!

CREATING WIGHTS

No spell creates a Wight. They are the natural evolution/decomposition of a Ghast (see pp. 44-45).

Rather than slowly fall apart in classic undead fashion, the Ghast's magically altered decay causes its skin to become waxy and airtight. This keeps the vile fluids that provide its Venom attack from reaching its skin. Instead, they mix with the volatile decomposition gases that build to incredible pressures within the Wight's body.

Certain processes invented by impatient Dark lords can accelerate the change. Conversely, taking damage in combat or other strenuous activity can knock enough pieces from the Ghast to dispel the structural integrity needed to become a Wight. In game terms, make a Ghast due to become a Wight roll vs. its current Hit Points. A failed roll means it will simply remain a Ghast till it completely falls apart.

Character Templates

A character template resembles a racial template, except that it describes a *profession* instead of a *race*. It is a list of attributes, advantages, disadvantages, and skills that a player can use in order to quickly build a specific type of character without neglecting important abilities or getting bogged down in the rules. The point costs of these abilities are listed, and the sum is given as the "template cost."

With most *GURPS* character templates, the player pays this cost, specifies the options he wants, writes those abilities down on his character sheet, and spends his remaining points to customize his character (see below). The following *GURPS Myth* templates (with the sole exception of the Archmage template) have *no* options – for they are designed to both serve as a template and illustrate the very specific set of abilities found in the computer *Myth* characters. Extra points may be spent to enhance these templates normally.

Templates are never required – they simply purchase many abilities at once, have no in-play effects, and offer no "package discount." *GURPS Myth* GMs may require them, because they can efficiently emulate the computer-game characters. If not required, templates can be treated as nothing more than recommendations, exactly like those listed in the *Character Types* sections of other *GURPS* books.

Skills

In the templates in this section, *primary skills* are skills that are absolutely required, and *secondary skills* are helpful skills that it's hard to imagine the character not having. The latter sets of skills are implied or can be reasonably assumed given the narrative thread of the computer *Myth* games, but aren't "coded" into the computer characters' performance. Skills are listed in the following format:

Skill Name (Difficulty) Relative Level [Point Cost]-Actual Level

Customizing Templates

Once the template has been purchased, the player may customize it by spending any remaining character points. The template does not influence how these points are spent. If the template has fewer disadvantages than the campaign permits, more may be taken, giving extra points to spend. Quirks are rarely listed on templates, and are always optional. They should be selected by the player.

Altering Templates

Templates are *guidelines,* not rules. When customizing a template, the player is free to alter any or all of the items that came with it. Subtracting items from a professional template may result in a character who will be regarded as incompetent, however.

Character Templates vs. Racial Templates

Racial templates, as found on pp. 36-67, differ from character templates in several ways. Racial templates use attribute modifiers instead of attribute levels, may include advantages unavailable on a less-than-racial basis, and include disadvantages that don't count against the campaign disadvantage limit.

Character templates can be used with any race, although the following are normally human professions in Myth. When using character templates with other races, simply add or subtract any racial attribute modifiers from the template's attribute levels. For instance, a character template listing ST 12 applied to a race with ST -1 would suggest ST 11. Should both templates share an advantage, skill, etc., simply rebate the appropriate number of points.

Evening the Playing Field

GURPS and *Myth* use differing factors in placing value on a character. These differences should be kept in mind when translating from one game to the other.

Most *GURPS* GMs expect a character writeup to include a significant number of non-combat advantages, skills, and spells, rounding out the character and giving the player hooks for roleplaying, as compared to mastering combat. Being oriented solely toward combat, *Myth* doesn't concern itself with any other abilities when valuing a character.

Conversely, *Myth* valuations take into account arms and armor, whereas a *GURPS* character's equipment falls completely outside his perceived value.

Point totals for the following templates straightforwardly reflect the points provided by the *Myth* conversion formula on p. 26, meaning that professions wearing heavy armor (Brigands and Warriors, primarily) essentially get "free" effectiveness when translated to *GURPS*. Given that these same professions are at the bottom of the *Myth* food chain and bear the brunt of melee combat in the setting, this advantage wasn't seen as system-shattering.

When assigning a *Myth* value to a translated *GURPS* character, GMs should keep in mind to deduct non-combat investments and factor in the standard equipment wielded by the character.

ARCHMAGES   365+ POINTS

Archmages overshadow "ordinary" mages as ordinary mages overshadow a peasant with the Ignite Fire knack. They seize center stage wherever they appear, taking on vast armies man to multitude, opening great fissures in the earth with the power of their magery, and ignoring pleas to slay dragons not out of fear but boredom.

Their methods of mastering magery tend to vary vastly from individual to individual, but some common traits can be determined, especially since Myth archmages tend to belong to one of two groups: the Avatara (see pp. 97-98) or the Fallen Lords (see pp. 99-102).

The following does *not* present a complete character. It merely provides a 365-point framework around which to fill in a respectable archmage. These should be considered the minimal stats for recognition as an archmage; see Chapter 5, *Magic in Myth*, for more information.

Attributes: ST 11 [10], DX 13 [30], IQ 14 [45], HT 11 [10].
Advantages: Literacy [10]; Magery 6 [85]; Status 5 [25]; Strong Will +4 [16]; *either* Extra Fatigue (Spellcasting only) +20 [40] *or* Fatigue Recovery +6 [40]; and 50 points in any combination of Allies or Ally Groups (representing loyal servitors, undead minions, etc.); Patrons; Reputations; Status +1 (total of 6); and Wealth.
Disadvantages: Duty (To empire, Dark lord, circle, etc., on 6 or less) [-5] and *one* of Absent Mindedness; severe Compulsive Behavior; great Destiny (Dark fate); upgrade Duty to Extremely Hazardous Duty; Fanaticism; Glory Hound; Greed; Low Empathy; or Weirdness Magnet [-15].
Primary Skills: Tactics (M/H) IQ-1 [2]-13 and Thaumatology (M/VH) IQ+6 [8]-20. Avatara must have a sword skill at (P/A) DX+2 [8]-15 or Fallen Lords must have Intimidation (M/A) IQ+3 [8]-17.
Secondary Skills: Heraldry (M/A) IQ-1 [1]-13; Spell Throwing (type) (P/E) DX+2 [4]-15; and Staff (P/H) DX-1 [2]-12.
Spells: At least 30 spells from 10 different colleges, among these *either* three spells at skill-20 *or* one spell at skill-25 [39+].
Languages: Bruig (M/A) IQ [0]-14.
Customization Notes: Increase everything! As mentioned, this represents the low end of the archmage spectrum. Most will possess higher IQ, better reserves of and/or ability to recover fatigue, many

more skills suitable to combat and the arcane arts as well as running a kingdom, scores of spells at very high skill levels, a private army or two, and a suite of language skills including several dead varieties for researching lost knowledge. Even Magery may be higher, though the advantage rarely will increase more than one or two additional levels beyond the generally accepted archmage "floor" of Magery 6. See Chapter 5, *Magic in Myth*, for lists of commonly available spells and other information on archmages in Myth.
GURPS Wizards can provide a great deal of inspiration; the Overlord (p. WI84) and Super Mage (p. WI116) templates portray similar character concepts, or many of the other templates can inspire creation of "themed" archmages.

ARCHMAGE NAMES

Archmages of the Light portrayed in Myth have all belonged to the Avatara (see pp. 97-98). Their simple names are shorn of any honorifics; everyone already knows who they are. Examples include Alric, Rabican, Mazzarin, Murgen, Maeldun, and Cu Roi.

Dark archmages have all been members of the Fallen Lords (pp. 99-102). Their names tend to be descriptive and/or evocative, as in Shiver, the Deceiver, the Watcher, and Soulblighter.

MAGUS OBLIGE

To be recognized as a true archmage, a wizard must possess a vast array of exceptional characteristics. Perhaps the most understated of these, and most important, are his social investments.

A true archmage wields Status equivalent to that of a duke (a minor archmage might be merely Status 5). He automatically commands attention at court, and foolish is the king or emperor who doesn't think carefully before ignoring an archmage's advice. Even the sort of archmage who spends decades tucked away on some mountain should possess this level of Status. If he ever does come down, the local sovereign will be that much more inclined to listen.

Status this high requires "infrastructure." Socially active or necromantic archmages will need retainers, while "lesser" archmages may draw their social distinction from a powerful archmage or ruler acting as their Patron. Most archmages, even the recluses, have considerable Wealth. Usually the recluses have the most outlandish Reputations, as well.

See p. 95 for examples of social "packages" specific to Myth.

SHIRTLESS SUCCESS STORIES

GURPS favors the armorclad, but barechested Berserks and similar warriors can overcome with smart fighting.

The Berserk disadvantage is a good start, if used wisely. Myth's Berserks attempt to use their nature as a weapon rather than a defect. They will maneuver cannily prior to engaging the enemy, summon up their berserk rage at the last moment and attempt to snuff it as soon as the swords stop swinging. Those few who fail to make their Will rolls will be wrestled down by their companions till they've had time to attempt another roll.

Berserks also learn a cat-quick fighting style requiring minimal encumbrance. To reflect this, their Increased Speed has a "Berserk Fatigue" limitation. This costs them fatigue equal to three times their encumbrance level at the end of a fight, plus the usual loss on p. B134. Most Berserks will pass out after fighting at heavy encumbrance! The limitation is worth -10% per multiple of encumbrance in fatigue loss.

Most Berserks, with Move 8, get two steps in combat (see p. CII72), so GMs might allow them two retreating defenses (p. B109) per turn if not berserking at the time. Their long swords and speed can allow them to stay out of range of shorter weapons. In tight quarters, the second rank can All-Out Attack behind the first.

BERSERK NAMES

Names advertise attributes or accomplishments: Bran of the Iron Skin, Hrungnir Bereft of Fear, Bram with Screaming Iron, Hervard of the Bloody Stump, Angtyr the Sword Lover, Tyrvard of the Silver Hand, Thyrm of the Mighty Blows, and Thrend Atop the Piled Dead.

BERSERK 175 POINTS

"Though Gwyon and his brothers all died they had succeeded in breaking the momentum of the Ghôls' charge . . . each scattering corpses until a step could not be taken without treading on one . . ."

– from the lore of Myth

The Berserks are several tribes of hardy clansmen who make their homes in the northern mountains and coastal lands. They tend to be brawny men with full beards, often pleated. Hair tends to be blond or reddish; eye color is most often blue, green, or gray.

The most noticeable trait of these warriors is their namesake disadvantage, which is so nearly universal among them that GMs should consider allowing it outside any cap on disadvantages in his campaign.

Berserks have spent a good deal of time among more polite societies, fighting side by side with the Legion. This affords them some small measure of respect, though ordinary folk still look upon them warily as wild and dangerous men. The informal accords between the great Berserk tribes and the Cath Bruig empire (both old and new) require the Berserks to come down from the mountains when the Legion deems the need has arose. Should a tribe of Berserks refuse to muster, the empire would have to reevaluate its longstanding policy of leaving the Berserks to their own governance.

Berserks spend a great deal of time shirtless in foul weather. This toughens them to the point where their average zone of comfort is a startling -7° to 90°.

They enter combat armed with greatswords and an attitude.

Attributes: ST 12 [20], DX 14 [45], IQ 12 [20], HT 14 [45].

Advantages: Increased Speed +1 (Berserk Fatigue as explained in sidebar, -30%) [18]; Magic Resistance +3 (vs. spells resisted by ST only, -50%) [3]; Semi-Literacy [5]; Strong Will +1 [4]; Temperature Tolerance +3 [3]; and Toughness +1 [10].

Disadvantages: Berserk [-15]; Duty (To Legion on 9 or less) [-5]; and Social Stigma (Useful barbarian) [-10].

Primary Skills: Tactics (M/H) IQ+1 [6]-13 and Two-Handed Sword (P/A) DX+1 [4]-15.

Secondary Skills: Boating (P/A) DX-1 [1]-13; Brawling (P/E) DX+1 [2]-15; Broadsword (P/A) DX [2]-14; Knife (P/E) DX [1]-14; Stealth (P/A) DX+1 [4]-15; Survival (Mountains) (M/A) IQ+2 [6]-14; Tracking-13 (M/A) IQ+1 [4]-13; and Wrestling (P/A) DX-1 [1]-13.

Languages: Berserk (M/A) IQ [0]-12 and Bruig (M/A) IQ-1 [1]-11.

Customization Notes: A PC Berserk can improve his combat performance in a variety of ways – first and foremost by purchasing Combat Reflexes, then by raising ST or DX, increasing his Increased Speed, etc. GMs might even allow Enhanced Dodge given their fighting style. As a point of cultural pride, they shouldn't wear armor. Non-combat improvements could include Area Knowledges and languages to reflect traveling with the Legion, a craft skill to reflect a peacetime profession, or Seamanship and all the skills related to it to indicate a past spent exploring the oceans around the continent of Myth.

Bowman   175 points

Bowmen are the newest, proudest addition to the Legion's arsenal. Handpicked and trained for years by an allied race (see *The fir'Bolg* sidebar), these soldiers find themselves handled a little more carefully than shock troops wielding sword and shield. Conversely, high demand for their services means that, even if not placed in harm's way quite so often as Warriors, they're just as often in harm's general vicinity.

Bowman wear cloth armor, and wield a longbow, large knife, and broadsword-sized falchion (2d+1 cutting damage only; 1 turn to ready after swing). They carry a quiver of 24 arrows, including one fire arrow soaked in the explosive liquid used in Dwarven grenades. The arrow doesn't explode or do extra damage, but will ignite most flammables (grass that isn't wet, dry wood, etc.) at its point of impact.

Attributes: ST 13 [30], DX 13 [30], IQ 11 [10], HT 11 [10].
Advantages: Acute Vision +3 [6]; Combat Reflexes [15]; Literacy [10]; and Patron (The Legion on 9 or less) [25].
Disadvantages: Duty (To Legion on 15 or less) [-15] and Fanaticism (Patriotism) [-15].
Primary Skills: Bow (P/H) DX+3 [24]-16; Broadsword (P/A) DX-1 [1]-12; Fast-Draw (Arrow) (P/E) DX+4 [8]-17*; and Tactics (M/H) IQ+1 [6]-12.
* Bonus of +1 for Combat Reflexes already applied.
Secondary Skills: Armoury/TL3 (Bows and arrows) (M/A) IQ+1 [4]-11/17; Brawling (P/E) DX+2 [4]-15; First Aid/TL3 (M/E) IQ+2 [4]-13; Jumping (P/E) DX+1 [2]-14; Knife (P/E) DX+1 [2]-14; Savoir-Faire (Military) (M/E) IQ+1 [2]-12; Stealth (P/A) DX+1 [4]-14; and Survival (Plains) (M/A) IQ+2 [6]-13.
Languages: fir'Bolg (M/A) IQ [2]-11 and Bruig (M/A) IQ [0]-11.
Customization Notes: While the average Human student doesn't reach his fir'Bolg teachers' level of skill, advanced students might have more woodcraft skills, higher Stealth, Survival (Woodlands), Tracking, etc. Many Bowmen enter the Legion with existing skill levels in Agronomy, Merchant, crafts, etc.

Bowman Names

Bowman have names common to the civilized lands of Myth, including: Jean, Cale, Denis, Matthieu, Guibert, Luis, Roger, Gobain, Philip, Otto, Thomas, Garin, Aubry, Clement, Alvar, Simone, Petrarch, Piers, Francis, Wyclif, Cipolla, John, Jerome, Jaques, Edward, Bartholomew, Walter, Gibouin, Guerri, Raoul, Bernier, Ybert, Amant, Herbert, Droon, Gerard, Henry, Bernard, Peter, Raymond, Leo, Michael, Charles, Olivier, Urban, Eustace, Gislebert, Godfrey, Albert, Victor, and Adrian.

The fir'Bolg

One of the more subtle mysteries of Myth are the fir'Bolg, the not-quite-human residents of The Ermine. These forest dwellers appear Human, but cannot interbreed with the more populous Human race! No one knows what separates the two breeds.

The fir'Bolg first developed archery, and remain its uncontested masters. When Balor invaded the west, the fir'Bolg set aside their longstanding differences with the Human kingdoms and brought their unique skills into the ranks of the Legion.

Since that war, they have sworn never to leave the Ermine again, but in exchange for this right they have begun teaching select legionnaires the way of the bow. About 1 in 20 Legion recruits is sent to one of the fir'Bolg's three war colleges in the Ermine: jo'Za-Thatal, wa'Ama-Tchal, and ai'Kijin-Tak.

There the legionnaires master their military trade – and not coincidentally strengthen the new ties between their races.

Fir'Bolg archers are distinguished by their very developed musculature, and garb of vest and long loincloth. Legion archers have taken to wearing facial hair in respect of the fir'Bolg custom of long mustaches.

CRIME AND PUNISHMENT

The *Myth* computer games don't deal much with law and order. GMs should assume a fairly medieval legal system, with "high justice" for crimes against the state and most other infractions committed by nobles, and "low justice" for mundane robberies, slayings, and such among the unwashed masses. This can be tweaked to fit the GM's whimsy however he pleases.

The Legion handles most law enforcement, a practical measure that keeps the troops in shape and acknowledges the powerful combat capability of many of the felons in Myth. As mentioned previously, the wars have left pockets of Dark combatants in civilized lands; most of these are still busily committing mayhem in their own interests.

Should peace prove lasting in a given campaign, the Legion might even go so far as to create a specialized police corps, teaching proper law-enforcement skills and dispatching armored investigators to combat crimes that require more than knocking someone upside the head. Members of this corps likely would have increased Military Rank, Legal Enforcement Powers at 10 or 15 points, and several law-enforcement-related skills, in addition to the Warrior template investments. They would make *very* worthy adversaries for a group of PC Brigands.

BRIGAND NAMES

The sort of men who defy their duty and take to the outlaw life generally pick up an unflattering nickname to suit them. Some samples include Gape, Lug, Hook, Mook, Gog, Punch, Jounce, Lech, Slog, Shlep, Widdy, Chug, Creep, Flump, Lurch, Rip, Scrieve, Truk, Lout, Jag, Jerk, Junk, Juke, Drivit, Pall, Muggle, Schuss, Scrooch, Gawk, Grimace, Worm, Leer, Dirge, Coze, Slug, Jabber, Quip, Squib, Bray, Tyro, Rasp, Blat, Crow, Grouse, Jape, Jeer, Scoff, Yobbo, Droog, Balump, Kaf, Smek, Nok, Fulsome, Pong, Rank, Scab, Feeb, Goon, Hoyden, Rube, Spas, Skite, Carper, Rake, Pug, Crud, Churl, Fink, Heel, Snipe, Skeeve, Foozle, and Blut.

The Legion works very hard to screen the men it turns into Warriors, enlisting them early in youth when it can and pushing them to the limit in their training. But no training can emulate the horrors and hardships of a legionnaire's life, and some number of them desert their duty.

Often they embrace banditry or a Dark lord's service as the only living left available to them, and this is what they become.

Brigands represent a very real threat to the empire and the causes of Light. Though most are unwashed thugs, those with Legion training can be tough and canny, and unlike most Dark agents they can walk amongst humanity unnoticed. During the wars, Brigands bolstered various Dark armies. Currently, they live lives of banditry or other outlaw activity. Some have gone so far as to carve remote lordships for themselves, prickling with defenses to stop the Legion force they know will eventually come.

Rumors have it that, since the war, a few Brigand captains have foraged east and south in search of training in spellcasting. This causes Legion generals more than a little concern. Their thinking (or conceit, some would say) is that one of the main reasons the Legion can stand up to powerful mages is that the average mage is so *impractical* about military matters. A powerful mage with the gritty, practical experience of a veteran Brigand would pose considerably more challenge than your average Warlock without the sense to put on some armor . . .

Brigands wear mail and pot helm, and carry a medium shield and broadsword. During the war with Soulblighter, respecting the heraldic needs of friend and foe alike, they exchanged their Legion-issue flatiron shields for circular ones. They don't always observe such niceties.

Their template suffers some minor skill decline as compared to the Warrior's because Brigands don't keep up their old regimen.

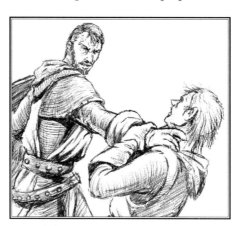

Attributes: ST 13 [30], DX 13 [30], IQ 11 [10], HT 12 [20].

Advantages: Combat Reflexes [15]; Increased Speed+1 [25]; and Literacy [10].

Disadvantages: Enemy (The Legion on 6 or less) [-20]; Social Stigma (Outlaw) [-15]; and Stubbornness [-5].

Primary Skills: Broadsword (P/A) DX+2 [8]-15; Running (P/H – HT) HT-3 [1/2]-9; and Tactics (M/H) IQ [4]-11.

Secondary Skills: Brawling (P/E) DX+2 [4]-15; Carousing (PA – HT) HT [2]-12; Climbing (P/A) DX [2]-13; Fast-Draw (Sword) (P/E) DX+1 [1]-14*; First Aid/TL3 (M/E) IQ+1 [2]-12; Gambling (M/A) IQ-1 [1]-10; Gesture (M/E) IQ+1 [2]-12; Knife (P/E) DX [1]-13; Orienteering (M/A) IQ [2]-11; Savoir-Faire (Military) (M/E) IQ-1 [1/2]-10; Scrounging (M/E) IQ+1 [2]-12; Shield (P/E) DX+3 [8]-16; Stealth (P/A) DX+1 [4]-14; and Survival (Plains) (M/A) IQ+2 [6]-13.

* Bonus of +1 for Combat Reflexes already applied.

Languages: Bruig (M/A) IQ [0]-11.

Customization Notes: More combat and survival-oriented skills will always prove useful, as would Thief/Spy skills for a particular trade (perhaps Boating for smuggling, etc.). Many Brigands still have Dark lords whom they serve; this relationship *might* count as a Patron, though likely not given the usual nature of Dark lords. Bowmen have Dark Archer defectors, as well. Start with the Bowman template, then apply differences similar to those displayed between this and the Warrior template. Primarily this is a matter of swapping disadvantages.

Heron Guard   175 Points

The warrior-sage order of Heron Guards serves the emperor of Cath Bruig as bodyguards and house troops. The order reaches back to the very first years of the empire countless centuries ago – as do some active Guardsmen themselves.

The order practices a religion bordering on philosophy, placing reverence in the emperor, honor, duty, and respect for the values of Light. Though their clerical devotion gives them increasing mastery of Healing spells, Heron Guards are anything but pacifists, willing – even eager – to end certain lives to improve others.

Though intelligent and of forceful personality, Herons lead secluded lives when not on assignment and quickly lose any worldly knowledge they may have possessed. This naive quality lowers their effective IQ score.

Older Herons have mastered the Halt Aging spell (see p. M51) and extend its benefits to all their brethren, greatly increasing their life spans. Given this, the order traditionally exhibited very little turnover. Most Herons died when Balor destroyed the empire and Muirthemne (see p. 21). The survivors took up a life of penance as Journeymen (see p. 74), of whom many have lived to see the empire revived and their order restored, though its ranks are much depleted. See p. 92 for details on the order.

In combat, Heron Guards wield a katanalike sword in each hand. Though initially untrained in off-hand fighting, their high skill allows competent handling of the second weapon. They wear armor resembling the traditional Japanese; see p. 82 for details. The order issues them one mandrake root (see p. 84) when on duty outside of Muirthemne.

Attributes: ST 13 [30], DX 14 [45], IQ 11 [10], HT 13 [30].

Advantages: Extra Hit Points +2 [10]; Literacy [10]; Power Investiture +3 [30]; and Strong Will +5 [20]. See p. 92 for other possible requirements.

Disadvantages: Discipline of Faith (Monasticism) [-10]; Extremely Hazardous Duty [-20]; and Fanaticism (Patriotism) [-15].

Primary Skills: Katana (P/A) DX+2 [8]-16; Running (P/H – HT) HT [4]-13; and Tactics (M/H) IQ-1 [2]-10.

Secondary Skills: Armoury/TL (Hand weapons) (M/A) IQ [2]-11; Fast-Draw (Sword) (P/E) DX+1 [2]-15; First Aid/TL3 (M/E) IQ+1 [2]-12; Heraldry (M/A) IQ-1 [1]-10; Judo (P/H) DX-2 [1]-12; Knife (P/E) DX [1]-14; Leadership (M/A) IQ [2]-11; Savoir-Faire (Military) (M/E) IQ [1]-11; and Theology (M/H) IQ [4]-11.

Spells: Lend Health-12 [1]; Lend Strength-12 [1]; Major Healing (VH)-12 [2]; and Minor Healing-12 [1].

Languages: Bruig (M/A) IQ [0]-11.

Customization Notes: The above represents a Heron Guard who's recently left training. A more experienced Heron might pursue martial-arts styles emphasizing off-hand weapon training; certainly he would seek a wider variety of spells and to improve his clerical bonus (through increased devotion to his "religion of state"). Any skills outside this list likely represent prior experience. The order excludes applicants with any of several mental and physical ailments (see p. 92), so the GM should carefully screen any additional disadvantages.

Every seven years, the Heron Guards stage a grand competition to select new recruits. Hundreds of warriors and other hopefuls from across the lands gather in Muirthemne to compete. Historically, the Guards have chosen fewer than six of these hopefuls at each competition, though war casualties may greatly increase these quotas for the next few tournaments.

The applicants are supposed to be competing for the honor of serving their emperor – and patriotism does drive a handful of them – but the Heron Guards' well-known longevity entices the majority to make their bid. Contestants with only this self-serving motive invariably fail to make the grade.

During the competition, the Guards put the contestants through a rigorous series of physical exercises, combat simulations, and military drills. They drill them on the fine points of the empire's noble houses and tactics, while running them across leagues of plains in the noonday sun.

Many applicants fall out as a result of this punishment, but to a large extent it's all a sham. The Guards aren't looking for someone who already possesses combat prowess and knows the difference between one duke's standard and another. These things they can teach. All they really seek is a will of iron. A clumsy and ignorant contestant who endures the combats and intensive questions with stoic face will impress them more than a virtuoso who flusters the first time he falters.

Once the Guards find that rare applicant with an unstoppable desire, only then do they begin molding him into a warrior and sage. By the time the next competition arrives in seven years, he might even meet standards.

Heron Guard/ Journeyman Names

New Heron Guards cast aside their birth name upon joining the deathless order. They take as their surname the year of their initiation as notated by the old calendar of the kings of Cath Bruig (predating the Acit El calendar reformation; see p. 18). Preceding this is a number denoting which member of that class an individual is. This is randomly assigned from one through the class' size. Older Herons, initiated during the empire's long prosperity, rarely have a number higher than six. Younger guards may be as high as 15, and even higher numbers might be seen as the order replaces its war dead.

Journeymen retain their Heron Guard names.

Examples include: Eight Flint Deer, Twelve Eagle Falling Sun, Six Motion Bloody Jaguar, Five Heron Waiting Cactus, Eight Pride Stalking Rabbit, Three Vulture Drum, Ten Stone Reed, Four Serpent Seeking Shadow, Seven Lizard Tongue, Nine Eagle Red Skull, One Flint Puma, Twelve Serpent Falling Eagle, Seven Wind Lizard, Nine Serpent Rising Puma, Seven Crocodile Rain, Six Coyote Flower, Thirteen Bloody Crocodile, Five Rabbit Fleeing Jaguar, Seven Jaguar White Flower, Five Obsidian Heron, One Serpent Green Talon, Seven Devil Puma, Five Monkey Bloody Stone, Six Vulture Dog Star, One Deer Burning Skull, Nine Serpent Bloody Sun, Eleven Vulture Fire Serpent, Ten Eagle Burning Stone, Seven Eagle Jaguar Claw, Twelve Flint Sun Collar, Twelve Devil Burning Wind, Thirteen Wind Moon Stone, and Fourteen Flint Moon Eagle.

Journeyman   250 Points

"Returning to the ruin Llancarfan had become in their absence, the emperor's deathless Heron Guards each tore nine gold tiles from the collapsed palace wall, every one the weight of a grown man, and hung them about their necks in penance for being absent when most needed."

– from the lore of Myth

When the empire fell every Heron Guard fell with it, save for 100 veterans on assignment elsewhere at the time. Emperorless, they took up the wandering penitent role of the Journeymen, and provided vast support to the subsequent wars.

Now Herons once again, the former Journeyman retain their skills if not their penitent ways. About 80 have survived to reform their order; see p. 92.

Journeyman carried a common shovel, treated in combat as a cheap great axe doing -1 damage. They wore a heavy (though not nearly as heavy as legend would have it) fur coat (see p. 82) adorned with nine gold tiles, whose worth was ignored by the wearers, but attracted the few bandits stupid enough to believe it real. (This gesture showed the weight of their guilt and their contempt for material values.) They usually carried six mandrake roots (see p. 84), as they spent their time hunting and enchanting these.

Attributes: ST 13 [30], DX 14 [45], IQ 11 [10], HT 13 [30].

Advantages: Extra Hit Points +2 [10]; Literacy [10]; Power Investiture +6 [60]; and Strong Will +5 [20]. Administrative Rank 1 [5] may also be needed; see p. 92.

Disadvantages: Discipline of Faith (Monasticism) [-10]; Enemy (Random bandits on 6 or less) [-10]; Fanaticism (Patriotism) [-15]; and Vow (Wear coat) [-10].

Primary Skills: Bard (M/A) IQ-1 [1]-10; Katana (P/A) DX+2 [8]-16; Running (P/H – HT) HT-1 [2]-12; Tactics (M/H) IQ-1 [2]-10; and Two-Handed Axe/Mace (P/A) DX+2 [8]-16.

Secondary Skills: Armoury/TL (Hand weapons) (M/A) IQ [2]-11; Fast-Draw (Sword) (P/E) DX+1 [2]-15; First Aid/TL3 (M/E) IQ+2 [4]-13; Heraldry (M/A) IQ-1 [1]-10; History (M/H) IQ+1 [6]-12; Judo (P/H) DX-2 [1]-12; Knife (P/E) DX [1]-14; Leadership (M/A) IQ+1 [4]-12; Literature (M/H) IQ [4]-11; Meditation (M/VH) IQ-2 [2]-9; Savoir-Faire (Military) (M/E) IQ [1]-11; Survival (Plains) (M/A) IQ+4 [10]-15; Teaching (M/A) IQ-1 [1]-10; Theology (M/H) IQ [4]-11; and Writing (M/A) IQ-1 [1]-10.

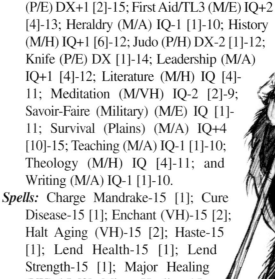

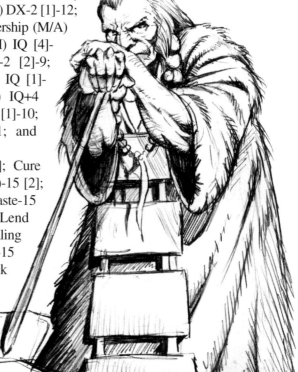

Spells: Charge Mandrake-15 [1]; Cure Disease-15 [1]; Enchant (VH)-15 [2]; Halt Aging (VH)-15 [2]; Haste-15 [1]; Lend Health-15 [1]; Lend Strength-15 [1]; Major Healing (VH)-15 [2]; Minor Healing-15 [1]; Powerstone-15 [1]; Quick March-15 [1]; and Sterilize-15 [1].

Languages: Bruig (M/A) IQ [0]-11.

WARLOCK   300 POINTS

". . . drawn to forbidden lore and others wise in the ways of the metaphysical sciences as a moth is to a flame . . . they are doomed by the very knowledge that gives them power over other men."

– from the lore of Myth

The Warlocks of the Scholomance have fought on both sides of the great wars between Light and Dark, following the shifting allegiances of the Deceiver, with whom they have an ancient alliance. They are grim master mages of breathtaking might, yet even so less than an archmage in the scope of their power.

Legend has it that a Scholomancer never grins but that those around him will regret it, and that this mighty circle trades their very souls for their arcane arts. (If the latter proves true, the template may require an additional disadvantage . . .)

Warlocks excel in battle, and stride into the hottest conflict armed with only their staff, a robe enchanted with Fortify +1, and their incredible skills. As a good offense, said skills provide a Warlock's best defense.

The Warlocks' alliance with Deceiver has no point cost on either side. Both the Scholomancers and former Fallen Lord deal at arm's length, and trust each other no more than they would expect a wise soul to trust themselves.

Attributes: ST 11 [10], DX 12 [20], IQ 14 [45], HT 11 [10].

Advantages: Extra Fatigue (Spellcasting only) +17 [34]; Fatigue Recovery +6 [40]; Literacy [10]; Magery 3 [35] with additional Magery (Fire college only) +5 [57]; and Strong Will +4 [16].

Disadvantages: Bully [-10]; Fanaticism (Self) [-15]; and Reduced Hit Points -1 [-5].

Primary Skills: Spell Throwing (Fireball) (P/E) DX+3 [8]-15 and Tactics (M/H) IQ-2 [1]-12.

Secondary Skills: Intimidation (M/A) IQ [2]-14; Knife (P/E) DX+1 [2]-13; Staff (P/H) DX [4]-12; and Thaumatology (M/VH) IQ+2/+7 [4]-16/21.

Spells: Cold-20 [1]; Confusion (VH)-15 [2]; Create Fire-20 [1]; Daze-15 [1]; Detect Magic-15 [1]; Enchant (VH)-15 [2]; Essential Flame-20 [1]; Explosive Fireball-20 [1]; Extinguish Fire-20 [1]; Find Weakness-15 [1]; Fireball-20 [1]; Fireproof-20 [1]; Foolishness-15 [1]; Heat-20 [1]; Ignite Fire-20 [1]; Lend Strength-15 [1]; Mass Confusion (VH)-15 [2]; Mental Stun-15 [1]; Purify Air-15 [1]; Recover Strength-20 [1]; Resist Cold-20 [1]; Resist Fire-20 [1]; Ring of Fire-20 [1]; Seek Earth-15 [1]; Seek Water-15 [1]; Sense Life-15 [1]; Shape Fire-20 [1]; Simple Illusion-15 [1]; and Staff-15 [1].

Languages: Bruig (M/A) IQ [0]-14.

Customization Notes: More and more spells are in order, particularly the other Fire spells! See p. 93 for further description of the circle that might inspire additional customization ideas.

The Warlocks of the Scholomance bear unusual names for the lands of Myth, which suits them since so little is known about the nature of their order. Some scholars theorize that their names suggest their origins lie somewhere beyond the known lands. Others counter that they likely take new names of obscure importance upon entering their order. A variant of this theory proposes that the powerful Dark entities that grant them their powers give them these names to denote the Warlock's servitude to them!

Some examples include Ceannard, Malairt, Admillin, Caithim, Aibistear, Abharsair, Braman, Breamas, Diabhol, Sgulanach, Miosguinn, Eireallach, Sgreataidh, Skrati, Uabh-bheist, uadh-chrith, Beithir, Be'imneach, Mairtrighim, Martad, Casgair, Fadhbhaim, Gonim, and Lollard.

A HARD LIVING

No one else goes through the sheer misery that a legionnaire routinely endures. Standing back to back hacking at undead hordes with pasty gibbets of rotting flesh flying about, plowing through mountain passes in the dead of winter, pulling your own severed hand off your weapon hilt so as to pick it back up with the other hand . . . the Legion turns its men into all that they can be, then routinely asks for more than that.

The average legionnaire takes a perverse pride in all of this. No one sacrifices more for empire, emperor, and Light – he knows it and he knows his superiors all the way up to Alric himself know it, too. He'll grumble and complain and bemoan his fate – but giving his all is why he picked up the sword in the first place, and why he'll likely die with it in hand as well.

Warriors begrudgingly respect Bowmen, as the only other arm of the Legion proper, but don't consider them proper "legionnaires." A real legionnaire knows that dirty jobs require getting dirty hands, something you can't do at bow's range.

WARRIOR NAMES

Ordinary men bear ordinary names, at least by the norms of human Myth society. These include Mauriac, Adalard, Aethelwulf, Curran, Derek, Ajax, Avis, Barret, Esme, Kenway, Bevan, Bevis, Montago, Moliere, Billie, Brenainn, Calhoun, Casey, Cathal, Aldwyn, Allard, Chadwick, Farrell, Aethel-weard, Garner, Cillian, Alyce, Conlan, Eadgar, Edmee, Beald, Brady, Cormac, Donagh, Bran, Brand, Duncan, Loring, Nealon, Ewan, Nels, Garwin, Kalevi, Kalwa, Neel, Kearney, Murrough, Niall, Bramwell, Mather, Malthus, Nola, Owen, Ramsay, Rand, Sigmund, Sloan, Thayer, Trahern, Ulrich, Vasya, Warner, Hector, Kay, Malory, Naram, Pelleas, Moore, Macaualy, Strephon, Tarquin, Alisander, Alexander, Berel the Unworthy, Clairemonde, Darras, Floridas, Gahalatine, Lucan, Melias, Tristram, Bors, Gareth, Kaherdin, Gaheris, Accolon, Sansloy, and Kearney.

WARRIOR 150 POINTS

The Heron Guards and Bowmen may have more prestige, but when someone has to face down 500 gibbering Ghôls heaving chunks of the lunch they procured at the orphanage, the Warriors of the Legion take the call.

The empire maintains the Legion as its core army, though it can draw upon its nobles' private armies for auxiliaries if need be. Beginning as early as when their voice breaks, Legion recruits undergo 18 months of harrowing training, leaving them superbly trained. More often than not, it's not enough.

Legionnaires wear mail and pot helm, and wield a medium shield and broadsword.

In peacetime, the Legion stays sharp by patrolling the empire, dealing with bandits, necromancers, and rampaging horrors alike with stern justice and sharp sword.

Attributes: ST 13 [30], DX 13 [30], IQ 11 [10], HT 12 [20].

Advantages: Combat Reflexes [15]; Fit [5]; Increased Speed+1 [25]; Literacy [10]; and Military Rank 1 [5].

Disadvantages: Extremely Hazardous Duty [-20]; Fanaticism (Patriotism) [-15]; and Stubbornness [-5].

Primary Skills: Broadsword (P/A) DX+2 [8]-15; Running (P/H – HT) HT [4]-12; and Tactics (M/H) IQ [4]-11.

Secondary Skills: Brawling (P/E) DX [1]-13; Climbing (P/A) DX [2]-13; Fast-Draw (Sword) (P/E) DX+1 [1]-14*; First Aid/TL3 (M/E) IQ+1 [2]-12; Gesture (M/E) IQ+1 [2]-12; Knife (P/E) DX [1]-13; Orienteering (M/A) IQ [2]-11; Savoir-Faire (Military) (M/E) IQ [1]-11; Shield (P/E) DX+3 [8]-16; Stealth (P/A) DX [2]-13; and Survival (Plains) (M/A) IQ [2]-11.

* Bonus of +1 for Combat Reflexes already applied.

Languages: Bruig (M/A) IQ [0]-11.

Customization Notes: Legionnaires provide all of the NCOs and officers for the entire Legion, so Military Rank is always appropriate, and all legionnaires are at least junior NCOs in relation to other military units. Better attributes and combat skills always prove handy.

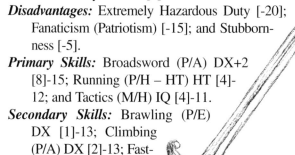

Supporting Cast

The following are commonly found in minor roles in Myth:

Peasant   10 points

The engine that keeps the human empires and kingdoms running is the peasant farmer. These sons of the earth lead a hard life, wrenching a living from the soil, enduring all too frequent raids from Dark horrors, and giving up promising sons at about age 14 to serve in the Legion.

Attributes: ST 10 [0], DX 10 [0], IQ 10 [0], HT 10 [0].

Advantages: Fit [5] or Semi-Literacy [5].

Disadvantages: Necrophobia [-10].

Primary Skills: Agronomy/TL3 (M/A) IQ+2 [6]-12 and Two-Handed Axe/Mace (P/A) DX [2]-10.

Secondary Skills: First Aid/TL3 (M/E) IQ [1]-10; Knife (P/E) DX+2 [4]-12; and Survival (Plains) (M/A) IQ [2]-10.

Languages: Bruig (M/A) IQ [0]-10.

Wolf

ST: 13	**Speed/Dodge:** 7/7	**Size:** 1
DX: 14	**PD/DR:** 1/1	**Weight:** 150-200 lbs.
IQ: 5	**Damage:** 1d-1 cut	**Habitats:** P, F
HT: 11	**Reach:** C	

The wolves of Myth are larger and sturdier than their real-life counterparts, with massive jaws that bite for 1d-1 cutting damage in close combat. They don't run particularly well for a canine, but given their aggressiveness they don't often need to.

Wolves are often found in the company of the bre'Unor (see pp. 36-37).

Cave Spider

ST: 16	**Speed/Dodge:** 8/7	**Size:** 1
DX: 14	**PD/DR:** 0/0	**Weight:** 75-90 lbs.
IQ: 4	**Damage:** 1d imp	**Habitats:** Sub
HT: 13	**Reach:** C	

These giant spiders inhabit many or most of the subterranean regions in Myth. A single cave spider doesn't represent much of a threat to an armed Warrior – but they are very rarely found in less than large groups. They are very aggressive, and once one has detected prey the victim can depend on every other spider in the immediate vicinity appearing within seconds.

Cave spiders can function perfectly well in sunlight; they simply prefer dark and cool homes. Mages with arachnid-control spells often use them as wartime scouts; their low height and natural talent gives them an effective Stealth skill of 17, and their high speed allows them to cover a lot of ground quickly.

Explosives have spectacular (if nauseating) impact when used against spiders. Treat them as possessing the Fragile disadvantage (see p. CI102).

The selection of professions portrayed in this chapter shouldn't be taken as indication that other traditional high-fantasy professions don't exist in the Myth setting. Assume that they do, but they simply didn't play as prominent of a role in the wars vs. Balor and Soulblighter.

Both the empire of Cath Bruig and the various kingdoms of Myth have a noble upper caste, so knights of Status 2+ will exist. The one weakness in Alric's martial leadership is that he underemploys cavalry, so assume that the only reason knightly warriors did not appear in **Myth** is because Alric preferred to rely on his professional infantry over his vassal horsemen.

While the Journeymen performed a clerical function during the wars, they left room for a more traditional clerical healer with an aversion to violence and much more powerful healing spells. Assume that these sorts simply tended to the wounded in the rear (when such existed) during the wars, leaving frontline work to the all-too-eager Journeymen.

A cataclysmic conflict represents a terrible time for thieves with the slightest shred of patriotism to ply their trade. Assume that light-fingered rogues prowl the cities and highways of the empire during peacetime, but simply lie low (or enlist!) when the authorities get distracted by Dark invasions.

In short, players should feel free to explore other character types than those already established in Myth. A Dwarf makes just as good a safecracker as he does a soldier.

4. Handle With Caution: the Equipment of Myth

Mighty magical artifacts and advanced Dwarven technologies add a lot of bang to the Myth setting.

The State of Technology

The world of Myth functions on a day-to-day basis at TL3, with some noteworthy exceptions.

Military

Most armed forces use "realistic" TL3 arms. Soldiers wield axes as often as swords, and rarely enjoy the luxury of head-to-toe heavy armor. The uniform equipping of the Legion's Warriors with chain, medium shield, and broadsword represents an enormous investment by the Cath Bruig empire. Many "backwoods" cultures – the Mauls and bre'Unor among them – employ crude implements of even lower TL. Some of these perform identically to TL3 versions (the Maul's maul); some do not (the bone weapons of the bre'Unor; see p. 37).

Plate armor is rare, though known; even great nobles tend to wear scale instead.

Missile weapons are underdeveloped. Only the fir'Bolg (see p. 71) and Legion utilize the bow. The crossbow is unknown. Siege engines don't exist, either.

In the place of classic medieval artillery, the Dwarves have developed cannon (treat as early TL4), which select Human and (ironically) Ghôl forces use more than the nearsighted Dwarves themselves. The Dwarves also forge muskets, but these have not caught on; interested parties will find them hard to locate and usually restricted. In combat, the Dwarves rely upon a liquid explosive that they've concocted and satchel charges (see pp. 80-81), but do not export these arms.

Civil

Most dwellings and public buildings utilize TL3 construction: mud and straw for a peasant's hut, stone for city walls, etc. Many public works are grandly sized or advanced in concept, but this likely represents magical refinements rather than higher-TL processes. (The appropriate Earth spells converting brick and mortar into a solid piece of stone can greatly improve performance, though they certainly would *not* make the appropriate Engineer skills obsolete.) Notably, the great cities of Myth usually feature immense walls 20′ high or more, and the Human-governed regions can build sophisticated dams. The Province utilizes windmill technology extensively.

Medical

Most care is TL3, with the Dwarves and state-of-the-art human caregivers at TL4. Given the power and efficiency of Healing spells, mundane medical science probably receives relatively little attention.

Eventually, in a race full of nearsighted gadgeteers, spectacles will be invented, increasing the cost of the Dwarven racial template by 15 points!

Magical

One of the more interesting aspects of Myth technology is the fusion of magical and technological properties in certain artifacts. It appears that Myth enchanters and gadgeteers may often combine their attentions in creating certain items.

This creates two significant exceptions to *GURPS* precedents. At least some magical items may be broken and not lose their enchantment, but only the ability to *use* it, and appropriately skilled non-spellcasters may repair this mundane damage thereby making the enchantment "active" again. For instance, the World Knots (see p. 85) scattered about the lands are complex mechanical constructs as well as powerful magical ones. They may be broken and rendered useless, but their enchantment remains intact, if dormant. A non-mage craftsman can repair this damage, at which time their teleportation enchantments become active again.

The particulars of this enchantment-gadgeteering crossover are subject to GM interpretation, but assume this as a default: Most magic items of simple construction – swords, staffs, armor, jewelry, etc. – follow the standard *GURPS* rules, and once broken lose their enchantments. Only complex devices can break with only a temporary loss of function. This must be *minor* damage; heavy damage will destroy the enchantments. At most, an item with several interlocking parts might be disassembled and still retain its enchantments in inactive status.

To repair a broken magical item *properly* (i.e., and restore its enchantments to active status), a craftsman must both make his mundane skill roll and one Thaumatology roll for each enchantment on the device. A critical failure on any roll destroys the device.

Mages detect broken magic items with suspended enchantments just as if they were in perfect condition.

Arms

To spice up combat, Myth introduces a variety of exotic arms beyond those in *GURPS Basic Set*.

Melee Weapons

The following weapons are described on the indicated pages, and included in the weapons table on p. 81.

Bre'Unor jawbone-axes – see p. 37.

Ghôl scythe – see p. 47.

Heron Guard's sword – this weapon is treated as a katana. The blade may be either straight or slightly curved like the Japanese example.

Journeyman's shovel – see p. 74.

Myrmidon gridaksma blades – see p. 53.

Explosives and Firearms

Dwarven Cocktail – The principal weapon wielded by the gadgeteer Dwarves is a bottle filled with an explosive liquid. They hold a fire-starting striker (1 lb., $40, needs $1 flint every week or so) in one hand, light the cocktail's fuse, and toss it. If the fuse remains lit the cocktail generally explodes on impact, causing 7d damage in the target and adjacent hexes, 2d-1 two or three hexes away, and 1d-2 four or five hexes out.

Fragmentation is normally 1d-3 cutting; in a normal room it would be 1d-2 and in a scrap yard 1d. The base chance of being hit by a fragment is 18 or less on 3d, -1 per yard from the detonation point, to a minimum of 3, out to 35 yards.

The cocktail fuses are simply soaked rags, and unreliable, giving Malf 14. Lower Malf to 12 in light rain or snow, 11 in snow-covered terrain or heavy snow, or -4 in heavy rain. An unlit cocktail will explode if it takes more than 2 points of explosive damage or 10 points of non-explosive crushing dam-

age! The Dwarves keep these weapons to themselves, and the explosive formula is a racial secret. $15, 1 lb.

Dwarven Satchel Charge – This canvas bag contains 2 lbs. of primitive black powder and is coated with a compound that causes it to explode from more than 2 hits of fire or explosive damage, or 10 hits of non-explosive crushing damage.

The Dwarves use their Engineer (Mining) skill to perform demolitions with these. The satchel charge does 7d damage just like the cocktail, except that it causes no fragmentation damage unless in a cluttered environment. $100, 3 lbs.

Dwarven Mortar – Fires a 5-pound explosive-filled iron shell, treated precisely as a Dwarven cocktail except that minimum fragmentation damage is 1d-2.

The mortar costs $2,000 and weighs 25 lbs. Each round costs $120.

Dwarven Muskets and Cannon – These weapons follow the standard rules for TL4 firearms; see p. 81.

Disgusting Innovations

Wight Bits – see p. 67. Some Dark lords find it more useful to purposely explode their Wights in a rear area, then stock the remains as ammunition for their Ghôl forces, who are more than glad to fling them at the opposing ranks.

Magic Weapons

Examples of these are listed among magic items in general on pp. 83-85. Mages enchant magic weapons normally as per *GURPS Magic*, but with the additional prerequisite that the weapon must have been used by a great warrior in performing great feats. The GM may rule that a given weapon's history will allow enchanting with up to (for instance) +2 in Accuracy and/or Puissance, while another weapon's history allows +5. This *will* increase the price and lower the availability of enchanted arms.

Myth Weapons Tables

Melee Weapons

Weapons are listed in groups, according to the skill required to use them. The skill's default level, and any defaults from other skills, are also shown. For swords, daggers, etc., the weight includes a good scabbard. Weapons which can be used in two ways have two separate lines – one for each type of attack.

Weapon	Type	Damage	Reach	Cost	Weight	Min ST	Special Notes
AXE/MACE (DX-5)†							
Ghôl scythe	cut	sw+2	1	$50	5 lbs.	12	1 turn to ready.
bre'Unor jawbone-axe	cut	sw+1	1	$24	4 lbs.	12	Throwable. 1 turn to ready. Cheap weapon.
KATANA (DX-5 or Broadsword-2)							
Heron Guard's sword	cut	sw+1/+2	1,2	$650	5 lbs.	11	Often of fine quality; add +1 to damage.
	imp	thr+1	1				
scabbarded	cr	sw+1/+2	1,2				Used to subdue.
SHORTSWORD (DX-5, Broadsword-2, or Force Sword-3)							
Gridaksma blade	cut	sw	1	$700	4 lbs.	10	Regular shortsword if broken *once*.
	imp	thr	1				
TWO-HANDED AXE/MACE (DX-5) *Requires two hands.†*							
Shovel	cut	sw+2	1, 2*	$40	8 lbs.	13	1 turn to ready.

* Must be *readied* for one turn to change from long to short grip or vice versa. †Becomes unready if used to parry.

Ranged Weapons

Weapons are listed in groups, according to the skill required to use them, along with skill defaults.

Weapon	Type	Damage	SS	Acc	½D	Max.	Cost	Weight	Min ST	Special Notes
AXE THROWING (DX-4)										
bre'Unor jawbone-axe	cut	sw+1	10	2	ST	ST×1½	$24	4 lbs.	11	Cheap weapon.
DX-3 or THROWING SKILL *(See p. B90)*										
Wight bits	special	see p. 67	13	0	–	ST×2	–	1 lb.	–	
Dwarven cocktail	exp	7d	13	0	–	ST×3½	$15	1 lb.	–	Malf. of 14.

Weapon	Malf.	Type	Damage	SS	Acc	½D*	Max	Wt	RoF	Shots	ST	Rcl	Costs	TL
BLACK POWDER WEAPONS (DX-4)														
Typical musket	14	Cr.	3d-2	16	3	90	630	11	1/60	1	10	-2	$1,000/$1	4
GUNNER/TL4 (Cannon) (DX-5 or other Gunner-4)														
Typical cannon	10	Cr.	6d×6	–	2	400	2,000	8,000	1/60	1	–	–	$20,000/$50	4
GUNNER/TL4 (Mortar) (DX-5 or other Gunner-4)														
Dwarven mortar	14	exp	7d	–	0	30	200	35	1/20	1	13	–	$2,000/$120	4

* Minimum range for mortar.

Armor

Most Myth combatants wear armor as described in *GURPS Basic Set*. Some special cases include:

Heron Guard Armor   see p. 73

see p. 73

The Heron Guards wear a suit of steel-scale and leather armor resembling that of the Japanese samurai, though not as lightly or inexpensively made. It provides PD 3, DR 4 on the head (though not the face), torso, arms, and legs. The boots protect the feet with PD 2, DR 2. The hands and face are left unprotected. A full suit weighs 38 lbs. and costs $1,200.

Journeyman's Coat   see p. 74

see p. 74

Journeymen wear a special fur coat adorned with heavy gold tiles. It provides a mundane PD 1, DR 3, +2 DR vs. crushing damage, to the arms, legs, and torso, as well as the head (though not the face) when the hood is worn.

The coat also bears a special enchantment that reduces *any* damage by 20% prior to applying it to DR! The Heron Guards keep this powerful enchantment a secret, and don't even apply it to their Heron armor even though they have provided the emperor a suit of armor enchanted with it. Given the sheer weight of gold ($1.88 million's worth . . .) and the powerful magic invested in these coats, they're essentially priceless. They weigh 100 lbs.

Sundry Goods

Along with the medieval fare found on p. B212, adventurers in Myth may be able to purchase the following goods:

Aconite

The fir'Bolg craft this weapon poison from a very toxic plant found in their home, the Ermine. Treat as wolfsbane on p. B132.

The forest dwellers don't often sell this substance to outsiders, but have provided it to the Legion's Bowmen on occasion.

Livestock   see p. B144

see p. B144

The world of Myth includes chickens, pigs, oxen, horses and other creatures familiar to a TL3 agricultural economy. The Human populace employs horses both as draft animals and mounts, though the latter usage remains relatively rare given Alric's refusal to employ cavalry in the Legion.

Most livestock costs will be close to those listed on p. B144, barring local economic swings. Saddle-trained horses will generally cost 20% more than the listed price, to reflect their relative rarity.

Nepenthe

Advanced healers use nepenthe, an opium-like drug, as a crude but effective anesthetic. It is expensive, incapacitating, and totally addictive, worth -40 points as an Addiction.

Those under its influence often appear dead, requiring a roll vs. IQ-5 or Physician (plus any Alertness bonuses) to detect signs of life.

Magic Items

From minor aids to Great War-tilting artifacts, the world of Myth displays a variety of magical items.

When costs are listed, these use the price established in *GURPS Magic Items 1* (100% "retail" markup over "wholesale" *Magic* price, or $50 × energy to create in most cases), but the listing of a cost doesn't imply that magic items often are found for sale. They're not.

Many of these items have avoided inquiring archmages for centuries. Assume Scryguard-25+ and similar measures are commonly associated with them.

Abraxas Stone

Also called fever stones, these nondescript totems provide powerful relief from the foul diseases that often accompany the undead. The average Abraxas Stone features Resist Disease-15 against all ailments and costs $125,000.

Anvil of Culwyeh

Little is known of this near-mythical artifact once wielded by Shiver and reportedly destroyed in Connacht's purge (see p. 20). Most scholars believe Shiver used the Anvil to forge wicked weapons empowered only for undead wielders, but a few of the greatest archmages hint that the name Anvil misleads: The artifact had nothing to do with weapon-crafting and bore no resemblance to a blacksmith's tool.

Whatever its real nature, the Anvil would elicit great concern and dread should rumors crop up that it survived Connacht's attentions.

Balmung

Generally regarded as the most powerful enchanted weapon in all of Myth, Balmung boasts a storied history dating back to the earliest days of the Cath Bruig empire. Alric currently owns the blade.

In addition to being a very fine broadsword, with +3 Accuracy and Puissance, Balmung features a variant Lightning attack. On any successful sword strike, this does 3d-3 additional lightning damage to the target, then arcs to any nearby targets as per the Dispersal Dream described on pp. 29-30.

Balmung does not distinguish friend from foe, other than that it will not attack its owner, so is best wielded by a great hero at good distance from his companions.

Rumor has it that Balmung possesses other great powers, including some disadvantages that

make even the mightiest archmage wary of unsheathing it too often. This suggests that Balmung may be intelligent, and that it attempts to seize control of its user.

No price can be placed on such an item.

Crom Cruach

The Ghôls sacrifice children (their own only when raiding has been poor . . .) to this gold idol to beg favor from their dark gods. Legend has it that Crom Cruach may be one of the original Rune Stones (see pp. 8 and 85).

Deceiver's Staff

In addition to the Staff enchantment, the Deceiver (see pp. 100-101) has enchanted his personal staff with Magic Resistance-15, providing up to +6 to his resistance rolls, and Power 3, making the effect cost no energy for a mage wielding the staff. (Those without magery must pay 1 fatigue per minute for +4 or 3 fatigue for +6.) The top of the staff features a skull, glowing with the light of a 30-point Powerstone imbedded within it. The Deceiver's Staff would fetch $182,530, assuming that it doesn't possess additional enchantments unknown to all but its creator.

Deep Fen Boots

These boots of fir'Bolg invention feature Walk on Water-15 and cost $25,000. Wearers can walk across water, bogs, quicksand, etc. for as long as they can maintain the spell.

Eblis Stones

Connacht reportedly destroyed these mighty war totems, but at least one of the original five survived to provide Alric the crucial edge he needed against Balor. That stone provided a ranged Total Paralysis spell, likely enchanted at skill-25+! Legend has it the other stones featured different effects, but each just as mighty. Given their historical significance and overwhelming reputation in battle, any surviving stones would be priceless.

Energon Cubes

This is another name for the unrechargeable Powerstone variant normally called a Manastone (see p. G42). Roughly, they cost as much as an equivalent Powerstone (see p. M22), less $15 per point of energy held. In this setting, it's customary to carve the gem into a cube shape prior to enchanting. Manastones are more common than Powerstones in Myth.

Gleaming Wands

The archmage Malagigi created these glowing sticks to end the long-ago Siege of the Seven Gates. The Gleaming Wands force the Mahir (see pp. 56-57) to become corporeal, temporarily losing their Shadow Form disadvantage. This is an area effect with a base cost of 3 and duration of 1 minute. Each Mahir in the area of effect receives a HT roll to resist the spell. The component spell to enchant Gleaming Wands has been lost in history.

Halcyon Stones

These two fragments of a single stone each gave the user great power over wind and weather (all Air and Water elemental spells at skill-20, with four levels of Power and Counterspell-20 only vs. the other stone's spells). The only known fragment was lost in Balor's sack of Muirthemne.

Ibis Crown of the Cath Bruig

Perhaps the greatest enchanted item in Myth's history, the Ibis Crown is a massive headpiece of bejeweled platinum possessing a vast inventory of powers. Its wearer, if a mage, can cast Fear, Bravery, Berserker, Daze, Sleep, Peaceful Sleep, Madness, Nightmare, Loyalty, Charm, Emotion Control, or Suggestion, all benefiting from the crown's four levels of Power and all at skill 20. Any wearer will enjoy a +2 to IQ up to a maximum of IQ 17. A Conceal Magic-20 spell gives any mage -10 to detect the crown's magical powers. The crown also has other powers, kept secret by the state.

When the Cath Bruig emperor Ceiscoran realized the power of the thing that his mages had crafted, he ordered the creation of 11 ordinary copies at huge expense to make stealing the original that much more difficult. The one true crown was lost when Balor sacked Muirthemne, but subsequently recovered by Alric.

Mandrake Roots
see p. 29

see p. 29

Heron Guards and Journeymen carry these to power their healing spells. Their order teaches them to never use their own fatigue to do so in combat, for fear they'll exhaust themselves.

These can be found for sale from time to time. A charged 7-point root costs about $750. Most of the expense reflects the difficulty of finding and procuring the root itself, which emits a ghastly shriek as it's unearthed that automatically slays any living digger.

A variety of tricks – involving undead minions or Earth spells if available, cheap trained dogs if not – will circumvent this unhappy side effect.

The Head

A treacherous counselor to the Avatara in the Great War against Balor, the Head was just that: a disembodied head perfectly preserved in mind, form, and function. It could think and speak. Research into ancient practices suggests that this enchantment was performed several times in the past – perhaps through some combination of Soul Jar and variants of the Preserve Food and Voices spells.

Heaven Stones

These sapphires are supposed to keep their owner safe from malign influences. Legend has it they wield the most power when held in the mouth. Treat as Moly amulets (Magic Resistance +1 to +5 vs. one college only; see *GURPS Magic Items 1*, pp. 116-117), with only half effect if not held in this fashion.

Maul of the Dwarven Kings

This incredibly heavy weapon boasted several Air spells in addition to high Accuracy and Puissance. The Dwarves will not say whether they retain the legendary artifact after the sacking of their cities, but were not prone to bring it out into public view even when they clearly did have possession.

Petrification Arrow

To defeat a Fallen Lord, Alric once created an arrow – tipped with the bone of the intended victim himself – that triggered a Flesh to Stone spell when it struck its target. The unusual choice of arrowhead materials suggests that at least a fragment of the victim's bone (obtained from a severed limb in this instance) is a prerequisite for this powerful enchantment. Further details appear to be known only to Alric and his trusted subordinates.

The Oriflamme

The royal standard of the house of Mabingion of Tyr, this cast a powerful combination of Bravery on the bearer's companions and Terror on his foes. It was lost early in the war against Balor, in a fortnight battle in the Bagrada Valley.

Quivers of Power

The fir'Bolg specialize in creating quivers of incredible magical power: Any arrow left in them for more than a day and *fired by the quiver's wearer* will be treated as if fired from a magical bow, regardless of the actual bow's properties! Enchantment costs are the same as for a bow of the same properties. Examples incorporating Accuracy, Puissance, Quick-Aim, and other standard weapon enchantments have all been seen.

Rune Stones

These are the original rune stones of Myth, landmark-sized monoliths thought to be fragments of the One Dream (see pp. 8, 95-96), barrows of the Callieach, or both. Their rough surfaces become reflective if an archmage taps them. Each apparently facilitates study and casting of a single dream, but archmages are extremely tightlipped about any additional properties. Their locations are kept secret by those who know them.

The Tain

The most powerful Gate artifact ever enchanted, the Tain resembled a jewel box of very strange design. Its holder could send those around him to another plane, a cavernous place of shadows seamlessly merging with walls.

Connacht commissioned the Tain to hold the thousands of creatures he desired to dispel from the lands. Its user could cast a powerful area version of Plane Shift Other (resisted by IQ+1) to transport those around him into the Tain. The secret to getting back out died with the two archmages who discovered it, shattering the Tain in the process. Each fragment of the Tain can still access the alternate plane to which the original led, though it's doubtful that a fragment boasts the ability to force creatures into that plane as the original did.

Tarnkappe

These capes incorporate a self-powered Hide spell. The Dwarves are known to have enchanted 12 of them.

Thalor's Eye

This isn't an enchanted item, but the magical legacy of a powerful Myrkridian mage-pack leader. The eye constantly casts Wither Plant with a 3-hex radius. Anyone who looks into its gaze must resist the eye's skill of 25 using HT (modified by Strong/Weak Will); the victim receives a +1 per yard between himself and the eye. If the victim loses, he takes 1 hit of damage per point by which he lost. Looking at the back of the eye is safe. This item has been lost in time.

The Total Codex

This indestructible book contains the fate of all things, and thus all of history. The book is infinitely long, though it appears of mundane size and weighs but 15 pounds. No one can turn to a specific fate upon opening it, though the great archmage Mazzarin could usually turn to a page near his own fate. Treat reading the Total Codex as casting a Divination spell at skill-30 with no prerequisites. Instrumental in the recent wars, the Total Codex is in Alric's possession.

Trabist's Mirror

Soulblighter used this artifact to gather up Shiver's spirit and make her corporeal once again. It might be an instrument casting or assisting Resurrection. It might cast or assist a spell to create powerful undead. No one got close enough to Shiver in her short second lifetime to divulge the mirror's function from her nature. The mirror currently is considered lost.

Wards

The fir'Bolg often wear jewelry enchanted with a Fortify variant that need not be enchanted on clothing or armor. The cost is twice that of standard Fortify enchantments.

World Knots

Scattered throughout Myth, these sites halve the energy cost and skill penalties to Teleport to a World Knot or from one toward the caster. They have a radius of 3, allowing 19 human-sized subjects to be teleported at one time while benefiting from their Beacon enchantments. Most possess no Name and can be used freely by any mage. All World Knots incorporate four curved pylons that must be intact for the Beacon enchantment to work.

5. Magic in Myth

More fearsome than the foulest fiend are the mighty mages of Myth, who wield power far beyond that usually portrayed in *GURPS*.

This chapter describes the general nature of spells and spellcasters in the Myth setting. For specifics on a particular sort of mage, see Chapter 3, *Denizens of Myth*.

Myth Magic Elements

GURPS Myth uses the *GURPS* magic system introduced in *Basic Set*, detailed in *Magic*, and further expanded in *Grimoire* and to a small extent in *Magic Items 1*. A few elements described in the above books have never manifested in the Myth setting; these are listed in this chapter. Conversely, Chapter 2 introduces several new options for mages. These, and the overall "style" of magery in Myth, are elaborated upon below.

FATIGUE

While Myth mages do employ Powerstones (and even more commonly single-use Manastones), most do not rely exclusively upon these aids. Rather, they develop the capacity to personally store and channel vast quantities of mana. A mage who could only harness mana equivalent to his ST probably would be regarded as "puny."

Extra Fatigue

Mages purchase this extra mana storage as specialized Extra Fatigue (see p. 27). The GM may want to consider a limit on how much Extra Fatigue a given mage can purchase, but if so it should be fairly liberal – an interesting and very conservative one would be up to 2 × the mage's Thaumatology skill. GMs should allow Myth mages to purchase Extra Fatigue after character creation – it's an acquired trait, just like the endurance gained in long-distance running in real life.

Recovering Fatigue

Many Myth mages also can channel more mana than the *GURPS* norm; that is, they recover spent fatigue much more quickly than even mastery of the Recover Strength spell enables. The Fatigue Recovery advantage on pp. 28-29 provides this ability. A high Fatigue Recovery allows the massive-fireball-every-half-minute performance seen in the *Myth* games. An important distinction: Though mages in *Myth* appear to recover spent mana regardless of what they spend their time doing between spells, in *GURPS Myth* a mage must still *rest* to recover fatigue no matter how quickly Fatigue Recovery allows him to do so.

MAGERY AND POWER INVESTITURE

Magery functions normally in Myth. An elaboration used here is that mages may purchase a "base" level of general Magery then add additional levels of a limited Magery on top of it. The mage then possesses a "split" bonus to spells, Thaumatology, sense mana, etc. as appropriate.

Power Investiture simply represents a religious or philosophical approach to Magery. It is cheaper than Magery, especially at higher levels. The fact that certain disciplines must be followed to retain access to spellcasting counteracts this discount; see p. 90.

Extended Magery

Many Myth mages possess Magery well past the normal three-level maximum (see p. 27). Since this represents outlandish talent, the GM should probably make Magery an attribute that can be increased after character creation. This variation from normal *GURPS* policy is assumed in the Myth setting description on pp. 90-91.

CAN I USE THIS IN OUR OTHER CAMPAIGN?

The answer probably is "No."

GURPS Myth empowers mages of far greater might than is the norm in *GURPS*. In doing so, it sidesteps many longstanding *GURPS* restrictions on spellcasting and sprints past them with nary a backward glance.

Many GMs will not want to introduce these measures into existing fantasy campaigns, and since it's their campaign they don't have to. Certainly a clunky continuity lapse would result from simultaneously lifting the standard Magery 3 cap, allowing unlimited Extra Fatigue, introducing more powerful spells, and above all permitting Fatigue Recovery. The 100-point mages before and after might look pretty similar, but the 400-point mages would look completely different.

A better gambit might be to ask for one or two of the above elements to be introduced, to loosen things up a bit and provide a few more design options. Many GMs will resist even this and, again, that's their right.

As a point of reference, the options in this book will "spice up" magic at least as much as *GURPS Grimoire* did to *GURPS Magic*. GMs who admire and embrace the exquisite checks and balances of *Magic* probably will want to tighten things up even in a *Myth* campaign. Those who found it refreshing to add *Grimoire* to their campaigns might consider using these additional options.

SPELLS OF MYTH

The following section explains which of the existing **GURPS Magic** and **Grimoire** spells have been seen in use in Myth, which of them probably exist given the nature of the setting, and which probably do *not* exist given the same.

GMs should feel perfectly free to introduce or forbid additional spells as they see fit, of course.

For several spells unique to Myth and guidelines on creating additional new spells, see pp. 29-31.

Animal

All spells of this college fit into the Myth setting, except for Shapeshifting and the spells related to it. Lycanthropylike effects are very rare in Myth (see *Soulblighter* on p. 100), nor do history and legend mention them. This college does not appear to be a favorite course of study, at least among more civilized mages.

Body Control

Many mages master Body Control spells in Myth, and nothing suggests that all the spells listed in **Magic** are not commonly known. Shrink, Enlarge, and their variants from **Grimoire** probably are not known. It would seem likely that Decapitation would be more popular if known (see sidebar, p. 104), but it would seem unsporting to deny Myth mages this flashy method of aggression.

Communication and Empathy

Almost certainly this college is underdeveloped in Myth. Truthsayer and Compel Truth probably do not exist at all, since the most powerful archmages seem no more able to parse falsehood from fact than an ordinary man would be. Especially in light of the prerequisite chain leaning heavily on these two spells, the GM could rule that the entire college simply does not exist!

Elemental

These colleges provide the meat and potatoes of the Myth mystical armaments. All spells should be available except the Summon and Create Elemental spells. Standard Elementals don't exist in Myth. Introducing the Acid spells from *Grimoire* would fit just fine with the existing Myth ambiance.

Enchantment

All of these spells should be available. Manastone from p. G42 will be very common. Note that Soul Stone on p. G42 may also be widely known among archmages, providing an alternative to the Extra Life discussed in the sidebar on p. 102.

Food

The *Myth* games deal very little with victuals, but likely the entirety of this college is known. In fact, Create Food and/or Monk's Banquet may be very common, given how little attention is paid to logistics. Alternatively, see *Food and Lodging* on p. 109.

Gate

Myth mages often master spells from this college, but only the spells dealing with teleportation are common. Planar spells are known, but not widely. Timeport and all spells related to time travel would be the private reserve of the most powerful archmages, if known at all.

Healing

Most likely all these spells are available.

Illusion and Creation

This appears to be another underdeveloped college, with few phantasms seen in the Myth setting. Likely the basic spells are known, but the Create spells either do not exist or are secrets held by a few archmages.

Knowledge

This appears to be a well-mastered college, particularly in divination. Wizard Eye and the like, though not specifically seen in Myth, fit perfectly into the feel of the computer games. So does the Projection spell from p. G61.

Light and Darkness

This college is known, though not very commonly pursued. The Dwarves appear to hold more interest than most.

Making and Breaking

These spells probably are very popular, especially in light of the enhanced durability of magic items as described on p. 79. Animate Object (see p. G67) could be made a prerequisite for the Stygian Knight variant of Golem on p. 61.

Meta-Spells

These spells are probably very common. The linking spells from *Magic* and various spell-manipulating spells from *Grimoire* can serve as vehicles for explaining many Myth effects, such as long-ranged or delayed versions of Regular spells.

Mind Control

Another well-mastered college, Mind Control may offer the second-most popular repertoire of offensive spells behind the Elemental colleges. All of these spells probably are common, with the single exception of Vigil (see p. G75), which probably does not exist since Alric himself does not appear to know it!

Movement

This college isn't as well-mastered as it might seem. Though many creatures levitate in Myth, most use a native ability or variant of Walk on Air (see p. M35) that doesn't actually require physical walking but outpaces Levitation substantially. Likely, though, most spells are available with the exceptions of Cloud-Walking and -Vaulting.

Necromantic

Less a college than cottage industry in Myth, the Necromantic arts are very well-developed. Note that most of these spells are still very much *illegal* in Light-ruled societies . . .

Plant

Urban mages rarely master this college and probably do not know where to find the advanced spells. The Forest Giants (see pp. 42-43) often specialize in this field.

Protection and Warning

Myth mages underutilize these spells to the point that even some basics – such as Iron Arm and Reverse Missiles – may not exist. If they do exist they aren't common knowledge.

Sound

Likely most or all of these spells are available, but the college simply isn't a favorite among most Myth mages.

Technological

This college has yet to flourish, but is simply waiting for an enterprising Dwarven researcher or 10 to develop it. The GM will want to introduce these spells with great care, though. While basic spells such as Seek Machine/TL won't do much harm and can add a little flair to a Dwarven mage, the same can't be said for the advanced spells. Combining Draw Power/TL with Enhanced Magery and Dwarven gadgeteers waiting to develop advanced power sources can create some jawdropping magical potential and place a campaign on tilt!

The Eldritch Path

The *Myth* games elaborate little on the process of mastering Magery, though certain assumptions appear to be built into the setting. This section describes how an ordinary mortal undertakes the journey from adept to mage to archmage in the Myth setting. It extrapolates heavily. GMs may freely edit.

All Applicants Welcome, Sort Of

No one is born to be a mage – i.e., with an innate Magery advantage – in Myth. Mages are made, honed through long and hard hours studying the intricacies of the thaumatological arts. Native ability will only manifest in the form of Knacks (see pp. M96-97) that a few rare children will display at birth. Even Knacks can be taught later in life as a sort of superspecialized spellcasting (see the bre'Unor racial template on pp. 36-37 for an example), though the process is difficult (charge double points after character creation, just as if increasing an attribute).

That means that theoretically anyone can pursue the thaumatological arts in Myth. In practice, it merely swaps one set of standards for another. In most *GURPS* settings, wizardly teachers gladly take Magery 3 pupils where they get them, since Magery must be innate and high levels rarely occur. A teacher will often overlook a promising applicant's background, political leanings, and mental makeup. These things can change over time, after all; Magery cannot.

In Myth, with the far wider talent pool, teachers of magic can practice far more discrimination. They will still require considerable IQ and Will in most cases, but they can also select based upon shared values. Does the applicant feel allegiance to the same causes, oppose the same factions, promote the same agendas? Practiced mages will attempt to invest their energies in likeminded pupils.

What follows from this is that guilds, circles, and schools of mages tend to thrive more in Myth than in other settings, because the membership tends to be less eclectic and fractious. (This doesn't mean that *no* infighting takes place; it simply tends to be less frequent and severe.) This in turn means that independent teachers – independent mages of any sort, for that matter – are less frequently encountered than in most *GURPS* settings. Most mages simply tend to stick with their guild/circle/school at least until its members have taught all they have to offer – and very few mages manage to embrace all the knowledge shared among their colleagues.

Finding a Teacher

Given these conditions, most aspiring mages will have to apply to an established guild, circle, or school, unless they happen to know one of the rare loners who's also in the market for a pupil. (In game terms, this means that GMs can limit mage PCs to the established "schools" in this book and any additional schools that he creates, should he for some reason feel the need to limit character concepts in this fashion.)

An organization that accepts the student almost certainly will require a Vow of loyalty or similar oath, though the vigor with which these measures are enforced varies considerably. The school also will want some other form of payment. For most, money will do. Others require far more precious commodities, up to and including a lien on the pupil's very soul . . .

When scouting schools, the prospective student will find that all of them fall into one of two basic camps, depending on how they approach spellcasting.

Methods of Magery

Most schools teach magic as a sort of science, if one that bends what little is known about the laws of nature at TL3. These schools may – most probably do – possess extensive religious, philosophical, and political beliefs, but these exist independent of the magical discipline itself. These schools teach Magery (often of a limited sort) and theoretically any spell known in Myth, though very few schools will offer such a wide selection and many will specialize in a particular college. Should a student or member leave the organization or take up new values, his spellcasting abilities will not change as a result.

Other schools teach a belief-based form of spellcasting. Often these aren't perceived as schools of magic at all, but rather as special interests that also teach spellcasting as a tool for members. The student or member's ability to cast spells hinges upon his remaining true to the religious beliefs or philosophies of the school that taught him. Should he falter in these values, his spellcasting ability will diminish. Should he lapse, so will it, though he will retain any knowledge of spells and be able to cast them in high or very high mana. These schools teach Power Investiture and usually offer a limited repertoire of spells. Note that in this setting Power Investiture doesn't always require an active deity behind it; what energizes it can be simply a particular state of mind.

For the vast majority of students – who shouldn't expect to become more than competent at wizardry – the belief-based disadvantages far outweigh the fact that it's slightly easier to learn spellcasting in this fashion. (In game terms, Power Investiture saves 5 points compared to Magery for the first three levels.) Therefore, most opt for a more "secular" Magery-teaching school unless firmly committed to the cause represented by a Power Investiture-teaching school.

School Days

Once a student has selected a school and it has selected him, he will settle down to an arduous course of study for the first several years. He will need to learn at least the first level of Magery and a few spells before even becoming handy around the place. With the normal *GURPS* study rates, this process alone will take more than 13 months even if attended to obsessively. In addition, some schools – particularly those of the Power Investiture branch – treat spellcasting as simply one of several courses of study to be tackled simultaneously! In game terms, this means that PCs who take up learning the wizardly arts after character creation will leave game play for a considerable period.

Standards vary widely between guilds, circles, schools, and the endless variety of other organizations, but in general a student isn't even considered a formal member of the school until he masters Magery 2. Indeed, many drop out before this point, giving the Myth setting about the same proportion of lower-Magery denizens as in other *GURPS* settings. At Magery 2, the school formally initiates the student as an adept (or similarly low title). Many wait till this point to administer the Vow of loyalty, as well, though the more cautious or paranoid do not. The student now has become more beholden to the school, and probably no longer can leave at his own whim.

Adepts spend more time attending to duties than to studies, but continue pursuing Magery 3. Reaching it provides only the first step toward obtaining the equivalent of journeyman rank. Most schools also require an extensive spell list and some level of Extra Fatigue to qualify. Many will require one or two levels of Fatigue Recovery as well. Obviously, passing from adept to journeyman can take as long as *decades*. Many dedicated souls never make it.

Service in Good Stead

Once the student reaches acknowledgement as a journeyman (equivalent titles can include graduate, layman, fellow, initiate, etc.), his formal studies end, though he may freely take advantage of the organization's resources to pursue independent studies at his own initiative. A period of service begins, instead. This may be as short as a few years. More than a few schools require that it last a lifetime, though the journeyman will be free to do as he pleases in any second or subsequent lifetimes . . .

Once this period of service ends, the former journeyman becomes accepted as a fully competent *mage*. He may pursue one of three paths. He may become a master or equivalent at the school, taking up full-time employment educating and leading young mages where he once learned. Qualifying for this usually requires Magery 4 and suitably higher levels in other journeyman prerequisites, as well as some skill in Teaching and Administration. He may become an associate (or equivalent title) of the organization, taking part in circle/guild/etc. politics but pursuing his own interests most of the time. In this case he will probably also be subject to guild service in certain circumstances. Or he may leave his school behind completely, though many schools don't officially allow this.

Most PCs will belong to one of the latter two categories upon beginning their *GURPS Myth* adventures.

In Game Terms

So what characteristics does a given adept or mage need? Common elements include:

Administrative Rank: Journeymen take Rank 1, masters take Rank 2+, and associates usually have no Administrative Rank.

Magery or Power Investiture: This will be 0-1 for a student, 2 for an adept, 3 for a journeyman, 3+ for a mage. Most schools don't allow studying through the next level till its actually obtained, so Magery 4+ adepts are very rare.

Status: This depends on the guild or circle's standing in the community. The average school has Status 0 adepts, Status 1 journeymen, and Status 2 mages. Status usually continues to keep pace with Magery after this, at Status equaling Magery-2.

Duty: Students usually have -10 points; adepts, journeymen, and masters -15 points; and associates -5 to 0 points.

Vow: This can be at any point level, including effectively 0 points, depending on the school. Some schools require students to take it; the others require adepts to do so.

CREATING CUSTOM SCHOOLS

GMs should feel free to invent new circles or guilds based on the guidelines in this section. In addition to the *In Game Terms* considerations above, he should add any unique advantages or disadvantages for all members. He should fully spell out the spells and additional characteristics needed to become an adept, journeyman, or master. Most importantly, he should describe the values that drive this particular organization. In Myth more than most settings, a mage wears his "school colors" for a long time. These values will define him to many observers.

Sample Schools

The *Myth* games provide two examples of magical schools, conveniently one each in the Magery-based and Power Investiture-based branches. The following pages explore these familiar character types as organizations rather than individuals.

Ideally, no attribute will be below 11. Any disadvantage that would minimize effectiveness as an elite soldier will also disqualify an individual (see *GURPS Special Ops*, pp. 50-51, for a discussion of what is allowed or prohibited, or the GM rules).

Cranes (Adepts)

After years of diligence, a trainee receives promotion to Crane Sentry (usually just called Cranes) upon reaching minimum ST 12, DX 13, IQ 11, and HT 12; Literacy and Power Investiture +2; Katana-14 and Tactics-9; and 1 point each in Lend Strength and Lend Health.

Heron Guards (Journeymen on)

A sentry becomes a true Heron Guard upon reaching the standards set by the character template on p. 73. The order "expects" this to take seven years, but a Heron Guard can take a little pride in reaching this level in that interval. Most take a bit longer.

Masters

A Heron Guard with seven years as a Heron; Leadership-12 and Teaching-10; and the Charge Mandrake spell at 15+ can apply for master status. This places him in nominal command of all "regular" Heron Guards, Cranes, and students.

Before the recent crisis, many preferred to forgo this distinction. They spent their time honing their martial and magic skills rather than teaching and leading others. Former Journeymen restoring the order will not make this choice, since the order obviously needs them teaching new recruits. This will require them to purchase Administrative Rank 1 as part of the character template on p. 74 in a campaign set after *Myth II: Soulblighter*.

And Beyond

The order has no equivalent of an associate – members do not graduate or retire, and service is for life, which can be a *very* long time (see p. 73). History has never recorded a Heron Guard attempting to leave the order, so the consequences of such a decision are not known.

Older Herons will improve their skills in line with the Heron Guard customization notes on p. 73 and/or Journeyman template on p. 74, with the exception that the Two-Handed Axe/Mace skill is unique to the former penitents.

THE HEROn GUARDS

The Herons serve the emperor of Cath Bruig with intense reverence akin to that expected of modern special forces. The order isn't really a "school," but it teaches Power Investiture-based spellcasting (among other skills) so qualifies for these purposes. It is based solely in Muirthemne, though Herons travel often.

Balor annihilated the order when he sacked Muirthemne, but it has recently been revived by the surviving Journeymen (see p. 74). They currently are debating how quickly to add students to replenish their ranks; historically they have been able to concentrate attention on a handful at a time (see p. 73) but circumstances may press them to speed up enrollment.

Overview

Heron Guards do not take a Vow or Duty to their order, but rather to the emperor. Their required disadvantages are listed on p. 73. Their Discipline of Faith prevents them from accruing the Status that would normally accompany their accomplishments. Their organizational structure is very flat. "Journeyman" Heron Guards require no Administrative Rank; masters take Rank 1. Decisions are generally communal, with the emperor as the only figure with extensive authority over the entire order.

Getting In

As detailed on p. 73, the order puts applicants through a rigorous competition. Successful candidates will possess Will 16+.

THE WARLOCKS OF THE SCHOLOMANCE

The Warlocks of the Scholomance represent one of the more straightforward magical circles, even by Myth standards. They have an agenda, but it's strictly one of accruing personal power. If they could be said to have an organizational philosophy, it's that might makes right and extra might makes privilege.

Though an astounding proportion of those entering the circle become incredibly powerful mages, they do so by ignoring the fine details of spellcasting's potential, concentrating solely on what will make them more fearsome in combat. For this reason, even mages of ostensibly lower Magery (albeit full Magery backed by a wide variety of spells) sniff disdainfully at any claim that a Warlock qualifies for archmage status. It takes far more than mastering battle spells to qualify for that lofty distinction.

If the Warlocks have a base of operations, they keep it to themselves. It might even be in the Untamed Lands or east of Gower.

Overview

Warlocks maintain an every-wizard-for-himself culture, so Duties and Vows vary widely; see below.

Given what little the public knows of them isn't flattering, Warlocks only gain Status equal to *full* Magery -3. This means new students and adepts will be treated little better than panhandlers, *especially* by full Warlocks.

An additional disadvantage may be required if the rumors that Warlocks bargain with Dark powers for their skill prove true; see p. 75.

Getting In

Applicants need only be literate and crave power at *any* cost. Somewhere along the way that's exactly what they'll pay . . . Joining the circle requires a -10-point Vow and -15-point Duty.

Embers (Adepts)

Upon attaining Magery 2 and the Fireball spell a student may pass muster as an adept, called an ember among the Warlocks. The Vow and Duty remain the same, but Status increases to -1.

Firebrands (Journeymen)

The Scholomancers' journeymen, called firebrands, must have Magery 3 *or* Magery 2 and two additional levels of Fire college-only Magery. Their Will must be at least 14 and their personal fatigue reserves for spellcasting 15+. They must have the Explosive Fireball spell at any level and Fireball at 15+.

Attaining Journeyman status requires purchasing Administrative Rank 1; Magery 3 will increase Status to 0.

Journeymen serve the guild till they reach Warlock competence, however long that takes.

Warlocks (Mages)

Full-fledged Warlocks must have Magery 3 and two additional levels of Fire college-only Magery. Will must be 16+ and personal spellcasting fatigue 20+. They must have at least two levels of Fatigue Recovery (three if skill in the Recover Strength spell is less than 15). They must know the Explosive Fireball and Ring of Fire spells at 16+.

At this point, as full-fledged mages, most Warlocks become "associates" of the circle, leaving its confines but staying in touch, if solely for the learning resources to increase their abilities. They lose their Administrative Rank, their Vow (which they only kept through fear previously, anyway), and their Duty (since they'll expect the circle to return any favor that they do for it). The circle expects associates to pay 20% of income as dues. They average more like 3%; this still suffices to fund the circle's operations.

Those few mages who decide to become masters in the circle keep their Vow and Duty, purchase Administrative Rank 2, and begin inflicting real terror on the embers and firebrands . . .

Rumor has it that many Warlocks have cut off association with their circle entirely. How the masters react to this move is unknown.

And Beyond

Most full Warlocks wander the world on a personal path toward more and more power. While they covet thaumatological knowledge and alliances with even greater mages (such as the Deceiver), they seem so bent upon these pursuits that they don't ever actually get around to using what they've learned in carving out a personal fiefdom or similar worldly goals. Perhaps this reflects a more arcane agenda invisible to outside eyes . . .

Wise mages keep in mind that as their powers grow ever stronger, the standards by which the rest of society judges them grow ever narrower. Ordinary people and the influential alike will react to increasingly powerful mages with increasingly powerful jealousy, envy, and most of all fear. While the opinion of a single ordinary man may be beneath an archmage's notice, the opinion of an entire city or state from lord to lackey can matter in ways that no number of 8d fireballs can cure . . .

In practical terms, this means that an archmage must show more restraint in using his powers than even an ordinary mage. For instance, a tailor might be forgiven using any measure to defend himself. An ordinary mage might be forgiven for casting a Missile spell on a crowded city street, as long as he didn't hurt any bystanders. An archmage likely would be criticized for taking *any* risk of collateral damage, no matter how slight. He probably would be criticized for taking any potentially lethal action, even against an assailant. Ostensibly this would be because a mage of his power should have plenty of non-lethal measures at his disposal. In reality it would be because *nobody* wants to establish the right of someone as powerful as an archmage to use lethal force.

This greater responsibility is perceived whether the archmage likes it or not, just as someone today with a concealed-carry permit would be treated far differently for using his pistol in a dispute than would a 110-pound middle-age accountant for using his fists. Wielding greater power heightens critical attention.

Applying this sort of realistic social feedback can help flesh out a society that challenges ordinary hero and archmage alike. It simply wouldn't be "polite" for an archmage to turn every problem into a smoldering grease spot, even if a knightly sort gets by with using his broadsword toward the same general result.

From one perspective this double standard isn't fair, but from another viewpoint this dynamic is all about fairness. It attempts to handicap powerful individuals in ways that the game stats won't reflect.

Archmages

Among the thousands of willful, talented individuals mastering magery, a handful will rise above the rest. These driven few will rapidly master every lesson, advancing their thaumatology at nigh the speed of thought, till they have consumed all knowledge that their circle or guild has to offer. At this point most settle in to a long, prosperous life as guildmaster or the equivalent.

The remaining few find that they've only just begun working up a thirst for knowledge. These rare souls – for no more than a few score walk the land at any one time – tend to leave behind their original associates and seek out mystical secrets to make an ordinary mage quake in dread.

They have taken up the road of the archmage.

The Definition of Archmagery

No dusty lexicon lists a set of minimum abilities to qualify as an archmage, so standards differ. The template on p. 69 describes a minimal competence; a mage displaying no more ability than portrayed there really wouldn't be seen as putting the "arch" in "mage." Getting results can influence this perception, however, because what really sets apart an archmage is the quality of the things he gets done.

Archmages can routinely overcome large numbers of ordinary combatants *and* delve into the past's deepest mysteries *and* walk into the most inhospitable environs unannounced (and unnoticed if desired) *and* act like it's all no big deal. Therefore a mage shrewdly using his minimal abilities might be acknowledged as an archmage by his peers, while many mages with characteristics far beyond those in the template will not be because they specialize in one or two activities. It's a judgment call, and generally those already acknowledged as archmages do the judging.

In general, at least Magery 5 is required to qualify for this distinction, and that would have to backed with a really impressive spell list and the ability to recover fatigue very quickly. By Magery 8, even a mage with no extra fatigue-related advantages who's studied in at least 10 colleges probably will make the grade.

Taking Up the Calling

Unlike standard mages in Myth, archmages do tend to be loners, with the noted past exceptions of the Avatara and the Fallen Lords, described later in this chapter. Their advanced studies leave them little time or patience to cater to the elementary needs of their former circle or guild. Many archmages devote all of their time to honing their mystical prowess, many seek worldly power, many hunt lost knowledge – see the sidebars for a variety of considerations applying to these pursuits.

Ultimately, though, most archmages sense that there's something more out there – that the mystical knowledge they've achieved serves as no more than a primer for the *real* power flowing through Myth. They begin searching for the dreams of Wyrd.

The Dreams of Wyrd

As described in Religion on pp. 8-9, 49 "dream" spells exist in Myth. These are ultrasecret and powerful spells that only archmages can hope to learn (see p. 31). Each has a great Rune Stone associated with it (see p. 85).

No one knows (or admits to knowing) exactly how to track down a dream spell. Most believe that if an archmage can find a dream's Rune Stone, it will divulge the dream, whether through a formula inscribed on its surface, telepathic inspiration, or some other method.

The problem is that most of the Rune Stones have never been located, and those who have tracked one down keep it as a most cherished secret. Not a single Rune Stone has fallen into common knowledge.

Given the difficulties, only a handful of dreams have been uncovered to date. Most archmages spend several lifetimes trying to uncover a single example. Some that have been found include:

Dispersal Dream

See pp. 29-30. Alric has mastered this dream, as apparently have all Shades! It appears that the location of this rune stone is the least secret of all, shared among these particularly powerful undead. Some question lingers of whether the Shades' spell is actually the Dispersal Dream – they don't actually advertise it as such (which may simply be because they *rarely* engage in professional chitchat with living archmages) and the special effects differ from Alric's version. Still, the spells' other properties are identical, and most scholars suggest that this spell – and perhaps all dreams – varies in appearance depending on the caster's aura.

Whisper Dream

Shiver possessed the secret to this dream that allowed her to walk into her victim's dreamscape and usually destroy him from within! She appears to have lost it the first time she died; certainly she was never seen to use it in her second incarnation and no one now openly wields it. Likely mastering it requires great expertise in the Mind Control college. Shiver possessed as much among her many talents.

As mentioned in their template (see p. 69), archmages must make a considerable investment in social advantages. This represents that – at least in Myth – nigh-omnipotence doesn't occur in a vacuum. The following elaborates the sort of "trappings" expected from Myth's archmages.

The Avatara

Any Avatara wielded the influence of a duke (Status 6) in Cath Bruig and the Province. Keeping up appearances at this level required an Avatara to be at least Very Wealthy. That's *before* the resources required to hire enchanting circles, but did pay for a host of mundane underlings.

A reclusive Avatara who lived and worked alone could trim his monthly cost of living, but if he was wise he'd spend the saved money on agents and representatives at various courts and in other key positions. This would maintain his Status even when he was off on his mountain. If he refused to make that investment, effective Status would decline by 1 for each month that he didn't pay his monthly cost of living. It would bounce back to 6 the moment he made a public appearance, but an Avatara simply could not meet the demands of urban life and fulfill his responsibilities to his circle without the infrastructure that the Status 6 maintenance costs implied.

The "base" Reputation for an Avatara was +2, but personal Reputation could modify this even into a Disadvantage.

Many Avatara would have additional social advantages as described on p. 69; the above represent the minimum.

Fallen Lords

The Avatara's Dark counterparts also wielded great influence, though this varied more depending on personal fortunes. Status 5-7 was usual.

Along with the Wealth to maintain Status, Fallen Lords often took Balor as a Patron whether they liked it or not.

Base Reputation for a Fallen Lord was -3, but note that most people would be far too *afraid* to display hostility toward one. Personal Reputation could modify this in either direction.

Politics in the Inner Circle

Some wags have suggested that the only reason for mages to form circles is so that they can keep their eye on the only people whom they fear. The observation bears a core of truth. For all the advantages of joining forces with one's contemporaries, that same circle will often serve to moderate an individual's ambitions.

Within the Nine – and assuredly within any reborn Avatara led by Alric – a fine balance between community and individual priorities existed. For instance, if an Avatara set off on an epic quest to recover some mighty artifact, he could keep it to himself *if* he didn't ask the circle's help in mounting the expedition, *if* the artifact didn't prove crucial to meeting some common need, and if a variety of other contingencies didn't manifest.

Opinions usually varied on whether circumstances required sharing of a new spell or similar resource, so an Avatara had to expect to defend his right to hoard an asset. More importantly, at least with Alric in charge, he had to know when to quit defending that right and meet the circle's demands. No two cases were alike, so a fine sense of politics served an Avatara well.

At least within the Nine Alric would not tolerate more than minimal infighting. Within the Fallen Lords, political maneuvering usually gave way to open warfare whenever Balor wasn't directly supervising things. Any Fallen Lord who expected to seize an asset for himself had to ensure his contemporaries heard nothing of it. The atmosphere was very much "every archfiend for himself," and the best that could be said of being a Fallen Lord is that it provided a bit better intelligence on one's rivals.

Any new manifestation of Dark archmages probably would share similar conditions.

These sorts of social dynamics should be applied to any circle or guild. A mage entering one of these groups will find himself trading three quarts of inconvenience for a gallon of convenience – and the GM can use circle/guild politics as a handy device for steering PC behavior.

Confinement Dream

This was used on the Watcher (see pp. 101-102) by *someone*, though precisely who remains a mystery. The Deceiver seems a likely culprit. This dream pinions the victim to an immediate surface *permanently*. Remove Curse may be attempted *once*, and anything less than critical success means some appendage remains stuck. Not much except condolences can be offered if it's the victim's head that remains attached, because amputation is the only option at this point. Also called the Binding Dream by some sources.

Rotting Mist Dream

Technically, this dream hasn't been uncovered, but at least some Ghôls know where to find the Crom Cruach idol (see p. 83) believed by many to be its Rune Stone.

The Other 45

The other dreams include unlife, compulsion, slow, fear, sun shower, shaking earth, daze, and 38 for which most archmages don't even possess a name! No scholar has been able to come up with even the beginnings of a map of how these eclectic concepts might fit into a 49-piece mosaic representing Wyrd.

The One Dream

Ultimately, collecting dream spells has the goal of obtaining all 49, no matter how distant that seems given current progress. Legend has it that the archmage who performs this incredible task will transcend into an advanced consciousness, perhaps even taking up an avatar role for Wyrd himself!

Simultaneously, this act will transform the nature of Myth, though exactly how is subject to much interpretation. Most clerics and scholars believe it would usher in an

era of Light triumphant. Others believe it would be an era of *harmony* between Light and Dark, rather than the current cycles. Those on the fringe foretell the end of the world as it is known, and a rebirth incorporating all that has been learned since Wyrd first felt inspired.

The Trow may have more solid information on what would transpire should the 49 dreams be united, but as usual they don't see fit to invest their time in educating mere mortals.

One serious catch in the above theories is the legendary evidence that a dream can be permanently *destroyed*, seemingly making it impossible to rejoin all 49. The stories usually state that destroying its Rune Stone will inflict this fate on a given dream, though a few hint that the Rune Stone must be destroyed and all practitioners of the dream dead. Theoretically, any number of dreams might already be destroyed, to which some scholars answer that only the remaining dreams need be joined, thereby drawing the One Dream that much closer! Much debate takes place over this topic, but only time will provide enough evidence to point toward a solid answer.

THE AVATARA

Based in a high tower near the heart of Madrigal, the Avatara (potential avatars) championed Light for centuries before Balor's arrival. The group was supposed to consist of the nine greatest archmages supporting Light's cause – and was often called The Nine – though membership fluctuated at times.

Most Avatara held civic responsibilities akin to a high noble, and their last leader, Alric, was a king. This further invested them in civilization's prosperity, though some complained that it slowed down their magical research.

·The Great War claimed every Avatara except Alric. He has yet to proclaim whether he intends to reconstitute the circle. Certainly most of the remaining archmages of Light would be honored to take this role.

The Ultimate Goal

While defending Light on a day-to-day basis, the Avatara held the goal of reconstituting the One Dream in order to secure a lasting victory for the causes of civilization and fulfill their avatar potential. When they could afford the investment, they spent their time seeking out clues to the location of the many dream spells they had not already mastered.

Place Hope in Spells, Faith in Steel

No one knows how the tradition started, but all potential Avatara had to demonstrate mastery of a sword to be accepted in the circle (see p. 69). Most commentators suggest that the skill merely served as a symbol, that an archmage who took the time to learn bladework would take the time to learn to use armies and use them well. Many a Light archmage has thought their time more efficiently used purely in spellcasting rather than in leading ordinary men and simply augmenting the soldiers' work with magery. Apparently one of the Avatara's shadowy founders did not want to see any of its members fall into this conceit.

Alric

Alric probably wasn't the most magically skilled of the Nine – perhaps Murgen claims that distinction – nor did he claim the greatest martial skills, an honor Rabican pursued with vigor. But he far and away represented (and continues to represent) the best all-around embodiment of the Avatara ideal.

Warrior, sage, mage, statesman, Alric was born to lead through sheer competence regardless of personal desire. He com-

In Myth, social circumstances prevent archmages from flogging the **GURPS Magic** enchantment rules senseless. While they certainly *could* set up assembly-line production of minor magic items, the motive largely has disappeared.

For starters, the average archmage wouldn't dream of personally using such a device. An archmage depending on a ring of Ignite Fire would create the same reaction as a modern surgeon reading each step of a procedure from a textbook during an operation. They should be able to just *do* these things; relying on little crutches will call their competency into question. (This also explains why the typical archmage enters combat with one individualized magic item of great power, whereas the typical experienced PC mage totes about an inventory of minor enchanted gear.)

In addition, the profits of quick-and-dirty enchantment can prove elusive, while the monthly cost of living for high Status does not. A Myth archmage could easily churn out four 100-energy magic items per day with just a few assistants, but that barely covers typical cost of living before expenses! Those who have attempted to cover this gap by retailing for themselves (thereby keeping the 100% typical markup) discover that being a merchant is a full-time, skilled job. Those who attempt to form more elaborate circles – using more assistants and Powerstones to create more costly items – discover that administrative snarls increase exponentially. Losing one assistant can shut down production for months while seeking a replacement. A huge inventory of Powerstones attracts thieves, requiring security across the large area they'll need to recharge.

Finally, it just doesn't enhance an archmage's standing to churn out minor items no matter how useful, anymore than a master chef would earn kudos for a really nice cheeseburger. Archmages find it simpler to earn their income through holding land (as a noble does) and/or from retainers to advise the local rulers. This involves far less risk and requires far less attention.

bines sterling leadership qualities with practical strategy and an overwhelming desire to see Light triumph despite the grimmest odds.

Alric ruled the Province when he led The Nine and now rules the Cath Bruig empire. He is a thin, elderly, bearded man. He wears especially enchanted armor (see p. 82). He usually carries an "ordinary" enchanted very fine broadsword, but wields Balmung (see p. 83) in dire circumstances. His best combat spell is the Dispersal Dream (see pp. 29-30), which he holds back till really necessary given its high energy cost. As emperor and the Light's greatest living archmage, he has access to a wide variety of powerful magical artifacts. There can be no doubt that he will shape the direction of Light's efforts for the years to come.

Rabican

Some of the Avatara paid little more than lip service to their circle's martial requirements. Not Rabican. This archmage routinely wore great helm and armor, and volunteered for assignments that his contemporaries dreaded. He proved that a Fallen Lord could be defeated – by making Shiver the first of them to fall – then himself fell in battle against the Watcher's forces, which had to unleash their mightiest magics to best him.

Before his death Rabican wrote of his dream duel with Shiver. Her mental assault conjured a mocking image of Moagim, the Dark lord of the Wind Age. Shiver seemed to taunt him with some relationship between Moagim and current events, but before her assault completely unveiled Rabican counterattacked and destroyed her.

This account rests among his personal papers, which lie yet uncataloged in The Nine's tower at Madrigal.

Murgen

Murgen was a particularly skilled sorcerer, with a knowledge of the Gate college and extraplanar affairs unmatched by any of his colleagues. He also was a polished diplomat. He died in forcing an exit from the Tain (see pp. 22 and 85).

Maeldun

Known for his persistent and stubborn nature, Maeldun never yielded to man, beast, or deity. Alric claimed his word was the stablest currency in all of Myth.

A native of Tyr, Maeldun destroyed the pirates of Leix after they sacked his city. In the Great War, he led Legion forces defending Cloudspine's passes from Balor. In the process he suffered wounds that eventually killed him.

Cu Roi

A steadfast if unspectacular Avatara, Cu Roi died in Murgen's company as they escaped the Tain.

The Others

While all household names, the other Avatara failed to seize the spotlight during the Great War. The GM should feel free to cut their sagas from whole cloth.

WHY ARCHMAGES SEEK THRONES

In a world full of powerful mages, spellcasters will fill many key positions. Sometimes this extends to the extent that mages make up *all* the nobility – as can be argued was the case with the Dark forces under Balor and the Fallen Lords.

Multiple reasons prompt these moves to seize power, the simplest being because the archmage can. No ordinary man can hope to harness the personal power that the average archmage wields, no matter how fine his sword arm or silver his tongue.

The opportunity to reshape society offers the most pressing temptation to take over local authority. As detailed in the *Wizardry and Polite Society* sidebar on p. 94, mundane rulers and societies often restrict an archmage's activities. Once on the throne, the archmage can greatly influence these factors. A necromancer-king may never get all his citizens to volunteer to become Ghasts, but he can abolish any laws making necromancy illegal. An Avatara-king may face an uprising if he tries to get everybody to spend all their waking hours assisting in ceremonial magic, but he might make participation an option in lieu of paying taxes!

In short, an archmage who takes a role in the power structure gets to make the rules, while an archmage who does not often finds the rules stacked against him. It just makes sense to divert part of one's towering intellect and ambition into the political venue.

THE FALLEN LORDS

Ironically, most of humanity knows far more about these evil archmages than of the Avatara, but then living nightmares do command more attention and gather about themselves more legends than selfless protectors do.

When the Fallen Lords first appeared, the Avatara mistakenly assumed that they consisted of Balor and servants that he empowered. Subsequent events proved that each Fallen Lord very much wielded his own power on his own behalf, and that Balor's "lieutenants" really made up a Dark circle remarkably similar to The Nine's own as led by Alric.

Of the seven original Fallen Lords, one now thrives, having returned to service with the Light. Four have died at least once apiece, and for now all evidence suggests they remain dead. Two disappeared after Balor's defeat.

Balor

The Leveller, the god who created himself, Connacht reborn: Nothing about Balor suggested that he was anything less than the Dark lord of a new age, destined to triumphantly usher in a new era of heartbreak and horror.

Clad in plate and wielding an exotic broadsword, Balor may have exemplified the perfect blend of mastering the martial and mystic. He rarely let his Dark emotions override his keen sense of strategy, subverting foes whose price proved less than that he would pay to slay them. He used mighty magics, though favoring "behind the scenes" spells that created formidable troops or effects but left him free to lead during the battle proper. And he possessed incredible prowess in a fight, sufficient to face any Avatara on at least equal terms.

Balor was only defeated by a combination of archmagery, a mighty artifact, and trickery. Anything less would not have sufficed.

Pawns or Partners

Balor made each of his six Fallen Lords into lieutenants, and entrusted each with an army. Their motives for following him, and subsequent loyalty, varied considerably. Light scholars believe that only Soulblighter followed Balor of his own accord, and indeed revered the Leveller. Shiver may have been loyal in her own way, so too the Watcher. The Deceiver most certainly was not, apparently entering his train only for the personal opportunities that it presented. The loyalties of the Lurker and the Voiceless One are but single facets of the bejeweled mysteries surrounding each.

Archmages who take up authority positions often regret it, and many would never consider such a move. Being a king and being an archmage are both full-time jobs with serious ramifications for incompetency. No one man can easily juggle both. More likely, the archmage-king will fail at both, often with fatal consequences.

In the case of archmagery, the standard is set by colleagues who focus their razor-sharp minds on practice and research 24 hours a day, 365 days a year. This leaves no room for the duties of a mayor, much less a king. Those juggling crown and thaumatology will find that once-equal rivals now outpace them in skill and knowledge. They wield spells the sorcerer-king would have no idea how to cast, have uncovered lost artifacts that he had no clue might surface, and have enchanted powerful additions to their arsenal that make his ceremonial +2 Puissance and +2 Accuracy broadsword look cheap in comparison.

Meanwhile, mundane rival rulers have set the same standards in their calling. Every hour not spent ruling creates one more case of a lesser noble placing his own interests above the ruler's. Every hour spent researching spells means a subordinate will answer a legal question against the ruler's desires, whether intentionally or not.

Archmages who don't keep up often find former rivals eager to settle old scores, and wielding new magics that make success a certainty. Kings who don't keep up often face pretenders who think they can do a better job – and probably *can*. The wisest examples of both professions realize it takes a truly towering individual to balance both duties with any degree of success.

Curbing the Appetite for Destruction

Just about every sidebar in this chapter has detailed realistic social dynamics that keep an archmage from just playing God with the mundane lives around him. That's because some balance of power must exist for most players to enjoy portraying just-plain-folks in the company of ultrapowerful individuals. Conversely, an archmage needs to have the *capacity* to cast ultra-powerful effects, simply because that's what defines an archmage. Therefore, this chapter offers several subtle-but-no-less-real social conventions that require archmages to use discretion in most circumstances.

That said, some players just won't get it. The ability to cast army-shattering spells will give them all the reason they need to routinely cast army-shattering spells.

If all the PCs are archmages, the GM can cater to this sort of eldritch free-for-all. He should be prepared for it to transform his setting, though. An archmage who answers his neighbor's property-line dispute by petrifying him in mid-sentence will usually be forced to get rid of the neighbor (and his kin) and take over his property. If any higher authority objects, he'll have to face off again, and so on. Forward momentum shakes up a lot of no-holds-barred campaigns, and the results often satisfy no one.

A common alternative is to threaten the impulse-control-challenged player with a bigger stick – an authoritative NPC whom the PC can't hope to best. This can get clumsy when the PC is supposed to wield the most individual power in the setting: Whom do you threaten an archmage with?

A better solution might be to highlight the consequences of the archmage's actions. Describe the orphaned children, shattered economies, and looks of disapproval in detail sufficient to make the point. If several such instances still don't get through, put together an NPC coalition to take the PC down by whatever means at hand.

Afterward, explain that they were only working in their own self-interest when confronted with a raging sociopath, and make the player create a Warrior for his replacement PC . . .

Soulblighter

First among Balor's lieutenants, at the time Soulblighter was the only Fallen Lord who wasn't an archmage – simply a magically augmented warrior of epic potential. Only his bloodlust matched his martial magnificence – swords and arrows would bounce off him by the score as he annihilated entire armies with his glaive. Soulblighter strove to leave no living thing in his wake.

After Balor's death, Soulblighter fled into the Untamed Lands and mastered magical skills awesome enough to shatter the Cloudspine. Most certainly by his return he qualified as an archmage of first rank, an unprecedented gain in skill over simply a handful of years. He wields the one example of a shapeshifting spell ever seen in Myth – the ability to turn into *several* normal crows. Unfortunately, the death of even one of these canceled his ability to use the spell.

Alric believes Soulblighter was the reincarnation of Damas, Connacht's lieutenant who led the ancient emperor's quest to rid Myth of magical artifacts. Some cryptic references have also called him Anshar, patron of the hanged. Alric bested Soulblighter at Tharsis to end the Fallen Lord's own campaign against Light.

The Deceiver

Loyalty isn't the Deceiver's forte. An ancient Avatara, he fell in with Balor at the earliest stages, only to return to the Light once Balor was slain and Soulblighter rampant! Balor himself gave the Avatara born Myrdred the name that all now call him.

A rare individual, the Deceiver combines an undentable self-confidence with the most calculating of minds and understated manner in magical combat. In short, he is more prone to knife a foe in the back than meet him in a head-to-head confrontation, which undoubtedly earned him the honorific "Source of the 500 Poisons."

The Deceiver very rarely deigns to explain himself, so scholars can only theorize that he joined the Fallen Lords simply because Balor appeared to be foreordained to win. He might also have appreciated the opportunity that it provided to keep an eye on his ancient foe, the Watcher, but this proved his temporary undoing when the Deceiver overreached himself in confronting the Watcher's army with his own.

The Deceiver nearly died in fleeing that fight – perhaps *did* die – but was revived at Alric's command. For reasons again left unexplained, he agreed to join the

Light efforts against Soulblighter. Given that the Deceiver appeared to embrace evil as readily as any born to it during his tenure as Fallen Lord, Alric's offer left many onlookers stunned. Others suggest that appearances were just that, and the Deceiver served the Light as a spy in Balor's ranks.

Myrdred does not look like much – an old and balding lecher, to be precise – and likes things that way. He prefers to be underestimated. Despite that, he displays fine negotiating skills (likely magically enhanced), having convinced the Trow to join him in switching to Light's service.

He wields more secret knowledge by far than any other archmage in Myth. In battle he favors his Cloudkill spell (see p. 29). He uses frequent Teleports to travel long distances alone when in a hurry.

He may possess the Confinement Dream but knows better than to brag of it. His list of enemies stretches forever. They don't need the temptation to wrest it from him.

Shiver

The mother of plagues and first lady of Fallen Lords, Shiver had practiced archmagery for untold time before joining Balor's forces. The Ghôls whisper of her long-ago exploits using the name Culwyeh, and even they are taken aback by the tales they tell. Among other exploits, she is credited with first fielding Wights.

At the time she served Balor, Shiver may have been the most powerful battle sorcerer striding the lands of Myth. She wielded an Earth-college exploding Missile spell that burrowed toward its target, a Light-and-Darkness-college Missile spell that had an area effect and could be maintained (!), a Light-and-Darkness spell similar to Ring of Fire (see p. 30), a skill with Fear that allowed massive castings, secret defensive sorceries, and most of all the Whisper Dream (also called the Nightmare Dream), a spell that forced the target into a surreal dream duel in which Shiver held all the cards. She served Balor well as a general spearheading his invasion, not so much for her strategic sense, but for the sheer impact her sorcery added to his vanguard.

Not even an archmage could stand up to her till Rabican learned of her one weakness – vanity. Setting a trap for her at huge risk, he allowed her to engage him with her Whisper Dream, then used his new knowledge to stun her long enough to use a massive Flame Jet to finish her.

Even as the smoke curled away from her ashes, Rabican could still feel her presence, and indeed death apparently didn't endure. Soulblighter either revived her or created an undead incarnation with Trabist's Mirror (see p. 85), but where once Shiver boasted a gauzy appearance at turns beautiful and bestial, she now appeared all too solid, withered, and injured. What vanity remained would find little solace in her new form. Instead, her new appearance drove Shiver to a constant state of shrieking rage.

Shiver assisted Soulblighter as she had Balor until the Deceiver gave her a second – perhaps even final – death. During this period she did not appear to wield the same great sorceries that she had previously possessed – but was still a ferocious opponent, taken lightly by no one.

The Watcher

A calculating and *ancient* archmage with a tendency to nurse musty grievances, the Watcher served Balor as well as did any Fallen Lord. His army kept moving forward despite the Deceiver's treachery. He then pursued Alric's ragtag forces with zeal even though he might have been tempted to seek out Myrdred's corpse, for among his hundreds of hatreds he cherished none more than that he held for his old foe.

CUTTING LOOSE

Every so often – usually on the battlefield – the circumstances align to place no stigma on an archmage unleashing his full powers.

At these moments, the wise archmage *really* cuts loose.

The issue extends beyond turning the 100 Thralls before the archmage into half-price cold cuts. The spellcaster should seek to annihilate them in style. The more he impresses onlookers, the more whispered tales he inspires, the less risk he runs that a foe or rival will come looking for him.

Despite all the difficulties of navigating mundane society and circle/guild politics, an archmage still is measured by the size of the smoking crater he leaves behind. Interested parties probably won't interpret an efficient application of minimal effort as keen tactics. They'll perceive it as evidence that the archmage has let his skills get rusty.

Extra Life and the Prudent Archmage

The path of the archmage requires incredible talents, yields awesome rewards, and usually makes incredible enemies. An insurance policy of similar scope makes up part of the complete package.

GURPS offers a variety of methods for cheating death. (So many, in fact, that an opponent who wants to ensure the archmage stays dead can't possibly hope to cover them all.) The simplest, though, might be the Extra Life advantage on p. CI36; it also might provide the most accurate portrayal of the genre. GMs should consider allowing archmages to purchase Extra Life even after character creation.

The points invested can represent research into magical loopholes in the nature of luck, decomposition, the soul's transition, or whatever explanation ends up fitting the circumstances in which the archmage returns. Exploiting one of these loopholes causes it to close up in reaction, which explains why the archmage must research yet another loophole (and pay the points again) to buy another Extra Life.

In *GURPS* terms, the Deceiver probably used an Extra Life to cheat death between the intramural battle waged in *Myth: The Fallen Lords* and his revival in *Myth II: Soulblighter*. Had he been slain again just after revival, odds are that the second time the condition would have stuck.

Some GMs might find it uncomfortable that Extra Life turns the ultimate PC failure into merely a speed bump on their career path. If so, limitations can be placed upon it: The mage's body must remain relatively intact, the head must remain attached to the body, purchasing an Extra Life requires an epic quest for knowledge that is more likely to kill the mage than provide the clues to avoiding same, etc. These probably shouldn't lower the cost of Extra Life – 25 points already is pretty cheap by archmage standards – but can simply represent "house rules" curbing its abuse.

His poisoned mind led his contemporaries to consider him unhinged, even by the standards of a Fallen Lord. It also led to his greatest triumph, when he laid a trap that caught the great Mazzarin (see below) in the Wind Age. This earned a reputation as the second- or third-most powerful sorcerer of his heyday.

As a necromancer first and foremost, he pursued the Unlife Dream with great vigor (see the *Rhi'anon* sidebar, p. 16), but reportedly never found it.

Despite his prowess, the Watcher nearly died in a long-ago encounter with the Deceiver. At other times, miscalculated acts of vengeance often led him to seek sanctuary in the Dire Marshes or other remote stretches, to let things cool down and allow time to obsess over his next move. Eventually he found himself pinned in one of his remote hideaways beneath Cloudspine by the Confinement Dream (see p. 96) till Balor freed him at the cost of an arm.

The Watcher also was called Bahlíal, mad goat of the fens. An arrow enchanted by Alric from the Fallen Lord's own bones proved his downfall.

The Lurker

Little is known of this Fallen Lord, or her fate. She specialized in weather and plant-control spells, and would "soften up" a target with seemingly natural catastrophes before announcing her presence and intent. The Lurker was also known as Bheil, the twice-born daughter of flood and famine.

The Voiceless One

Perhaps the most mysterious of the Fallen Lords, the Voiceless One slipped through the night on missions that even Balor could not be sure he fully understood. Her name was Ravanna, and she was called the loveless child of the unwed dawn.

An alert Heron reported back to Alric that the Deceiver called Shiver "Ravanna" in his final confrontation with her, and that immediately afterward she quit taunting him and began unloading her mightiest magics at the Deceiver instead. Alric suspects this would indicate some sort of strange relationship between Shiver and the Voiceless One, but the Deceiver has remained true to form and enlightened no one.

It is known that Balor revived the Voiceless One from eternal sleep. It could be that Shiver and she are the same, Shiver was on her *second* and *third* lives in Balor's and Soulblighter's wars respectively, and the last Fallen Lord has yet to be revealed!

One Other

Of all the archmages destined to become legends who took part in the Great War, none would compare to the following individual.

Mazzarin

Widely acknowledged as the greatest archmage to ever walk the lands of Myth, Mazzarin possessed phenomenal magical gifts; see *The Total Codex* on p. 85 for one

example. Legend has him proving instrumental in forming the Avatara and – among dozens of other great deeds – providing the enchantments that would back Connacht's wars against the Trow. By the time Connacht first laid hands on one of these artifacts Mazzarin had been dead for decades, slain in an ambush laid by the Watcher and thousands of his Thralls. Still, many doubt death can hold its grip on such a man.

6. CAMPAIGNING in MYTH

The *Myth* games blend high fantasy with horror, frequent injections of humor, and a realistic respect for terrain and weather. So does *GURPS Myth*, but gently tweaking this mix can create an entirely new atmosphere worth exploring.

Combat in *Myth* possesses a distinct style. The following measures can help emulate it in *GURPS*:

Let chaos reign – *GURPS* battles tend to be fairly clinical, since everyone moves in turn and possesses fairly precise knowledge of what their options are, the risk they face, etc. Battles in *Myth* tend to be much more messy, with units heading the wrong direction, throwing explosives at the wrong time, and generally screwing up in real time.

To simulate this, the GM could have NPC units act more erratically than normal. Having them make Vision rolls to spot a new adversary is a good start. They should also try to fire through occupied hexes, throw Dwarven cocktails too close to allies, get too far away from (or too close to) supporting units, and generally let the PCs take nothing for granted in friend or foe's behavior.

Special effects – The GM should go all-out in describing the blow-by-blow of a *GURPS Myth* combat, to evoke the rather cinematic special effects seen in the *Myth* games. A good, garish description of a death wound always spices things up.

Heady Business

Even a casual review of the Myth setting shows that many combatants have an excessive interest in decapitating the competition. Part of this is practical: Decapitation may prevent certain wizardly death-cheating devices from working, heads form the components for certain magical items or processes, and the Ghôls reason that if they have a foe's head and hands tucked in their bag he won't be doing them much harm.

Showmanship also plays a role. Decapitating a foe on a Myth battlefield roughly equates to throwing down a tomahawk slam dunk in the NBA. Style points count.

This chapter explores how to emulate the flavor of *Myth* and *Myth II*, and how to approach variant campaigns, background issues, and mass combat.

Campaign Style

This entire book has attempted to set a tone emulating what's found in the *Myth* games. A "by-the-book" campaign would take itself with utter seriousness during the climactic scenes, entirely less so during the lulls. (Conveniently, many roleplaying campaigns naturally fall into this pattern.) Climax means combat, which includes a mix of archmages on one end competing with awesome offensive spells and ordinary grunts on the other trying simply to endure the myriad horrors and come through in one piece.

HIGH FANTASY

Ignoring the commoners in the Legion and concentrating on the archmages, Trow, and other high-point characters can create an interesting high-fantasy campaign. The smoking battlefields become less of a risk and more of a forum for showing off one's latest spell.

A subdued sense of horror can still exist. Though throngs of Thralls no longer will intimidate, even archmages should feel a little tingling along the spine when dealing with the dream spells (see pp. 95-96), because even the greatest of them have only a slight idea of what they're doing. The Trow may know a great deal more – but they're really just powerful puppets in this play and may be all too aware that the future holds horrors for them that they're powerless to circumvent.

Humor will be a little harder to maintain. All these sorts of characters tend to take themselves seriously even in the bathtub.

Areas to Explore

The first thing an archmage has to consider is his relationship with the general public and his peers, as explored thoroughly in Chapter 5. Neither will allow him to just go and muck about with potentially world-shattering energies. Peers, especially, can provide a fascinating "inner politics" campaign – see the Fallen Lords descriptions in Chapter 5 for a complex weave of relationships that will be hard to beat.

The Trow provide a convenient tool for defining the world's destiny in a given *GURPS Myth* campaign – they can always already know any given fact! Trow players should keep in mind that they probably are incapable of acting in their own best interest when the fate-of-the-world issues come into play. They don't earn their tragic gravity without paying a price, but handled well they make the perfect high-fantasy salt to the archmages' pepper.

HORROR

Some *Myth* designers originally intended to create more of a horror game.

It doesn't take much tweaking. Players should take the roles of ordinary Warriors, Bowmen, Berserks, and such. The GM should surround them with countless undead, then lovingly describe the infections and amputations they suffer, ensure they're aware that every fallen comrade becomes a potential foe, make them race long distances on foot against tireless undead, make them fight at night, and generally heap on the misery.

This sounds adversarial – and in a way it is – but it's hard to place the PCs in mortal fear for their lives without placing them in mortal fear for their lives. Hopeless circumstances and a host of gruesome details are the main ingredients of *Myth*-style horror.

A horror campaign can still retain elements of high fantasy, of course, by exploring the goals and fortunes of NPC archmages. The humor probably should be toned down a bit, since too much of it will ruin the effect the campaign is trying to create.

Areas to Explore

The GM can introduce a few horror-heavy sessions in a campaign simply by dumping the PCs in a situation seemingly over their heads as described above. Extended horror campaigns *need* epic goals, though – something valuable enough for an ordinary patriot to repeatedly run near certain risk of death, and challenging enough that an archmage needs an army in support to obtain it. Otherwise, the rational sorts just walk away proclaiming, "Let Therios the Lightning Master tackle it. My personal limit is four Ghasts a day." The campaign has to be sweeping enough to routinely occupy the more powerful NPCs elsewhere. In other words, there's no use waiting for back-up. See *The Final Act* sidebar on p. 107 for discussion of a campaign this lofty.

Humor

Myth has fun with itself (particularly in the secret levels and netplay games), and *GURPS Myth* can, too. Players who don't mind their high fantasy or horror interrupted by the occasional Dwarf using satchel charges to obtain supper (and bragging about his recipe for Blasted Bits Stew) can take this as far as they like.

You Are Here

Areas to Explore

Myth's Dwarves, of course, just beg for black humor. Humans and Ghôls also seem to be picking up their careless ways with high explosives, suggesting a variety of scenes bringing to mind *Butch Cassidy and the Sundance Kid*. Subtle or not-so-subtle nods to popular culture also follow the existing style. See the *Pulping Factions* sidebar on p. 106 for a fairly heavy-handed nod to a popular film rapidly going cult that would make for a wild *GURPS Myth* campaign. The occasional Brigand with a broadsword engraved "Bad (expletive of choice)" would be perfectly in order, here. Lots of Dwarves should be named Zed and end up dead, having bled, covered in red . . .

Other Styles

See the *Mixing Genres with Myth* sidebar on pp. 108-109 for several crossovers that will almost certainly change the style of a campaign.

Delicate Touch

In any *GURPS Myth* campaign, but particularly one emphasizing horror, an indelicate GM can find himself routinely overwhelming the PCs by opposing them with undead even at close to 1-to-1 ratios. That's because *GURPS Myth* undead are exceedingly *tough*, but are supposed to be played exceedingly *stupid*.

This means that if their overlord orders them to kill anyone who approaches within 40 yards, they'll close on anyone within that perimeter, but go back to their duty stations if the intruder subsequently leaves that perimeter. A lone, patient Bowman could slay them all from 41+ yards unless their orders foresee that contingency. A lone, risk-taking Dwarf (and there's no such thing as a Dwarf that doesn't take risk) can sprint up, lob a grenade, sprint back, and ready another grenade till the job's done.

This also means that, even if scores of fiends are within eyesight, the undead tend to attack in smaller groups that are more easily handled.

The GM should provide every opportunity and incentive for PCs facing the undead to innovate. Narrowing the odds through clever tactics is the essence of Myth.

This sort of style also must be applied to any use of *GURPS*' mass-combat rules (see pp. 110-111). At face value, a Thrall is far tougher than a Warrior, and their respective Troop Strength values reflect this. The "average" undead forces have been given inferior quality to Legion units to partially reflect their difference in brainpower. The rest of the gap should be closed by Strategy modifiers, partly portraying horrid undead tactics and partly portraying clever Legion tactics should the players provide them.

The racial and character templates provide a variety of adventure hooks. Here are some similar but more general ideas for starting a campaign:

The Trow Menace

Alric has decided that the revived Trow represent the primary threat to his empire. He sends a fact-finding mission to the Trow lands. This party should include a few Berserks (because they know the terrain and the Trow best), a few mages with a variety of information-related spells, a few Warriors to represent the Legion properly, and any other specialists that Alric deems necessary. The mission may engage in diplomacy, espionage, covert military action, or any combination thereof – there's just no way of knowing till they reach the Trow domains and determine what the Trow are really doing.

Money to Burn

The Dwarves have decided to take a greater hand in shaping Human society as the rebuilding after Soulblighter's rampage reaches high gear. They intend to introduce more TL4 innovations to humanity, and the player-characters are intermediaries in this process, whether as Dwarven inventors or merchants, Human merchants, or Legion officers in charge of procuring what the Dwarves have to offer.

This initiative should provide plenty of opportunity to form superheavy high-tech Legion units and make obscene profits – provided things don't get out of hand and nobody loses any fingers or toes.

Pulping Factions

Disarmament and economic dislocation have left Muirthemne full of bad-boy veterans with no visible means of support. Crime soars and demand for nepenthe (see p. 82) booms as people try to make ends meet and forget the horrors they've endured. Legionnaires turned gangsters aren't going to show a lot of subtlety in their intramural disputes when they're used to dodging fireballs the size of a hay cart. Think Myth gone *noir*.

Continued on next page . . .

Campaign Topics

Related to but distinct from style is a campaign's topic. Basically, what do the PCs spend their time doing during gameplay? The *Myth* computer games deal with combat, pure and simple. A *GURPS Myth* campaign should strive for more.

Military Campaigns

Beyond the swordplay, campaigns centered on the Legion can delve into several areas. Centering a campaign on the intense training required to form a Warrior or Bowman can prove interesting. Fielding such a vast force at TL3 would certainly create huge logistics problems that the empire seems to have smoothed out, but this probably requires several innovative supply sergeants using every trick in the book. Soldiers seek promotion, and a campaign centered on PCs grappling with ever-increasing responsibilities as they rise in the ranks wouldn't need to include too many battles to challenge the players.

Wizardly Campaigns

Chapter 5 describes quite enough pursuits to keep the sharpest archmage busy. But many matters less spectacular than negotiating with kings and mastering dream spells interfere with archmagery – and provide good campaign hooks. All archmages require some logistics of their own, and necromancers in particular face a heavy challenge when there's so much competition for the latest fresh corpse. The fine art of grave-robbing can provide an interesting if macabre campaign theme. A Light archmage will often find himself called upon to solve a host of mundane problems for those around him. Ending a drought or particularly vile curse may stump one who routinely defeats Shades. Wise archmages also pay some attention to the brick and mortar housing them. A good subplot can hinge upon the planning and construction of a home worthy and secure enough for someone so exalted.

Gadgeteer Campaigns

The Dwarves were on a technological tear before their losses in the Great War brought their attention to the here-and-now. Once the Ghôl issue is settled, one way or another, where will their bent for gadgeteering lead? The difference between TL4 and TL5 is particularly large, particularly when viewed with TL3 eyes. A campaign could center on Dwarven PCs harnessing steam technology, perhaps in conjunction with magical enhancements. Or they could create a mechanical computer in the mode of *The Difference Engine*, perhaps with the intent to use it in calculating the locations of Rune Stones. Or the PCs could be humans trying to pick up the knack of gadgeteering from their Dwarven allies.

Scholarly Campaigns

Not everyone wields a sword, even in Myth. A world so driven by mystical secrets and great destinies has its share of scholars. PC scholars might be complete pacifists, but still need to undertake a harrowing journey into the Untamed Lands to procure a scroll promising to crack open the secrets of the One True Dream. A wise Myth ruler realizes that his scholars can provide more utility in predicting upcoming crises than his troops can in reacting to them after the fact. Plenty of tension can result from the need to provide the best military intelligence, along the lines of Tom Clancy's best-sellers featuring Jack Ryan.

Trade Campaigns

In some eyes, civilization simply exists to facilitate trade. Though the Great War and Soulblighter's onslaught placed mercantile matters in a long shadow, the reconstruction will bring them back to the forefront. An excellent campaign can center upon the fine art of profit-seeking in this environment. Dwarven high-tech might be a prized commodity – or it might be shunned, given everyone's memories of how their petards tended to hoist friend and foe alike. Intelligent application of a few minor magics can provide a lot of leverage to the savvy merchant; what meat vendor wouldn't want to know Preserve Food? Raw materials can prove difficult to procure; see the *Forest Giant Adventure Seeds* on p. 43 for one example. Conversely, what fabulous prizes could a race like the Trow offer in exchange to the merchant who comes up with a commodity that they would desire?

The Ways of the World

Exploring non-battlefield matters in Myth requires knowing a bit about how the rest of the world works. Here are some general descriptions to get things going. Many of these topics have already been addressed elsewhere, but references exist here to provide a convenient clearinghouse.

The Basics of Life

The following assumes a campaign based in the empire of Cath Bruig. Other lands tend to feature considerably more anarchy.

Taxes

Imperial taxes average 5% of income. Local nobility levy a wide range of taxes, from 2% to 30%. Mages and guildsmen often pay dues to their professional association ranging from 3% to 20% of income.

For convenience, the standard costs of living already include tax payments on *ordinary* income in Myth, but adventurers will find collectors assessing the highest possible brackets on any loot, and appraising non-monetary goods at the highest possible retail.

The Final Act

This campaign copies the original epic scope of both **Myth** games, adding a third chapter to this cycle's grand conflict between Light and Dark.

The PCs can be from any variety of backgrounds. What ties them together is the growing, horrific realization that the true Dark lord of this cycle has yet to appear!

As described on p. 24, the results of the Great War and Soulblighter's return concern the scholars of Myth, for the simple reason that it was the Dark's turn to triumph. In hand with this, the sages speculate that every Dark lord is a Light hero reborn, and vice versa, and where last victory was known then bitter defeat will be sown.

Therefore, knowing which Dark lord Alric once was would provide some clue as to his destiny in this cycle. The one hint present is Alric's continued distaste for any association with horses – he won't employ cavalry nor mount one of the beasts. This would be understandable in the reincarnation of a Dark lord whose quarters are still theoretically being dragged about by four mythical steeds, as is the case with Moagim (see p. 20). Since Moagim knew victory (though at considerable personal cost), it follows that Alric must meet defeat. Through sheer force of will, magery, and military acumen he simply has been delaying the inevitable.

Will the pent-up pressures of fate manifest in a third Dark invasion to make the first two pale in comparison? Will the certain knowledge that he must eventually fail snap Alric's iron will and push him into insanity – perhaps driving him to become the true Dark lord himself? Or does the hole that Alric has poked in the gods' tapestry give Light a slim chance to unravel the cycle once and forever, perhaps requiring that a small band of heroes quest eastward to confront the Dark at its source?

Whatever the answers, they'll be written on a grand scale if this epic campaign theme is pursued.

Military Service

The Legion employs full-time commissioners who scour the empire for suitable young men, about 14 or 15 years old. In peacetime, service is strictly voluntary. In war, impressment is practiced, and the Legion might even offer minor criminals with the right stuff the chance to enlist rather than suffer a standard sentence.

Imperial nobles maintain traditional medieval forces, serving as patron to a few or several knightly types and requiring their peasantry to serve in levies on demand.

See p. 73 for the Heron Guards' practices.

Law and Order

See the *Crime and Punishment* sidebar on p. 72.

Medical Care

See p. 79. Note that quality of medical care can vary very widely, depending on whether a mage is around or not. A nasty disease can be an inconvenience or a sure, slow death. Losing a hand or foot isn't a great tragedy in the sense that eventually a mage can be found to replace it, but only if the critically injured character can survive long enough to reach the closest source of this aid . . .

Food, Shelter, Clothes

All basic needs are assumed in the monthly cost of living, and Status defines "basic." A Status 6 archmage should be allowed to build a really nice tower and claim it's all part of the $10,000 he shells out monthly. The equivalent duke's basic food includes a few cooks and table servants. The GM rules whether a given PC is attempting to exceed the quality of goods defined by his Status and must pay extra for the privilege.

TRAVEL

Most high adventure requires taking to the roads, and most crises begin along the extensive borders of the empire as well.

Restrictions

The empire never has restricted travel. Given the hazards routinely faced by travelers throughout much of Cath Bruig's history, the reasoning goes that no civil penalty would deter someone already willing to face them.

Food and Lodging

When in the field in the Province or more settled regions of Cath Bruig west of Cloudspine, the Legion generally does not carry provisions with it. Instead, the unit commander writes vouchers for foodstuffs at villages along the way. (The vouchers are submitted against tax obligations in return.) Similarly, the Legion tends to put itself up for the night in villages along its route of travel when it can. Lodging troops, unlike feeding them, is considered a civic duty and not usually compensated.

In wilder regions, a baggage caravan will accompany Legion units. The soldiers themselves rarely carry more than immediate rations (about one day's worth), to leave them unencumbered, minimally fatigued, and ready for action at a moment's notice.

Other forces in a Light army will take advantage of the Legion's supply system.

Among Dark forces, undead units don't require any food or lodging, of course. Living Dark races usually can live off the land, though with varying side-effects: Ghôls often wander off their course while scavenging. Mauls will halt for several days to gorge on rich hunting before marching several more eating very little along the way. Myrkridia spend a good deal of every day stalking game, which eats considerably into the time in which they may be put to military matters.

Civilian travelers generally follow the Legion model – depending on the frequently encountered villages within the Province, carrying their own supplies elsewhere – but they must pay for all services unless possessing a Claim to Hospitality (see p. CI21). This will apply to many nobles in their own lands, mages at guild halls, etc.

Potable water usually lies within easy traveling distance throughout the Human-inhabited lands of Myth, with the notable exception of the Barrier (see p. 14).

Hazards

Lingering Dark forces pose the greatest threat to travelers, from a couple of emaciated Mauls to yet another Dark army laying waste to everything in its miles-wide path. Brigands and various bandits of lesser caliber become increasingly common the farther west that travelers explore, save in the immediate area of Muirthemne.

See pp. 11-17 for descriptions of the terrain of Myth, which may be assumed to present the routine difficulties described on pp. B187-188. In particular, *The Three Passes* sidebar on p. 11 describes crossing Cloudspine, and *The Mysteries of the Arbors* sidebar on p. 15 details passing through one of the great forests.

In campaigns faithful to the *Myth* games, travel should never be undertaken lightly.

Weather and terrain play large roles in *Myth* combat. This sidebar provides broad guidelines for both. The sidebar on p. 111 reminds GMs how to factor weather and terrain in *GURPS*.

In general, Myth summers are dry and clear. Roll a 3 on 3d to determine that it's raining at any given time. If it is, roll 1d. On a 1 or 2, it's a heavy rain.

Spring and fall are much wetter. Roll 1d in the morning; a 1 means it's foggy. Roll 3d to determine current precipitation. On a 5 it's a light rain, on a 4 it's heavy rain, and on a 3 it's snow (usually light). Fog rarely coexists with heavy rain or snow, though.

In the winter, fog is less common (roll a 2 on 2d). Roll 3d for precipitation. On a 5 it's light snow, on a 4 heavy snow, and on a 3 light rain.

Local factors will heavily modify weather, of course.

Terrain is based on the map (see p. 10) rather than die rolls, with the important clarification that local variation are very often present. Even the dense forests and mountain passes will have small clearings of level ground. Most of the open land will feature frequent copses of trees, with the exception of the Barrier. An adventurer seeking dry ground in the Dire Marsh should have to make a Survival, Naturalist, Area Knowledge, or Geology roll to find it – and there may very well not be any in the general vicinity – but the GM should not simply assume as much.

Mass Combat

GMs may want to conduct battles the size of those in the *Myth* games – or even much larger – using the mass-combat rules on pp. CII112-124. Here's the Myth-specific information required. Also see the *Delicate Touch* sidebar on p. 105.

The Armies

None of the units in Myth use a hard-and-fast organizational structure, but here are some rules of thumb:

The Legion will usually deploy in squads of 10 men, companies of 100 men, and battalions of 1,000 men. Subunits exist at each level – such as files consisting of two or three squads – but these vary within different Legion units more than the above standards.

Casualties can alter squad size even when 10 is the goal,

of course. Recruits are added to a depleted squad so as to make it oversized and let the "learning curve" and law of averages bring it back down to the standard 10 men. It's the sort of grimly practical touch that lets a legionnaire know precisely where he stands . . .

Bowmen are deployed in smaller units, usually four or six men each.

Dwarves are deployed individually, or in squads of three.

Brigands and *Dark Archers* follow their Legion models.

Thralls are deployed in large, irregular squads usually of every corpse raised in a particular Mass Thrall casting (see pp. 30 and 63). These tend to range from eight to 25 creatures. A few engagements can greatly reduce average squad size.

Soulless and *Stygian Knights* usually deploy in squads of four.

Ghasts are not organized on military lines.

Other units either fight as individuals (Trow, especially) or use light infantry tactics that don't require much military organization (particularly Ghôls).

Myth Units

Archmages usually aren't counted among troop strength, though an Avatara wading in would provide an average 34 TS. They usually provide 5 to 16 Exceptional Strength points apiece.

Berserks (MI): Treat as medium infantry given their specialized tactics and ability to handle damage. Base TS is 4. Usually of veteran quality (TS 6).

Bowmen (LI): Base TS is 6. Usually of average quality. Rarely will they make up more than 10% of the TS of a Legion force of any great size. Too few of them exist.

Bre'Unor (LI): Base TS is 6. Usually of average quality.

Brigands (MI): Base TS is 4. Usually of seasoned quality (TS 4.8).

Cannons (CA): Usual crew is 6. Base TS is 50. Usually of average quality for humans or raw quality (TS 25) for Ghôls. Cannons can make up no more than 10% of TS for a field army or 50% for a fortification.

Cave Spiders (II): Base TS is 4. Usually of average quality.

Dwarves (LI): Base TS is 12. Even rarer than Bowmen, they rarely make up more than 5% of the TS of a medium- or large-sized force. In siege situations, they add +10 to base TS if in the attacking force. *Mortar Dwarves* have a base TS of 34. *Pathfinders* have a base TS of 18. Usually of average quality; they also count as Special Forces (see p. CII120).

Fetch (LI): Base TS is 28. Usually of average quality. Also provides 2 Exceptional Strength points.

Forest Giants (HI): Base TS is 36. Usually of average quality.

Ghasts (II): Base TS is 8. Usually of green quality (TS 6.4).

Ghôls (LI): Base TS is 5. Usually of average quality.

Heron Guards (MI): Base TS is 4. Usually of veteran quality (TS 6).

Journeymen (HI): Base TS is 5. Usually of veteran quality (TS 7.5).

Mauls (MI): Base TS is 12. Usually of average quality.

Myrkridia (LI): Base TS is 11. Usually of average quality. *Large Myrkridia (MI):* Base TS is 14. Usually of seasoned quality (TS 16.8). Also provides 2 Exceptional Strength points.

Myrmidons (LI): Base TS is 11. Usually of average quality.

Peasants (R): Treat as rabble with base TS of 1. Usually of average quality.

Shades (MI): Base TS is 34. Usually of average quality. Also provides 5 Exceptional Strength points.

Shadows (HI): Treat as heavy infantry given their special ability to resist damage; base TS is 11. Usually of average quality.

Soulless (LI): Base TS is 6. Usually of green quality (TS 4.8).

Stygian Knights (HI): Base TS is 9. Usually of green quality (TS 7.2).

Thralls (LI): Base TS is 11. Usually of green quality (TS 8.8).

Trow (HI): Base TS is 32. Usually of veteran quality (TS 48).

Warlocks (LI): Base TS is 28. Usually of average quality. Also provides 3 Exceptional Strength points.

Warriors (MI): Base TS is 4. Usually of veteran quality (TS 6).

Wights (II): Base TS is 30. Usually of green quality (TS 24).

Wolves (II): Base TS is 3. Usually of average quality.

Special Units

In calculating special-unit superiority, cavalry usually can be ignored, since it's extremely rare in Myth. For artillery, Cannons and Mortar Dwarves count.

For missile weapons, count the TS of all Bowmen, Dwarves, Pathfinders, Fetch, Large Myrkridia, Shades, Soulless, Warlocks, and Wights.

Berserks, Cave Spiders, and Ghôls *neutralize* missile-weapon superiority (i.e., their TS counts as missile weapons only to the point that it offsets an opponent's missile strength). *Exception:* The missile superiority provided by Wights can only be offset by *true* missile units.

GMs often overlook environmental factors in **GURPS**, but these play a large role in the Myth setting. After determining local conditions with the aid of the sidebar on p. 110, the following sources explain their impact on regular combat. The GM should apply appropriate Strategy modifiers in mass combat.

Rain and snow – The No. 1 impact of precipitation in Myth is that it makes Dwarven weapons even more risky (but also see *Fog,* below). See p. 80 for the reduction to their Malf in precipitation. Keep in mind that an unlit Dwarven cocktail lying in the snow will explode if another cocktail goes off near enough – it can be easy to lose track of the duds and set off a chain reaction damaging one's own allies!

Wet bowstrings can cripple archers as well. Legion Bowmen are professionals and keep their bows out of the rain till needed. Extended firing in rain eventually will render a bow useless till the string is replaced.

Terrain – Pp. B117 and B123-124 explain fighting at different heights, not just because of terrain but also when flying characters are involved. Woods add penalties described in *Fog,* below. Water hazards and bad footing are found on p. B107.

Light – The darkness penalties on p. B92 *do* apply to effective weapon skills, so that even a moderate penalty can play havoc with military efficiency. Overcast moonless nights are best left to those Dark races with Night Vision.

Fog – Along with precipitation and smoke, this imposes Vision penalties that Night Vision and related advantages won't cancel. Dense smoke imposes up to -1 per yard. Dense forest, thick fog, blizzards, and water generally impose -1 per 5 yards. Light rain or snow, or open woods, impose roughly -1 per 50 yards. This penalty impacts effective weapon skill.

The combined penalty from all factors described in *Fog* and *Light* can't exceed -10 (utter darkness). At this level, actions that can be performed blind (i.e., combat) take the -10 while those that require some level of sight (i.e., spotting enemy units) become impossible.

7. E-Roleplaying

Tools like the editing programs included with *Myth II* add a new dimension to roleplaying.

This chapter deals with "e-roleplaying" – the adaptation of the latest information technology to tabletop roleplaying – first in general and then specifically in the case of merging *Myth*'s combat engine with *GURPS*.

Myth and *GURPS* players alike will find ways to enrich their gaming here.

Roleplaying's Changing Face

As computers grow increasingly powerful – and the Internet transforms from "What's that?" to "Can I get cable-modem service?" – the traditional forms of roleplaying have transformed as well.

Some computerized roleplaying games have made the transition from solitary play emphasizing combat and/or puzzle-solving to massive online environments shared by thousands of players, albeit still emphasizing combat and puzzle-solving. In the meantime, traditional "tabletop" players have grafted computer technology into their version of roleplaying, with its increased and more complex plot structure and social interaction that has yet to be realized in a fully "computerized" game. This chapter furthers the hybridization of the tabletop game.

Types of E-Campaigns

Most electronic versions of tabletop roleplaying games have embraced one of the following three formats:

E-Mail

The most popular e-roleplaying format, e-mail negates the No. 1 difficulty with keeping a campaign going: All the players don't have to be in the same location nor even playing at once. Most campaigns feature weekly rounds in which the GM posts a move for the NPCs and general background, then the players each post their PC's move in response. Some GMs convert the posts into a format resembling serialized fiction; a search of the Web can unveil several examples.

The main drawbacks include that play takes a long time, especially if frequent combat of *GURPS*ian complexity is involved, and that less-than-severe "turn discipline" can result in one player posting a response to a turn two back from another player at the same time.

Chat

Chat forums, in which everyone logs on at once and types commentary onto a shared screen, offer less convenience than e-mail, in that everyone must play at once though they can still be spread across the globe. In return, it promotes more sophisticated interaction and faster play because there's not as much lag between actions and responses. Lulls in the action provide opportunity for the same sort of table chatter as in tabletop gaming, though in a chat environment the distraction isn't as easily blocked out as in person.

Its main drawback is that it challenges many GMs to keep up with several players typing rather than speaking. Some players have difficulty staying online, as well.

The E-Player

E-campaigns create player needs other than the obvious online access and at least hunt-and-peck typing.

When posting, the e-player can help the GM by thinking ahead a step or two and giving his PC's reactions. For instance, instead of just "I pump the bartender for the map's location with Fast-Talk," go ahead and add on "If he tells me, I call Jocko. Otherwise, I grab him by the shirt and use Intimidation."

Punctuality remains just as important online. Holding up a weekly six-hour tabletop marathon by 15 minutes is one thing. Holding up an e-mail campaign by being late with every other posting actually can be worse.

The E-GM

A hard job gets harder when adding the responsibilities of an e-campaign to the already impressive workload of a good tabletop GM.

In addition to filling interesting worlds with interesting PCs and adventure hooks galore, an e-GM usually must master certain skills. He needs to excel at typing, especially in a chat format, unless using voice technology. He should master any software used to conduct his campaign, whether this means the available commands in a chat forum or the intricacies of getting multiple players together in a real-time combat engine such as *Myth*. And he'll need to be good at improvising, because chances are good the game just won't run as smoothly as a tabletop experience would.

Against these added burdens, he'll enjoy several advantages over tabletop gaming. He'll literally be able to comb the world for the players he wants, and new jobs or semesters will no longer require experienced players to abandon his campaign.

Most popular roleplaying games have online forums dedicated to discussing them; advertising the startup of a campaign in these forums will often prove sufficient to find enough players. Several web sites specialize in linking e-mail GMs and players. This greater access to good roleplayers probably has inspired the creation of more e-campaigns than any other factor.

Computer Assisted

This method follows the tabletop model – everyone physically in one place at one time – but replaces some portion of the usual stacked books and dice and figurines with a computer die-rolling utility, reference library, etc. Handled skillfully, it can greatly reduce reference and bookkeeping time, leaving more of a session for the fun stuff.

The only drawbacks are that the GM must invest in the price of a laptop and in the time spent converting resources to a format usable on his computer.

Making the Message Fit the Media

Choosing the right kind of campaign generally depends upon player availability. Can all the players be in the same spot at once? If not, can they all be online at once? Most GMs and players prefer the most immediate format available, if not tabletop then chat, if not chat then e-mail. Given the number of PBEM (play-by-e-mail) campaigns currently under way, it's obvious that e-mail is better than nothing at all.

Once the choice has been made, certain format-specific measures can mold a tabletop roleplaying system and tabletop customs to operate more smoothly in the new environment.

What's Added to the Game

E-campaigns can add a lot to the traditional tabletop experience.

In combat, online forums such as *Myth* can contribute tons of additional tension to the simplest brawl, putting players on the spot to react *right now,* just as their warriors need to. The added splash of animated icons and explosions and richly detailed maps will also put the most elaborate miniatures to shame.

In social situations, most formats allow more intrigue, because they enable completely secret player-to-player or player-to-GM dialog. There's no "Jane just passed a note to the GM, so she must be getting ready to sneak off with the Lost Mace of Thrace." Behind-the-back dealings can be a lot of fun in an e-campaign, with the caution that they can get out of hand. Just as two people in an online forum will flame (verbally abuse) each other in ways they would never imagine if face to face, players in an e-campaign may be more likely to stab each other in the back.

E-forums can also provide the GM more room to steer the campaign while appearing to steer it less. At the tabletop, players usually know when they've surprised the GM and when he's introduced ad hoc elements to keep things on a preplanned course. Chat and e-mail conceal these elements.

Finally, electronic formats can be very friendly to those with hearing or other physical impairments. Being able to play from their own home at their own pace can provide a great deal more opportunity to enjoy the game.

E-Mail Campaigns

As mentioned, detailed combat can slow down an e-mail campaign, often intolerably. E-mail campaigns should feature little combat, use a very simple combat system, or break combat off into a different format such as chat or the *Myth* engine. The latter move would require players to be online at once, but only for the combat episodes.

PBEM GMs may also want to set up standards for when a player drops out of communication – in tabletop or chat games, a player either plays in a session or he doesn't, but in e-mail campaigns he might go on vacation just as the emperor's assassins drop through the ceiling tiles. The GM should consider reserving the right to "play out" the character during the interim to keep the game moving. Players probably will not like agreeing to this stipulation, but it may motivate them to keep up with the campaign.

Chat Campaigns

Where PBEM GMs enjoy an unprecedented luxury of disorganization and taking their time, chat GMs will need to display frightening efficiency. They will be juggling the main narrative thread, one or two private player communications, rules references, and maintenance of any mapping system, all while typing every communication.

A simple roleplaying system helps here, too, or at least one that the GM has mastered. While combat is less restricted than in e-mail, systems that feature detailed mapping (placing heavy emphasis on character facing, objects in the environment, etc.) will pose a challenge without sophisticated utilities to support the GM. On the plus side, utilities of this nature are being developed by a number of Internet interests at the time of publication, often coupled with voice technology that will allow the GM and players to speak to one another in real time in a web-based playing forum.

Computer-Assisted Campaigns

Computer-assisted gaming doesn't really place any new restrictions on a campaign – its whole purpose is to reduce some of the logistics – but the GM should keep in mind that it won't do to become so immersed in the support system that he loses sight of the game itself. A computer might allow the GM to track the bleeding of all 47 Orcs that the PCs just ran off, but even if it takes no more than a few seconds that probably won't enhance the game.

FUDGE FACTOR

"Fudging" is the GM practice of altering the outcome when the dice say a PC slipped on a banana peel and suffered a fatal concussion in his big confrontation with the Chief Bad Guy, or something similarly out of place or discordant. It generally stems from the logic that novel or movie heroes usually end up dangling but not falling from rope bridges, so if the dice say that a PC falls then the story won't be "right." So the GM fudges, either lying about a concealed roll or inserting something like a flying NPC who rescues the falling hero.

GMs should keep fudging in mind when deciding which forum suits their style. GMs who fudge will find e-mail and basic chat rooms the perfect forums. In these forums, even if the GM does roll dice to determine an outcome, he usually doesn't bother expressing it in so many words. A roll of 14 by a pirate with Shortsword-13 becomes "The corsair's cutlass slashes the air just before your face as you leap back and . . ." in his posting.

Adding a die-rolling command to a chat forum – and odds are that someone in a medium-sized or large roleplaying group will know how to do this – turns chat from very fudge friendly to very fudge unfriendly. Combat engines such as *Myth* are even less friendly, because they'll kill a PC as readily as an NPC and well before a GM can intervene. Even players who know that their GM fudges for them and don't mind will find it less enjoyable when prefaced by, "That didn't really happen."

GMs should consider their personal fudge factor carefully before choosing an e-forum for their campaign.

Many tabletop roleplayers consider e-roleplaying a poor substitute for the face-to-face experience. An e-forum provides less opportunity to joke and chat, because the joking and chatting intrudes more into the game, and often because the players – at least initially – aren't as familiar with each other as a personal encounter would require them to be. Some find their ability to express their character's personality reduced, because they're less comfortable with writing than telling/acting. Emotions usually heighten when shared between several people physically together, so the thrill of a climactic moment can seem muted in comparison when read alone in one's study. And, of course, there's little sharing of pizza and cola, or opportunity to show off one's latest miniature.

A GM who keeps these limitations in mind can do much to reduce them. In a chat-based campaign, he should encourage players to talk among themselves before taking a few minutes to analyze a situation. He should rev up the "literary" quality of his postings as big scenes reach their climax. And he should introduce little encounters and subplots intended to flesh out PCs' characters till the players get the hang of doing this on their own initiative.

Despite the best GM, a good roleplayer in the literal sense of the word – someone who enjoys these games for the opportunity to step into other characters and act out their lives – may never be satisfied by an e-campaign, at least till the future day when we can plug into virtual realities with fully rendered avatars. Fortunately for e-roleplaying's infancy, not all of us are good roleplayers by this definition, nor want to be. Some people play the games for the same reason that most games are played – to cooperate and compete in a forum where all the death wounds and treacheries evaporate once the game is over or suspended. For these people, less interested in acting than pure roleplayers, e-roleplaying may prove superior to the tabletop.

GURPS-Myth Synthesis

Although a few other systems might dare to challenge the claim, *GURPS* can be called the most detailed tabletop roleplaying system ever printed. At the time of this printing, *Myth II* can make just as serious a claim of being the most player-empowered computer roleplaying system ever published.

Myth can couple with any sort of *GURPS* campaign, whether tabletop, chat, or e-mail, provided the right equipment and software is in place. *GURPS* can add new dimensions to solitary or network play of *Myth* as well.

The following section provides *GURPS* players with basic guidelines for converting characters to *Myth*. *Myth* players can learn *GURPS* by downloading *GURPS Lite* (**www.sjgames.com/gurps/lite/**). Though *GURPS Myth* includes many character elements not seen in *GURPS Lite* (additional advantages, skills, rules refinements, etc.), 90% of what you'll need to know is there.

BEST OF BOTH WORLDS

A lot of the fun in roleplaying is that players get invested in their character's fortune as much as they would those of any movie or novel hero. They *care* how he fares, and feel the tension when he's in the midst of life-or-death situations. After all, to a large extent he's an extension of the player himself.

Real-time adventure games such as *Myth* offer similar feedback. The immediacy of real time puts players in a "you are there" mind frame. An animated fireball cruising toward his forces with a muted, menacing roar impresses peril upon the player more than any verbal description could. A horde of undead rising from a riverbed quits being a large but abstract threat and becomes . . . a horde of undead.

Coupling the two emotional investments can double the thrills.

In addition, the GM gets to "play" more than in a tabletop setting. He puts more work (though, with proper organization, not *that* much more work) into designing the scenario, but once it's set up the software does all the heavy lifting. He's free to operate the NPCs with no more responsibility than the players have.

Should this sound like fun, the first step is overcoming *Fear* and *Loathing*, or at least coming to grips with them.

Before You Tinker

In shop class, this is the part where the teacher introduces the religion of safety goggles. We don't have to exercise the same care because we're immortal as long as we have our *Myth II* CD from which to reinstall, and we certainly should have it.

Still, back up your saved games and anything else you don't want to be bothered to reinstall. The following process resembles Introduction to Surgery 101; we'll be tinkering in a variety of *Myth II*'s innards. You have the responsibility to ensure that nothing irreplaceable requires replacing.

Fear

Fear is the object-editor for *Myth II*, wherein one creates or alters characters, monsters, animals, magic items, and anything else that isn't nailed down in the setting. (*Loathing* is the map editor, in which the terrain is created or altered and the objects are placed for a given scenario, discussed on p. 126.) Both are included in *Myth II*. Doing a lot of work in *Loathing* is optional. Creating custom PCs, NPCs, and items – the reason for this exercise – will require some goodly amount of time spent in *Fear*.

This chapter *isn't* about learning how to use *Fear*. The *Myth II* CD includes extensive HTML documentation for the program. *Fear* doesn't require any programming knowledge; it's a "tag" editor that distills everything into type-in values or pull-down menus. *Hundreds* of values and menus. As mentioned before, don't let the vast number of settings intimidate. *Fear* is fairly simple, even if the game engine is not.

The Conversion

The following section walks through translating a *GURPS* character into a *Myth* character via *Fear*. It uses the same conversion rules used to create the racial and character templates in this book, only in reverse, of course. It assumes some working familiarity with *Fear*. If you can't follow a particular topic, please consult *Fear* and its documentation.

At no time are these rules hard and fast; they're merely guidelines. The two game systems are very different, sharing only the trait that you can do just about anything you want to do with either of them. Many of these rules present rigid either-or situations (either you get 1 with ST 16+ or else you get 0, for instance) where *GURPS* would provide a scale. This is to preserve the accuracy of the conversions; see the *Baseline vs. New Model* sidebar on p. 118 for more information.

Monsters

Every animate creature is a "monster" in *Fear*, whether fair or foul of face. Most inanimate objects are, too. In this folder are the metafiles that tie together all the smaller files, called tags, that define a *Myth* character class, type of object, or custom-crafted PC. To start creating a PC, highlight the file for his "base" template (berserk for a Berserk, ghol for a Ghôl, or the closest possible for a custom concept) and duplicate it. Type in the character name for the file name. A master menu (tag file) for the "monster" appears; altering its settings (tags) will make a unique character.

What's in it for *Myth*

Myth fans who have learned the intricacies of *Fear* and *Loathing* frontward and backward undoubtedly have noticed one minor failing: There's no guidelines for comparatively valuing new character concepts. Does a Death Hussars Flaming Ghôl cost 6 or 8 points? What about those electrified rodents your kid brother insisted that you design?

GURPS provides the hobby's most extensive system to comparatively value character concepts, no matter how differing in abilities. Using *GURPS Myth* and the *GURPS* core books, you can place a precise value on it *all*.

GURPS also provides a platform for roleplaying the *Myth* setting outside of combat scenarios. With it you can determine precisely what it is Berserks do when they're not dismembering Myrkridia, how Warlocks make a living throwing massive fireballs when they're not being paid to do battle, and just precisely how stupid is a Maul? The system will take you anywhere your curiosity leads you.

Some of you, though able to build a new *Myth* map in your sleep, will find *GURPS* overwhelming when first investigated. The same advice applies as given in the sidebar on p. 116 aimed at *GURPS* players starting up *Fear*: It's not nearly as hard as it looks. A few basic concepts will get you up and running, and you might discover entirely new facets of your netplay buddies once you recruit them into a in-tandem chat-room roleplaying campaign.

Baseline or New Model

The formulas we used to convert *Myth*'s characters to *GURPS* templates in this book are the same ones presented in this chapter. Taking one of the templates in this book and processing it with the formulas presented here will produce a conversion 90% identical to the original.

A more accurate *GURPS*-to-*Myth* conversion could be created by ignoring the precedents established by the existing *Myth* characters. The "baseline" that the existing characters set doesn't always follow the same design philosophies as *GURPS*, whereas a "new model" of character creation in *Myth* could come much closer.

A "new model" approach bears the primary disadvantage of invalidating all the existing *Myth* characters as "incompatible" with the new system. A thorough GM would want to redesign all of them to set this right, an imposing task.

The primary advantage to building a new model for *GURPS*-to-*Myth* conversion is incorporating the incremental increases that are a staple of *GURPS* design. As mentioned elsewhere, *Myth* characteristics sometimes use an "all or nothing" approach, even when the characteristic could support an incremental increase. For instance, *Myth* characters usually have full or no resistance to a particular kind of spell, where a "new model" conversion could give characters a value equivalent to the percentage chance of their resistance roll failing per p. B45 (0.259 for Will 12, 0.5 for Will 10, etc.).

The above example also illustrates the primary restriction that no new-model conversion will overcome: In places where *GURPS* offers a resistance roll to counter all-or-nothing effects, the GM will have to be satisfied with effects that always impact the target, but are reduced by a percentage reflecting his resistance in *GURPS*. No conversion will be 100% pure.

Basic Attributes

Starting in the monster menu's upper-left corner are the following settings:

Collection – sets the animation that the character will use. Usually left alone, but see *Collections* on pp. 125-126.

Object Tag – points to a collection of statistics that defines the character's body. These are wrapped up in the Object Tag, a file created on pp. 123-124. Set this to the new Object Tag created for the character after it's been created.

Size – set to reflect any racial Inconvenient Size.

Visibility – the misleading name actually refers to the character's vision, not how easy he is to spot. Most are Farsighted. Those with Bad Sight or Vision rolls of 7 or less are Nearsighted. Those with no vision have None.

Class – set to Melee, Missile, or Suicide according to character's favored mode of attack.

Allegiance – usually Light, but often won't impact play.

Local Projectile Group and Map Action Tag – leave at No Tag unless you know why you're using these.

Attacks

The *Attacks* box starts out with *Desired Projectile Volume*; this lets a character pick up things to throw. If the character doesn't use Throwing skill like this, just leave it at None. Normal thrown items are Small, but powerful creatures or Weapon Masters might be able to use Large or Unwieldy items.

The scrolling window lists the character's attacks. A character can use no more than three attacks – a standard missile attack, a standard melee attack, and a "special" attack. Wizards with dozens of offensive options will have to pick their favorite trio.

Double-clicking on an attack opens its menu. It's far simpler to modify the existing attacks than create new ones; duplicate and modify what's there, then delete the original in your custom character.

An attack's menu includes:

Projectile – this is the attack's payload, the damage and related effects that it does. This data is bundled into a Projectile tag file, found in the Projectiles folder in *Fear* and customized on pp. 124-125. Set this to point to your custom projectile once it's been created.

Minimum and Maximum Range – all melee attacks have Minimum Range 0, and a Maximum Range of 1 for range C, 1.199 for 1-hex reach, 1.4 for 2 hexes, or 2 for 3 hexes. Ranged weapons have a Minimum Range; set at 0 on up as preferred, generally 3-5. (Take care that explosive-attack users know not to throw it so closely as to catch themselves in the blast!) Maximum Range should be considered to reflect when it's prudent to open fire, not simply a weapon's Max. For fairly unlimited ammo (Soulless javelins, arrows, bullets) it's around 20, for bulky and/or expensive ammo (axes, grenades, knives) it's 10-12, for rare ammo (improvised weapons, costly spells) it can be as low as 8. This number shouldn't exceed two-thirds of a ranged attack's Max; it often will be much lower.

Repetitions – set to attack's Rate of Fire.

Miss Fraction – for melee attacks look up the character's skill level with the attack as a percentile chance on the p. B45 chart. Subtract that number from 100, then divide by 100. The result goes here, but put in a 0 for skill 16+. For ranged attacks, use this to represent a weapon with a Malf number in the same fashion as for melee weapons; set to 0 for weapons with 16+ or no Malf. Ranged-weapon *skill* actually factors into *Myth* performance below.

Initial Velocity – only applies to ranged attacks; ignore for melee attacks. The first value is usually 0.1 for missile spells, 0.15-0.19 for thrown weapons, and 0.24 for arrows. The second value is the first value +0 for missile spells, +0.01-0.02 for thrown weapons, and +0.02 for arrows.

Initial Velocity Error – only applies to ranged attacks; ignore for melee attacks. Subtract from 19 the **GURPS** attack's skill level and Acc. Subtract 4 if it's an explosive or area attack. Add 1 for every 5 full points of *Maximum Range*, above. Multiply the result by 0.002.

Velocity Experience Delta – set to 0. Modify Initial Velocity Error manually as a **GURPS** character improves through experience.

Recovery Time – this very important stat usually determines who hits first, which means that it encompasses some of the importance of an active defense in **GURPS**, which also usually determines who hits first. The game-play effects also are very similar, in that characters with very low Recovery Time can emerge from some repeated one-on-one combats relatively untouched, just like characters with very high active defenses. To give a more accurate feel to the conversion, this formula takes weapon speed and active defenses *both* into account.

The rule-of-thumb figure is reached by subtracting one-tenth of the character's best active defense *when using this attack* from 1.5. (For instance, a character with Parry-12 and PD 4 would subtract 1.6, for a result of -0.1.) Add 0.2 for every turn it takes to ready the weapon between attacks. Those fighting primarily as Berserks receive *no* active defense, but subtract 1.5 to represent their immediate combat advantages. The result should be GM-adjusted to reflect character combat abilities that aren't so simply quantified. This *can* be a negative number.

Recovery Time Experience Delta – set to 0. See *Velocity Experience Delta*, above.

Mana Cost – if the attack is a spell, determine how much energy will be used in casting it (this figure can't be varied while within a *Myth* combat). Divide this figure by (the caster's fatigue usable for the spell minus 3). Multiply the result by 100 (80 for a Shadow) and type it in here. For example, a Magery 5 wizard normally

HEROES

Myth includes "Hero" versions of several character types. To create these, call up the Monster tag/file for the particular Hero and look up its *Cost*. Turn to p. 26 and find the corresponding **GURPS** point total on the chart.

Use the basic version of the race or character type as the base package for the Hero. The Hero will cost more, so quite a few points will be left over. Simply spend these points on improving combat abilities in any manner.

Enterprising GMs or players may explore the Heroes' Monster tag/files in *Fear* to get an impression of how these improvements should be made – but often enough a "literal" translation involves nothing more than adding ludicrous amounts of Extra Hit Points!

Myth is designed to be fast, furious, and fun – which is the way it should be, unless one's handcrafted PC is the champion of Light in the middle of that throng of Thralls! The high mortality rate of the game as designed may put off some roleplayers.

Before overreacting, the GM should first ensure that PC mortality is not resulting from poor gameplay rather than the inherent viciousness of the setting. **Myth** requires skill to play well – and skilled players can preserve forces with great efficiency. Rather than implement some of the following solutions for poor players, only to have them turn later scenarios into cakewalks as their **Myth** skills improve, tone down the lethality of early battles to give them time to master the medium.

If body counts are still too high, the simplest solution is to take an "NPC cannon fodder" approach. Allow all PCs to take up to 60% *Absorbed Fraction* in their Monster tag/file. Do the same for major NPCs. Any PCs or major NPCs with existing *Absorbed Fraction* settings should multiply their existing value by (1-the universal value) then add the result to the universal value. For instance, in the above example, a Journeyman with an existing 20% *Absorbed Fraction* would multiply 0.2 by (1 minus the setting that all PCs enjoy, or 0.4), then add the result (0.08) to 0.6 and take a 68% *Absorbed Fraction*. This will allow the PCs to hack their way through minor NPCs, but offer no advantage over major foes.

A variation of this solution is to give players an *Absorbed Fraction* rating equivalent to the odds of their making their best Active Defense roll per p. B45 (0.838 for skill+PD 13, etc.). The current conversion undervalues active defense somewhat; this will *considerably* overvalue it but make PCs very, very tough. Dividing the value by 2 or 3 might be prudent. Inflicting a counteracting *increase* to the *Explosive Damage* suffered in their Object tag/file's Effects Modifiers might also be wise.

Another – albeit challenging – solution is to design a new model of *GURPS* conversion per the sidebar on p. 118 to better reflect the typical lethality of *GURPS* combat.

casts full-strength 5d fireballs with his Explosive Fireball-20. This costs him 8 fatigue. He has 15 fatigue. Subtracting 3 (to represent the "exhaustion" line mages shouldn't lightly cross) from 15 leaves 12; 8 divided by 12 is 0.666; 0.666 multiplied by 100 rounds to 67. Enter 67 here.

Attack Flags– mostly these are matters of player or GM choice. A ranged attack that normally isn't aimed checks the *Does Not Require Firing Solution* button, but be sure and not include Acc in the *Initial Velocity Error* calculation on p. 119.

Projectile Groups

These call up the animations associated with various actions. Leave them alone unless you want to play with different "looks."

String Lists

You should create unique string lists for your character and change these pull-down menus to call upon them, so as to give him his own name and description.

Distances

These are described in the *Fear* documentation and usually left alone. They will determine an unattended character's behavior, however. Altering these can transform hordes that rush to the enemy at first sight in a great cluster into iron-disciplined legions that stand firmly in ranks, even watching the slaughter of nearby allies till given the order to attack.

Ammunition

These specifications are used to keep track of very special ammunition. (More mundane ammunition inventory is factored into *Minimum and Maximum Range* on p. 118.) Any special ammunition will need to be created as a projectile; see pp. 124-125.

Those Unlabeled Things on the Right

Left Handed Fraction – 0 for righties, 1 for lefties.

Turning Speed – base value is 100 for DX 7 or less, 110 for DX 8, 200 for DX 9, 220 for DX 10-14, 260 for DX 15, 270 for DX 16, or 300 for DX 17+. Subtract 20 for heavy or greater encumbrance. Subtract 40 for a character that primarily flies or

levitates. Subtract 40 for large Inconvenient Size. The GM may want to introduce additional modifiers.

Hard Death System Shock – mostly a special effect left at base value, usually 0.75.

Flinch System Shock – this is a subtle but important stat combining elements of Stun and Shock. Add together HT and any Strong/Weak Will. Give the character -1 point if this is 10 or less, 0 points for 11-14, 1 point for 15, or 2 points for 16+. Then add 1 for High Pain Threshold, 2 for Unfazeable, or 5 for *both* advantages. Several other advantages and disadvantages could apply to the formula, but didn't come up in these conversions.

If this result is 0 or less then *Flinch System Shock* is 0, if 1 then 0.005, if 2 then 0.01, if 3 then 0.12, if 4 then 0.2, if 5+ then 0.3.

Absorbed Fraction – usually 0 but see *Journeyman's Coat* on p. 82.

Healing Fraction – set at 8 divided by the character's racial basic HT, which usually makes it 0.8. This is 0 for the undead or others with the Unhealing disadvantage.

Combined Power – this was never enabled in **Myth II**. Leave it alone or set it to 0.

Longest Range – set to the *Maximum Range* of the character's longest attack, or the *Activation* figure under *Distances*, whichever is higher.

Experience Point Value – set to 0, since you don't want instant-experience increases in a **GURPS** simulation.

Cost – look up the character's **GURPS** point total on the p. 26 table, rounding up to the closest figure. Enter the corresponding **Myth** point cost.

Pathfinding Radius – set at 0.15 for human-sized units, 0.30 for large units or units that use large swung weapons that realistically would not fight shoulder to shoulder.

Maximum Mana – this is always 100 for spellcasters, except for the basic Shadow (Mahir) unit, which was set at 80 for reasons too arcane for mere mortals. Non-magic users set this at 0. So can magic users with normal **GURPS** recharge rates (since they won't be recharging any mana during the course of a single combat) *and* who only use one spell in combat – they might count their fatigue as *Ammunition* (see p. 120) instead, which simplifies bookkeeping a bit.

Mana Recharge Rate – add up a spellcaster's total fatigue and subtract 3. Calculate how long it would take him to recover this much fatigue, in minutes. Divide 0.0555 by this number and place the result here.

Berserk System Shock – leave at 0.00.

Berserk Vitality – if the character has the Berserk disadvantage, subtract his Will score from 13. Multiply by 0.125 and put the result here. Otherwise, set at 0.

Edit Sequences . . .

These are animation routines associated with the original type of character on which the unique character is based. Normally, they'll be left alone. None of them have any bearing on character performance.

Edit Sounds . . .

As per *Edit Sequences . . .* above.

Edit Terrain Parameters . . .

This calls up a menu defining the character's Move and terrain modifiers to his Move. Do *not* drop fractions from the character's **GURPS** Move before subtracting 2.5, then dividing by 125 and placing the result in the *Base Movement Speed* box. If this formula would result in a Move of 0 or less, type in 0.001. Usually the terrain

ARMOR OPTIONS

Related to the issue of *Improving the Odds* in the sidebar on p. 120 is the complex issue of portraying armor in a **GURPS**-to-**Myth** conversion.

Myth offers several armorlike effects: the *Absorbed Fraction* tag in the Monster tag/file and the *Minimum Damage* tag and various Effect Modifiers (see p. 123) in the Object tag/file. None of these precisely mimic **GURPS** DR (much less PD), and the existing **Myth** characters don't consistently use them in the manners that would most straightforwardly translate to or from **GURPS**.

GMs exploring a "new model" for conversion (see sidebar, p. 118) should pay particular attention to the many possibilities provided by this variety of armor effects. The formulas presented in this chapter could be vastly improved upon once the necessity of a "baseline" translation is discarded.

Likewise, GMs who don't care for any of the options given for improving the odds should look at these tags first when coming up with their own solution. They present a lot of potential for modeling a variety of effects.

Making it Fit

As implied in the section on conversions, **Myth** and **GURPS** approach certain "game board conventions" differently. An enterprising GM may want to experiment with changing these variables.

The most noticeable difference is that **Myth** features a much narrower range band between the shortest- and longest-ranged missile weapons. An arrow travels roughly twice as far as the average thrown weapon, and no farther than a Soulless' javelin.

This conversion assumes that **Myth** range takes into account factors beyond **GURPS'** Max statistic. Ammunition supply (limited supplies making it advisable to hold fire till the target is relatively close) is mentioned. The value could be looked at as reflecting a "realistic" range given routine skill levels of 11-14. For instance, the above javelin and a longbow share the same Acc, thus the same effective skill at close range (till the javelin's 1/2 Dam range is exceeded).

This range does bear great importance in **Myth** – an expert player will ruthlessly leverage the difference between his troops with *Maximum Range* 12 weapons and opposing forces with range 10. GMs experimenting with more **GURPS**like range increments will discover that changes can have profound impact on game play.

Another variable is the linear-measurement conversion. Different formulas in the main text use different conversion standards, each in an attempt to best translate that particular statistic. A "universal" conversion, which some GMs may prefer, would be roughly 0.6 **Myth** units to 1 **GURPS** hex.

modifiers will be left alone, unless (for instance) designing a Berserk who also levitates. In such a case, you should call up the *Terrain Parameters* for a character with the new mode of travel, then copy those over to the unique character's statistics.

Edit Flags . . .

Translates Continuously – check this only for units that glide or float, moving across the landscape without moving their bodies.

Holds With Clear Shot – this is a matter of tactical preference, though the GM may rule that characters with low Tactics scores must leave it unchecked.

Floats – check this for levitating creatures, or flying creatures that always remain nap of the earth. Note that even though Shades (see pp. 54-55) use Walk on Air to levitate, their version of the spell doesn't require the special effect of actually moving their legs.

Flies – check this for high-flying units. Setting these units up in *Loathing* requires a bit more work.

Allows Projectiles to Pass Through – if checked, this allows 100% blow-through of any attack hitting the character, but the attack will still damage the character! See *Is Not Solid*, below.

Experience Proportional to Damage – check for characters with the Berserk disadvantage.

Is Anti-Missile Unit – check for characters that single out opposing missile units in combat.

Is Anti-Missile Target – archers and other missile units (including Missile-spell casting mages) must check this unless for some reason opposing forces would not realize that they possess a ranged attack.

Turns to Stone When Killed – mostly a special effect, best left at the race's normal setting.

Concentrates on a Single Target – generally it's better to have this checked on, though the GM may require a minimum Tactics skill for the privilege.

Is Undead – is fairly self-explanatory. Check for units with the Unhealing disadvantage at -30 points.

Cannot Be Autotargeted – this keeps computer-controlled characters from attacking the character when turned on (other players can still target him). Though not really used in **GURPS Myth**, it could be just the thing for that psionic with the Power-30 Aspect . . .

Is Giant Sized – check for characters with large Inconvenient Size.

Does Not Respect Visibility – check this for inanimate objects, whether part of the scenery or a character with the Sessile disadvantage. Once spotted, others will always know where they are.

Is Not Solid – check for characters with Insubstantiality or Shadow Form. Note that explosions and area-effect attacks will still harm them. See *Objects* on pp. 123-124 to provide immunity to these attacks.

Leaves Contrail – mostly a special effect; check if the character leaves some sort of trailing effect in his wake.

Invisible on Overhead Map – check for characters with Stealth 18+, Invisibility Art 16+, Invisibility, the Hide spell at -3 or better, or similar effects.

Cannot Be Healed – check if character has -30 points in Unhealing.

Does Not Drop Ammo When Dying – check if the sort of ammo being counted in the *Ammunition* data (see p. 120) isn't represented by physical objects that could be scavenged from a corpse.

Inanimate Object – check for a Sessile character or inanimate object.

Is Skittish – leave unchecked. It's non-functioning.

Objects

Now that the basic character is complete, close the Monsters tag file and go into the Objects folder in *Fear*. Just as you did for the Monsters file, find the Object tag/file for the race or character type upon which your character is based (or closest approximation for a unique concept) and duplicate it, naming the duplicate with the character's name.

Here we'll define how much abuse the character can take. When finished, we'll go back to the Monster tag/file and set its *Object Tag* to the new Object file.

Basic Attributes

Gravity, Terminal Velocity, and Elastic Coefficient – just leave these alone unless playing with the Bouncing advantage or something equally unusual.

Max. Vitality – for a unique character these two numbers will be the same. They represent how much abuse the character can take. We're also going to factor in the advantages of a high Move, in that a Step of greater than 1 can avoid some melee attacks without requiring any active defenses (which are covered in *Recovery Time* on p. 119) or allow a slightly better Dodge and Retreat against explosions (see p. CII54) that makes all the difference in the world.

Begin by taking the character's DR and adding 3.25 for a Move less than 8, 4.75 for Move 8-9, 5.5 for Move 10, 6 for Move 15, or 6.25 for Move 16+. Square this. Add 2×HT. Add any Extra Hit Points or subtract any Reduced Hit Points. Subtract 5 for the Fragile disadvantage. Divide the result by 169. Place this figure in both *Max. Vitality* fields.

Scale Fraction – usually left at normal setting for character's race. If, for instance, using a Berserk as the basis to create a 30′ giant, divide the new character's height by 6, then set these values at the square root of that result (the relative heights of units in *Myth* are skewed toward the standard height of a Human). The above giant would enter a 2.24 in both *Scale Fraction* fields and be quite the sight on the battlefield.

Minimum Damage – this field would be used to represent *GURPS*-like armor in a conversion system created from scratch (see *Baseline vs. New Model* sidebar on p. 118). As it is, leave it set at 0.

Draw Selection Box and *Draw Vitality Box* – always have these checked on.

Maintains Constant Height Above Mesh – this should be checked off for most characters, except those that fly (but *not* those that simply levitate just off the ground, as do all standard *Myth* characters that don't walk).

Ignore Model and Object Collisions – leave this unchecked unless the character has the Insubstantiality advantage.

Effect Modifiers

These settings further distinguish the differing damage a character will take from different forms of attack. For the most part, *Myth* uses them to model the same effects that *GURPS* models by having high DR shrug off low-level attacks. The following formulas are even rougher than normal. The GM should feel free to adjust values accordingly.

Slashing Damage – Multiply the character's PD by his DR that applies to cutting *or* impaling damage, whichever value is worse for both PD and DR. Use a minimum of 1 for either value. If the result is 24 or less then this value is 1, if 25-29 then 0.598, if 30-39 then 0.5, if 40-47 then 0.445, if 48-53 then 0.125, if 54+ then 0.

Kinetic Damage – Use the above calculations but with PD and DR that apply to crushing damage.

Explosive Damage – add together natural DR and DR from magical resources. A value less than 3 is 1, 3 gives 0.748, 4 gives 0.5, 5 gives 0.299, 6 gives 0.15, 7 gives 0.1, or 8+ gives 0.047.

Experienced *GURPS* players know that not all point investments are created equal. Raising certain characteristics increases survivability and lethality more than increasing others. High DX, high IQ, and the best active defense possible will take your PC far.

This conversion to the *Myth* platform turns many of those assumptions on their heads (which may be reason enough to convert for some GMs). Those seeking to regain their lost edge should consider the following points of comparison:

Active defenses – the standard conversion undervalues "normal" active-defense levels a bit, and high ones a lot. In this conversion, lots of plain old DR is the best defense.

Low-ST weapons – puny characters with weapons that often bounce off *GURPS* armor receive new life in *Myth*. The standard formula folds DR into the overall *Vitality* of a character, with the result that existing armor effects might reduce the damage done by a dagger, but by no greater proportion than they would reduce a greatsword's damage. It still hurts.

Weapon skill – becomes a bit more important, with the most efficient melee attacks at skill 16. Characters with skill 12-14 will feel the difference more sharply than in *GURPS*.

Movement – speed kills in *Myth*, where the maps are large and faster characters can dictate certain terms in combat. This characteristic takes on proportionally more importance.

Socializing

A campaign based on the *Myth* engine probably will emphasize combat for the obvious reason that that's what *Myth* does.

Even the players most loudly proclaiming "Let's get it on!" will want to engage their PCs in a social activity from time to time, if for nothing more than to buy a better sword, or bully the local lord into telling them which path leads to the Castle of Shattered Hope.

That's where the information at the beginning of this chapter comes into play. Depending on physical proximity of players and how much of the mutually shared "time window" is already taken up in *Myth*, the GM may want to build a more traditional e-campaign in conjunction with using *Myth* as the combat engine.

If the campaign originated in getting together to play *Myth*, the GM should consider building a campaign where routine, episodic combat makes sense (for instance, a gladiatorial campaign). It can be hard to rationalize routine bouts in a more freeform campaign. Conversely, if the players don't expect regular *Myth* sessions, but do expect long and involved sessions when they do get together, the GM should break up the planned combat into a series of ongoing skirmishes. Unless measures such as a new model of conversion (see sidebar, p. 118) have been implemented, a single *Myth* combat won't last long enough to fill hours of gameplay, no matter how many forces involved.

Multiplayer *Myth* does provide chat capability, but GMs and players should avoid attempting to operate an entire roleplaying campaign with this capacity over the Internet. *Myth*'s publisher Bungie provides the resources to play over the Internet, and this would be akin to "hogging a party line." Another consideration is that – even in a local-network game – attempting a great deal of roleplaying while a fight is ongoing may be unwise. Unlike in tabletop systems and comic books, the action doesn't stop while a PC delivers a lengthy speech! "The hordes of Ancrofanx spill over yonder hills, set upon reclaiming this fair city; we must sally forth to turn back this vile tide" probably should be truncated to "3 o'clock, Dwarf! Smoke 'em!"

Electrical Damage – if DR that applies to electrical attacks is less than 5 then this is 1, if 5 then 0.25, if 6 then 0.21, if 7 then 0.195, and if 8+ then 0.047. GMs should adjust these figures freely.

Fire Damage – apply the formula for *Electrical Damage* to DR that resists flames.

Paralysis – 1 unless ST-based resistance to spells is 16-17, in which case it's 0.5. If ST-based resistance is 18+ or the character has Invulnerability to spells resisted by ST, set to 0.

Stone – as per *Paralysis*, but based on HT.

Gas Damage – set to 1 for most characters, 0 for those with Immunity to Poison. The Breath-Holding advantage or similarly non-constant measures (such as protective spells) should provide some intermediary value by GM ruling.

Confusion – as per *Paralysis*, but based on IQ.

Projectiles

The next step is to create the damage and special effects for each of the character's attacks. Enter the Projectiles folder and open the tag/file for the first attack possessed by the unit on which the unique character is based. (You may need to go back to the Monster tag/file and look up this name if you didn't write it down.) Make a duplicate. Once done, repeat the process if the character has a second or third attack.

Once finished, go back to the Monster file and point the *Projectile* tag for each attack to the proper new Projectile tag/file you've just created.

Projectiles have several tags (*Collection, Object Tag, Lightning Tag*, etc.) that you can just leave as is, as long as you started out with something similar (a sword swing for a custom sword swing, a Warlock's fireball for a regular Fireball, etc.). These can be a lot of fun to play with (creating new Lightning effects, switching out the form of a Fireball for a Stone Missile, etc.), but this is the no-frills tour. Consult the *Fear* documentation for a variety of ideas of how to enhance your game with these tags. *Exception*: The Fetch's lightning and some other attacks have an ability to "jump" to nearby targets as described for the Dispersal Dream on pp. 29-30. For a standard *GURPS* lightning attack using this attack as a template, be sure to set the *Nearby Target Radius* to 0.

The only two menu items that our *GURPS* conversion absolutely requires dealing with are the following:

Edit Damage . . .

Type – defines the kind of damage as one of several fairly self-explanatory classifications. *Slashing Metal* is used for both impaling and cutting weapon attacks, *Slashing Claws* for natural (or non-metal) impaling and cutting attacks, and *Kinetic* for non-explosive crushing damage.

Damage – for a *GURPS* cutting attack, find the average basic damage done by counting each die as 3.5; for instance, 2d-2 average 5 hits of damage. Divide this by 10.36, then square the result. In our 2d-2 example, the division yields 0.483 squared to 0.233. The first *Damage* field should be 90% of this value, the second 110% of it.

For impaling attacks, multiply the average **GURPS** basic damage by 1.35 before applying the formula. For crushing attacks, divide the average damage by 1.35 first, *unless* it's a really powerful attack (where the **GURPS** damage multipliers start losing relevance). For 5d+ crushing attacks divide by 1.3, for 6d+ divide by 1.25, for 7d+ divide by 1.2, for 8d+ divide by 1.15, for 9d+ divide by 1.1, for 10d+ divide by 1.05, and for 11d or heavier crushing attacks don't divide at all.

Radius – this should be 0 for non-explosive or area attacks. Set both these fields to 57% of the **GURPS** radius in which an attack does more than 1d of damage. Remember to count the center hex as 1, the ring of 7 hexes beyond that as 2, and so on.

Rate of Expansion – this usually should be left alone, but can be used to create some interesting explosive or area-effect limitations beyond the standard **GURPS** rules. A very slowly expanding explosive attack could be outrun by some targets, for instance.

Damage to Velocity – usually this should be 1 or close to 1; leave at "base" setting unless tinkering.

Damage Flags – these can create a variety of effects, including conversion of **GURPS** attacks not specifically addressed in this book. Most are self-explanatory or can be referenced in the *Fear* documentation. Note that the paralysis, stunning, and similar effects are in addition to standard damage in the case of these flags. To represent a spell that does *only* stunning or related damage, change the *Type* of damage as described on p. 124. The normal amount of stunning potential for a standard weapon attack is already assumed; don't check *Can Stun* to represent it. *Can Stun* appears to be an unenabled tag, anyway – as is the often-checked *Cannot Be Blocked* in a game engine without any mechanics for blocking . . .

Edit Flags . . .

These will usually be left as is, again assuming that a similar attack was used as the basis for the customization. Keep in mind that the *Is Guided* flag (in conjunction with a *Guided Turning Speed* back on the main *Projectiles* menu) can be used for attacks that aren't guided in **GURPS**. Attacks such as the Warlock's fireball look cool cruising along relatively slowly toward the target – but they wouldn't hit very often without the guidance enabled to correct their course as the targets dive for cover.

Start out by leaving guidance unchanged, then as you notice that the fireballs hit a little too often (which they will in comparison to **GURPS** missile spells), you can start turning guidance off and speeding up the projectile (in the attack's *Initial Velocity* tags reached via the character's main Monster menu) to suit your tastes.

COLLECTIONS

We're getting very close now. We've defined our **GURPS** character in terms the **Myth** engine understands. Right now, he's going to look exactly like any other member of the character type he's based on, whether Berserk, or Trow, or Warrior.

Fear does offer some limited ability to set him apart. The groups of sprites that make up the animated image of a **Myth** character are called a Collection. Building new Collections is beyond the scope of *Fear*'s abilities, but we can swap out Collections or create a custom-colored Collection Reference (a tag/file that essentially takes a standard Collection and tweaks it in one or more variations) to set our unique character apart.

To swap out existing Collections, simply go to the *Collection* tag in the character's main Monster menu and pull up the one you want. The *Collection* tag is slightly misnamed – it actually calls up the standard **Myth** Collection Reference for that race or character class. This means that if you want to use the Ghôl, for instance, doing this means your character will appear as any one of five differently colored "stock" Ghôls every time you call up the game. This won't make most of us happy.

THE NEXT GEN

Any discussion of something computer- or Internet-based usually evolves from the present to the future tense. Enough about what we can do now, what will be able to do in the next version? Here are some things to look for:

Voice technology – The fact that "shooting off his fingers" evokes a considerably different image than "shooting off his mouth" says what needs to be said about the relative ease of typewritten vs. verbal communication. Any time players can just talk, a game runs more smoothly and quickly. It's less labor, too. This technology exists, though with great room for improvement, and many experts expect to see it incorporated into e-roleplaying products.

More generic utilities – Many Internet startups are developing e-forums for tabletop roleplaying supported by mapping features, die-rollers, and more. Some are up and running. These will only improve as time goes on.

The professional GM – Perhaps no more than a "wish-list" item at this point, many observers say the weak link in e-roleplaying is the extra effort required of a fan-GM, and that no matter how good the graphics get, an online forum won't go over the top till it incorporates a professional GM creating adventure behind the scenes. People cost much more than software, so this is nowhere near a sure thing.

Instead, to custom-color and lock in your Collection Reference, go into *Fear*'s Collection References folder and call up the Collection Reference you want to base it on. Make a duplicate. Delete every *Permutation* except the first. Double-click on the colored *Hue Change* squares to play with the coloring till satisfied. (To change the size, use the *Scale Fraction* settings in the character's Object menu as described on p. 123). Hit OK, then go back to the character's main Monster menu. Reference the *base* Collection Reference (*not* your customized Collection Reference; then again, you won't find it here) under the *Collection* tag. We'll access the custom Collection Reference in *Units*, below.

Units

All that's left now is to create a Unit that *Loathing* can see. Go into *Fear*'s Unit folder and create a new tag named for your character. In the *Monster* pulldown point it to your custom Monster tag/file. This causes the *Collection Reference* pulldown to appear. Your custom Collection Reference will be among the choices (assuming you remembered to point your Monster tag/file to the original Collection Reference tag upon which it's based). Choose your custom Collection Reference tag/file.

That's it. Quit *Fear*.

Loathing

Building custom maps in *Loathing* isn't for the fainthearted. Beginners should just stick to the netplay maps provided. Those who want to play solo against the computer can use the **Myth II** scenario maps, but changes will be permanent. (This can be a lot of fun. Challenge yourself to design and convert a 400- or 500-point **GURPS** character to singlehandedly handle one of the standard missions. The first few can be easy, but even updating the character for earned experience won't keep the latter missions from being huge challenges.)

To install your new custom characters in *Loathing*, call up the desired scenario or netplay map, double-click on the little character icon in the tool box, hit Add when the menu comes up, and proceed as instructed.

To go back to playing standard **Myth II** scenarios, use your backup or reinstall from the CD.

Troubleshooting

Any process incorporating computers or character design generally sees weird things happen, and combining the two pretty much guarantees trouble. Once you design a custom character, insert him in *Loathing*, then fire up **Myth II**, you'll probably find one or more bugs. Perhaps the character's legs won't move as he walks (altering the standard *Collection* tag and tag/file can cause special-effects bugs like this). Perhaps he's far more (or less) powerful than he really should be. Don't be afraid to go back into *Fear* and "debug" your work, ignoring the formulas in this chapter if need arise.

GURPS Myth RESOURCES

Every **GURPS Myth** player, from the simply computer-savvy to the professional programmer, can contribute to his fellows' enjoyment of the game by contributing the resources they've created to the **GURPS Myth** database at **www.sjgames.com/gurps/books/myth/**.

This database will contain all of the plug-in files or related resources donated by other players, providing you a chance to access instant NPCs, new maps, conversion tips, and more!

Similar resources already exist at **www.bungie.com**. Materials there include maps galore and a set of files to convert **Myth II** into a squad-level modern infantry combat game! As other third-party developers explore the **Myth** engine, these resources may increase, so stop by Bungie's website often.

To contribute a resource to the **GURPS Myth** database, e-mail submissions to our game-aids coordinator at gameaids@sjgames.com.

INDEX